Doing Time Together

Doing Time Together

*Love and Family in the
Shadow of the Prison*

MEGAN COMFORT

The University of Chicago Press   Chicago and London

MEGAN COMFORT is a sociologist at the Center for AIDS Prevention Studies at the University of California, San Francisco. She
received her PhD in 2003 from the London School of Economics and
Political Science and was awarded the Robert McKenzie Prize for her
dissertation. This is her first book.

The University of Chicago Press, Chicago 60637
The University of Chicago Press, Ltd., London
© 2008 by The University of Chicago
All rights reserved. Published 2008
Printed in the United States of America

16 15 14 13 12 11 10   3 4 5
ISBN-13: 978–0–226–11462–0 (cloth)
ISBN-13: 978–0–226–11463–7 (paper)
ISBN-10: 0–226–11462–7 (cloth)
ISBN-10: 0–226–11463–5 (paper)

Library of Congress Cataloging-in-Publication Data

Comfort, Megan.
    Doing time together : love and family in the shadow of the prison /
Megan Comfort.
        p. cm.
    Includes bibliographical references and index.
    ISBN-13: 978-0-226-11462-0 (cloth : alk. paper)
    ISBN-10: 0-226-11462-7 (cloth : alk. paper)
    ISBN-13: 978-0-226-11463-7 (pbk. : alk. paper)
    ISBN-10: 0-226-11463-5 (pbk. : alk. paper)
    1. Prisoners—Family relationships—California—San Quentin.
2. Prisoners' spouses—California—San Quentin.   3. Conjugal
visits—California—San Quentin.   4. California State Prison at San
Quentin. I. Title.
    HV8886.U5C66 2008
    362.82'9509749—dc22

                                                    2007000359

Pour Loïc,
pour tout et pour toujours

Contents

Acknowledgments

I am immeasurably grateful to the women who participated in this research by sharing their time, space, thoughts, and experiences with me. Without their generosity, this book would not exist, and I offer them my heartfelt thanks. I am particularly indebted to Queenie and Sarah, who provided feedback, fact checking, and encouragement from my early days of field observations up to the very last months of writing and editing. In addition, I appreciate my correspondence over the years with L.M., J.C., M.A., and J.M., who enabled me to get a sense of aspects of life "inside" and were particularly informative regarding issues addressed in chapter 3.

This book grew out of my PhD dissertation at the London School of Economics and Political Science, where I was supported by an Overseas Research Student award from the Committee of Vice-Chancellors and Principals of the Universities of the United Kingdom. A dissertation award from the Harry Frank Guggenheim Foundation greatly facilitated the final year of writing. When I arrived at LSE, Paul Rock reached out to me, becoming my supervisor and giving me the scholarly engagement I needed to stay for the long haul. At the end of my time there, Richard Sparks and Janet Foster were stimulating and insightful as my examiners in the dissertation defense. My warm thanks to all three, along with Stan Cohen, David Downes, and Leslie Sklair, for broadening my intellectual and cultural horizons.

Jack Katz graciously provided detailed comments on early drafts of several chapters, and Pat Carlen offered a close reading of key arguments in chapter 5. Thanks are due as well to Ursula Castellano, Rachel Condry, Alice Goffman, Olga Jubany-Baucells, Kim Koester, Barbara Mason, Kathleen McCartney, Josh Page, Gretchen Purser, Sharon Shalev, Nicolas Sheon, Wayne Steward, Scott Stumbo, David Sweeney, and Chris Wildeman for reading and commenting on various versions. I also benefited from feedback on presentations of this work at different stages: a seminar hosted by Rick Fantasia at Smith College; the "Gender, Race, and Incarceration: Activism and Scholarship" conference organized by Mary Katzenstein and Barry Maxwell at Cornell University; the "The Prison, the Asylum, and the Street" conference coordinated by Manuela Ivone Cunha and Cristiana Bastos at the Instituto de Ciências Sociais da Universidade de Lisboa; the "Strategies for Harm Reduction: Penal System and Drug Policy" conference held by the Universidade Federal Fluminense and the Instituto Carioca de Criminologia, in Rio de Janeiro, Brazil, to which I was invited by Vera Malaguti and Nilo Batista; and sessions of the American Sociological Association and the American Society for Criminology.

At the University of Chicago Press, Doug Mitchell lived up to every wonderful thing I had ever heard about him, and more. Tim McGovern and Mary Gehl made the sailing beautifully smooth, and John Raymond was attentive to every tree in a dense forest. David Garland and an anonymous reviewer offered helpful feedback and timely encouragement for the final revisions of the manuscript. A preliminary version of chapter 4 appeared as "'Papa's House': The Prison as Domestic and Social Satellite," in *Ethnography* 31, no. 4 (2002): 467–99. An early version of chapter 2 was published as "In the Tube at San Quentin: The 'Secondary Prisonization' of Women Visiting Inmates," in *Journal of Contemporary Ethnography* 32, no. 1 (2003): 77–107. And a portion of chapter 5 appeared as "'C'est plein de mecs bien en taule!': Incarcération de masse aux États-Unis et ambivalence des épouses," in *Actes de la recherche en sciences sociales* 169 (2007): 22–47. I thank the publishers of each of these journals for their permission to include that material here. I also am grateful to Paul Willis, Jody Miller, Franck Poupeau, Etienne Ollion, and these journals' anonymous reviewers for their assistance in clarifying and strengthening several core arguments.

My colleagues at the Center for AIDS Prevention Studies at the University of California, San Francisco, continually inspire me with the commitment and compassion they bring to heartbreakingly difficult work. Olga Grinstead has been a cherished mentor since day one of my involvement with women visitors at San Quentin. Barry Zack supplied me with that most precious of commodities during field work: a quiet interview room. Many times over the years, Harold Atkins and Xochitl Fierro have thoughtfully shared their perspectives on central issues, and my high school English teacher and friend, Patricia Ludwig, meticulously copyedited the entire manuscript before I sent it for review. For love, robust support, and timely distractions I am beholden to my family: Randy Comfort, Josh Comfort (who also produced the graphics for figures 2.1 and 2.4) and Kate Culligan, and Justin, Mathew, Susan, Loren, Emmett, Mollie, *et toute ma famille française*. And, for more than I ever could say, I dedicate this book with love to Loïc Wacquant.

ONE

Outside the Prison Walls

Toward the end of visiting hours today, Grace, who is married to a man serving a life sentence, came out of the prison.[1] *I've seen Grace visiting at San Quentin since 1995. She always greets me warmly but has never really opened up to me about her personal life—so I was particularly intrigued when she said excitedly, "I have a present in the gift shop! Come on, you can come get it with me." The gift shop (or "hobby shop," as it is officially called by the San Quentin authorities) is located just outside the main gate of the prison and is staffed by one highly trusted inmate decked out in a blindingly bright yellow jumpsuit (an outfit mandated after a hobby shop worker wearing the customary prison attire of a chambray shirt and blue jeans walked away from his post and into the "free" world unnoticed). This peculiar store consists of a dimly lit sallow room with three long display cases arranged like a horseshoe. Inside the cases and hanging on the walls are hundreds of objects crafted by prisoners, available for purchase by anyone who takes a fancy to them: paintings, drawings, earrings, note cards, clocks, and other trinkets produced by those inmates lucky enough to be permitted to engage in such "hobbies" behind the walls.*

As we strolled the short distance to the shop, Grace explained that her wedding anniversary was this week and her husband had made a gift for her that she could now retrieve. Before I could ask any questions we reached the front of the shop and came upon the prisoner-worker standing outside the door, smoking. Visibly eager to claim her present, Grace told the worker that she had a gift to collect but added kindly, "You

---

1. Grace is a pseudonym, as are the names of all the participants.

can finish your cigarette first." The man smiled shyly and took a few more self-conscious puffs, then stubbed out the cigarette and headed into the shop. Once inside he seemed a little uncertain of what to do, so Grace coached him through the process of giving her the correct form to fill out and of locating her gift, noting wryly, "I've done this a few times before." She signed the paperwork, and the inmate handed over a package about double the size of a shoe box, which Grace clutched to her chest. "I already know what it is," she told me, her voice quickening with anticipation. "Come on, we can go to the car and open it."

We walked over to the parking lot, and she set the gift on the hood of her car, unlocked the vehicle's door and threw her jacket inside, then pulled a pocket knife out of the glove compartment and began slitting open the box. Tearing away the protective packaging, Grace lifted out a wooden jewelry box, the general style of which I recognized from the others on display in the hobby shop. It was beautifully made, and Grace commented happily on the luster of the orange-colored wood and the obvious attention to detail. We both stood there admiring it, and then she opened the lid, revealing that it doubled as a music box: a tune began to tinkle, and I recognized it as a popular ballad for lovers, "Unchained Melody": "Oh, my love, my darling / I've hungered for your touch, a long lonely time / And time goes by, so slowly and time can do so much."

While I was listening to the little chimes, I stole a glance at Grace and saw that she was teary eyed. Without saying anything, she set down the box and turned and wrapped her arms around me. We stood there hugging each other, much harder and longer than I'd ever hugged her before, and the tightness of her clutch overwhelmed me with sadness. My melancholy was keenly intensified by the gray misty December weather, a fitting backdrop for the bleak scene: a lone woman with only a graduate student conducting her fieldwork for company, opening her anniversary gift on the hood of a car in a deserted prison parking lot, having just said good-bye to her husband before leaving him behind to be locked back into his cell . . . as he likely would be for a great many anniversaries to come.

Constructed with convict labor between 1852 and 1856, San Quentin State Prison is the oldest penitentiary in California and occupies 432 acres of prime real estate in Marin County on the northern shores of San Francisco Bay. In the summer of 1995 I arrived at San Quentin as an employee of a nonprofit organization and began working with women who came to the facility to visit one of the approximately six

Figure 1.1 Sign at front gate of San Quentin

thousand men incarcerated there. My primary duty was to coordinate an HIV-prevention intervention designed for women with incarcerated male partners, a program that took place directly outside the prison gates in a house owned by the nonprofit organization, which served as the San Quentin visiting center. My efforts to conduct health education and program evaluation were routinely interspersed with the provision of the more mundane services offered by the visiting center: lending clothes to people who were "inappropriately" dressed for their visits, caring for children whose mothers could not or did not want to bring them onto the prison grounds, and explaining the intricate visiting policies and procedures to newcomers.

When I accepted the job with the nonprofit I had long been interested in working *in* a prison without working *for* a prison. Being at the visiting center seemed an ideal stepping-stone toward what I really aspired to do—find a position where the action was, as it were, "on the inside." I had never given much thought to the families, loved ones, and friends of prisoners. My undergraduate classes in crime and delinquency had focused exclusively on the people who were committing felonies, going to court, spending years behind bars—it was the issues surrounding the perpetrators that were understood to be compelling and important, not the tribulations of the people they left behind. Yet as the months passed, I found myself increasingly intrigued by the hundreds of visitors, the vast majority of them women, who entered San Quentin's walls each week to maintain a connection with someone the state had ordered removed from the general public—and typically from the visitor's very home. Who were these women, and why were they here?

These ostensibly simple questions evolved into the starting point for my doctoral research. I left the nonprofit in 1997 to begin graduate school, returning to San Quentin three years later to conduct nine months of intensive fieldwork as I tried to make sociological sense of the innumerable conversations and observations that had remained with me from my first experiences at the visiting center. Coming back to the prison in 1999 (when I carried out three months of preliminary fieldwork) and 2000, I frequently encountered longtime visitors—and sometimes entire families—who remembered me by name, greeted me with hugs, and reminisced with me about the births of children now waist high, former staff from the visiting center, and other bits of gossip from "the good old days." Along with this social continuity there was also an odd physical time warp: the decor of the visiting center was nearly identical to how it had been when I had left several years earlier, with details such as flyers on bulletin boards, health-education posters, information binders, and other items I had created and arranged still in place. Notably, two large compositions of photographs, including pictures of me with prisoners' children, continued to dominate the walls of the living room.

Yet my return to the study site also felt distinctly unfamiliar, primarily in that my role as a service provider was over and my desire to investigate and dissect was my sole purpose for being there. Rather than having every minute of my time consumed by tasks and responsibilities, I now spent long hours sitting, waiting, watching. As the months went on, I began to understand that in addition to asking who the women visitors were and why they came to visit, it was critical to question how their interactions with the penitentiary transformed their daily routines and social lives. From the thick of this analysis, I could hardly fathom that at one time I had wanted only to study those who inhabited the prison and felt uninspired by those who lived outside its walls. Instead, I found myself grinning in hearty agreement one day when a visitor, who had greeted me on her way into the prison, paused on her way out six hours later and exclaimed, "You picked a helluva topic, Megan!"

Women Partners of Prisoners in the Context of Mass Incarceration

No study of a prison-related subject in this country can begin without a discussion of the meteoric rise of "mass incarceration" in the United States. San Quentin is the oldest of the thirty-three state prisons in California (twelve built before 1965 and the remaining twenty-one since 1984), which collectively housed 160,369 inmates in August 2006 (California Department of Corrections and Rehabilitation 2006).[2] At year-end 2005, California boasted the second-largest prison population in the United States, ranking just after the federal system, although this status is more attributable to California's sizeable population than to an especially punitive streak. California's 2005 imprisonment rate of 466 prisoners per 100,000 residents was just over the national average for states of 435 and far behind the country's top three states: Louisiana (797), Texas (691), and Mississippi (660) (Harrison and Beck 2006b). Importantly, the imprisonment rate refers exclusively to convicts confined in prisons and does not include people detained in city and county jails. The midyear 2005 *incarceration* rate for California was 682 prison or jail inmates per 100,000 residents, while the national incarceration rate for 2005 reached 738, bringing the nation's carceral population to an all-time high of 2,186,230 inmates (Harrison and Beck 2006a).[3]

The United States as a whole has been engaged in a continuous and now-infamous rise in incarceration since the mid-1970s, before which the imprisonment rate had hovered around a stable mean of 110

2. Counting those held in correctional camps and other facilities brought the state total to 170,994 (California Department of Corrections and Rehabilitation 2006).

3. This figure includes people confined in jails (operated on a local level by counties or cities and holding new arrestees awaiting trial, plus convicts sentenced to under one year of detention); state prisons (run by each state's Department of Corrections and containing felons serving more than one year as well as most parole violators); and federal prisons (controlled by the Federal Bureau of Prisons and inhabited by offenders convicted of federal crimes). It does not include temporary holding facilities (such as police lockups) or juvenile facilities. Recalculated by gender, the national incarceration rate is 129 female inmates per 100,000 women and 1,366 male inmates per 100,000 men (Harrison and Beck 2006a).

inmates per 100,000 residents for a half century (Tonry 2001, 8). From 1980 to 2000 the number of people behind bars increased by *at least* thirty-five thousand each year (the "low" from 1983–84), with typical years bringing in fifty-five thousand to seventy-five thousand additional inmates and high periods (like the peak from 1989–90) topping the previous count by 127,500 (calculated using figures from Bureau of Justice Statistics 2003; see appendix 3 in this book). As a result, today the United States is a penal outlier among its "peer" nations, which—despite significant rises in their own carceral rates (see Wacquant 1999)—confine their residents at levels similar to or below those of pre-Nixon America. For example, contrast the U.S. incarceration rate of 738 inmates per 100,000 residents to that of 68 for Norway, 88 for France, 95 for Germany, 102 for Italy, 107 for Canada, 128 for the Netherlands, and 147 for England and Wales. Even the Russian Federation, at 606, no longer challenges the United States as the world's top incarcerator (all rates from International Centre for Prison Studies 2006).

David Garland (2001, 1–2) notes that, in the tradition of the Great Confinement in seventeenth-century Europe and the Soviet Union's gulag archipelago, such an extraordinary transformation in U.S. carceral policies and profile "deserves a name of its own. . . . America now has 'mass imprisonment'—a new name to describe an altogether new phenomenon." He argues that mass incarceration's two distinct features are "a rate of imprisonment and a size of prison population that are markedly above the historical and comparative norm for societies of this type" and "the social concentration of imprisonment's effects . . . [due to] the systematic imprisonment of whole groups of the population." The latter refers to the staggeringly disproportionate confinement of African American men. The national incarceration rates of black men of all ages are five to seven times higher than those for white men in the same age groups; among men ages twenty-five to twenty-nine, 11.9 percent of African Americans were behind bars in 2005, compared to 3.9 percent of Hispanics and 1.7 percent of whites (Harrison and Beck 2006a). Becky Pettit and Bruce Western (2004, 160–61) calculated that 20 percent of black men and nearly 60 percent of black male high school dropouts born between 1965 and 1969 had been to prison at least once by 1999. The finding that "recent birth cohorts of black men are more likely to have prison records (22.4%) than military records (17.4%) or bachelor's degrees (12.5%)" leads these authors to conclude that "prison time [has] indeed become modal for young black men who failed to graduate from high school" (Pettit and Western 2004, 161, 164).[4]

When considering the impact of mass incarceration on women, the predominant impulse among researchers has been to examine the predicament of female inmates. Although men constitute 93 percent of the prison population, the annual rate of growth for women in prison has averaged higher than that for men since 1995 (4.6% vs. 3.0%), with 107,518 women state and federal prisoners at year-end 2005 (Harrison and Beck 2006b). The female populations in the United States and western Europe are nearly equivalent in number, yet in 2000 the number of imprisoned women in the United States was six times greater than that of their counterparts in the European Union (Council of Europe 2002). Research on female inmates further points out that women often suffer gender-specific ordeals such as grossly inadequate gynecological or obstetrics care, physical and sexual abuse at the hands of correctional officers, lengthy sentences for minimal criminal involvement as "drug mules" for male traffickers, and severe trauma over separation from and loss of custody of their children (Richie 1996; Owen 1998; Hairston 1999; Chesney-Lind 2002; Richie 2002). Yet concentrating exclusively on female convicts overlooks millions of women whose lives are directly affected by the criminal justice system on a daily basis: the wives, girlfriends, mothers, daughters, and other female kin and intimates of prisoners who, through their contact with loved ones and close associates caught in the revolving door of corrections, experience restricted rights, diminished resources, social marginalization, and other consequences of penal confinement, even though they are legally innocent and dwell outside of the prison walls.

In this book, I combine participant observation in the visitor-waiting area at San Quentin State Prison and in-depth interviews with fifty women whose male partner is behind bars to document how the incarceration of a partner infiltrates and distorts women's personal, domestic, and social worlds. Drawing on my previous work with women visitors, I determined that it was vital to explore the experiences of

4. For more on the U.S. "imprisonment binge," see John Irwin and James Austin's (2000) study investigating the social and civil profile of offenders, the conditions of their confinement, and the social and economic costs of mass incarceration; Michael Tonry (1995) dissects the crime-and-sentencing policies propelling the escalation, with a particular focus on the impact of the war on drugs on African Americans; Jerome Miller (1996) documents racial bias in the criminal justice system and investigates the devastating consequences of young black men's absorption into it; David Cole (1999) analyzes the U.S. justice system's "affirmative dependency" on inequality, which results in disproportionate numbers of poor and black people residing behind bars.

women in romantic relationships with prisoners separately from those of the other relations of convicts because, as will be demonstrated in the ensuing chapters, the incarceration-specific dynamics that develop within couples are distinctively shaped by heterosexual partnership norms and thus differ greatly from, for example, a mother's reactions to her son's lawbreaking.

No exact figure exists as to how many women are affected by a partner's incarceration, but even a conservative estimate indicates that this population vastly outnumbers that of women behind bars: the *Survey of Inmates of State and Federal Correctional Facilities* (Bureau of Justice Statistics 1997) reports that one-fifth of prisoners are married, meaning that about 278,000 women (20% of 1.39 million male prisoners) have a husband in a penitentiary. However, legal marital status is an unreliable indicator of being involved in a romantic relationship—particularly for prisoners, the majority of whom are young adults—because the overall marriage rates have been declining and the median age of first marriage has been increasing in the United States over the last several decades (see Becker 1991; Fields and Casper 2001). Indeed, some studies have found that upward of 50 percent of men entering penal facilities consider themselves to be in heterosexual relationships (Jorgensen, Hernandez, and Warren 1986; Carlson and Cervera 1991a; Grinstead et al. 1999). Also, 1.39 million men are in prison in the United States on any given day, but 13 million male bodies pass through the correctional system each year (Bureau of Justice Statistics 2003). If anywhere from 20 percent to 50 percent of those men are in heterosexual relationships then 2.5 million to 6.5 million women annually experience the incarceration of their partners—or roughly twenty to sixty times the number of women who are themselves behind bars. This suggests that when it comes to understanding the impact of U.S. penal policy on women, studying female inmates is just the tip of a deeply submerged iceberg.

Recapturing Sociological Ambivalence

The following is a summary of the major works and lines of inquiry that have marked the study of families of prisoners over the last five decades, highlighting the need to dispassionately consider the penitentiary as a social institution when examining its repercussive effects. Appendix 2 contains a more detailed orientation to the literature on prisoners' families.

Researchers in the United States and the United Kingdom began examining the impact of incarceration on family members in the 1960s and 1970s, with the concerns of women prisoners and their children (Zalba 1964; Gibbs 1971) and the role of the family in rehabilitation (Fenton and Fenton 1961; Glaser 1964; Holt and Miller 1972) receiving early attention. The most extensive and systematic study from this period is Pauline Morris's *Prisoners and Their Families* (1965), which reported on interviews with 588 wives of male inmates in England and Wales. A striking aspect of Morris's impressively thorough and carefully researched book is her acknowledgement that family responses to incarceration fluctuate according to an array of interpersonal, cultural, economic, and offense-specific factors. She pays particular attention to family relationships *before* incarceration, examining the ways in which the imprisonment of a parent or spouse could trigger, exacerbate, or alleviate difficulties within the home. Morris introduces three important distinctions: (1) there are separate effects on families resulting from criminality as opposed to incarceration; (2) confinement may not represent a crisis for all families; and (3) households can suffer from numerous troubles *prior to* men's imprisonment (Morris 1965, 23–25,89–90,160–200; see also Thompson and Morris 1972, 3).

As the U.S. carceral population underwent its heady ascent from the late 1970s through the 1990s, the publications on convicts' relations remained sporadic, consisting of conceptually isolated works from a smattering of disciplines, most notably psychology (e.g., Daniel and Barrett 1981; Hannon, Martin, and Martin 1984) and social work (e.g., Bakker, Morris, and Janus 1978; Lowenstein 1986). The bulk of this research departs significantly from Morris's tenor in that it adopts a prosecutorial approach by portraying the correctional system as a monolithically negative force in the lives of inmates and their families. Authors frequently present prisoners' kin and intimates as de facto "hidden victims of crime" (Bakker, Morris, and Janus 1978; see also Matthews 1983; Shaw 1987; Light 1993) or people "sentenced by association" (Blake 1990), while asserting categorically that incarceration "causes traumatic separation leading to family dismemberment" (Carlson and Cervera 1991b, 279) or constitutes a "crisis of a death-like loss" (Jorgensen, Hernandez, and Warren 1986, 52). Meanwhile, imprisoned mothers continued to receive preferential treatment in the study of children of inmates (Bloom 1995; Johnston 1995; Jose-Kampfner 1995; Richie 2002), with the notable exceptions of Creasie Finney Hairston's writings on family-centered programming for men (1995, 1998) and Anne Nurse's (2002) extensive study of juvenile fathers in the California Youth Authority system.

The attention paid to incarcerated mothers did not result in equal consideration of female partners of prisoners: only two monographs on the female partners of male prisoners had been published by the mid-1990s, Laura Fishman's *Women at the Wall* (1990) and Lori Girshick's *Soledad Women* (1996). Although significant for their treatment of women as individuals affected by incarceration outside of their roles as the bearers and guardians of children, both studies suffer from methodological and analytical flaws that considerably weaken the authority of their findings and their core arguments. In particular, Fishman's sample of thirty wives of prisoners contained exclusively white women living in Vermont, a predominantly rural state with an imprisonment rate one-third of the national rate around the time of her study (Bureau of Justice Statistics 1995). Among Girshick's twenty-five participants, recruited from a California state prison, just five women were African American and three were Hispanic, with the rest being white. In both cases, such dramatic imbalance in sampling for work on a subject deeply rooted in ethnic social division is highly problematic, especially when neither author engages these issues in her analysis.

By the turn of the millennium, the subject of prisoners' families had benefited from little sociological development or theoretical grounding beyond that established by Pauline Morris thirty-five years earlier. John Hagan, with Ronit Dinovitzer (1999) and Juleigh Petty Coleman (2001), redressed this deficit by applying the concept of social capital—"the resources that can be drawn on to facilitate relationships and initiatives" (Hagan and Dinovitzer 1999, 123)—to the study of the impact of imprisonment on families. Hagan and his coauthors also introduced a research agenda for the study of the "collateral consequences" (1999)—or, indeed, the "collateral damage" (2001, 352)—of imprisonment on families both during and after confinement. Calling for longitudinal studies that include broad family networks, that control for changes before and after incarceration as well as for differences between custodial and noncustodial sentences, and that involve comprehensive measurements of background factors such as income, employment, and violence in the home, they hypothesize that such research would show a marked decrease in social capital and hence the erosion of family stability among people affected by their own or their kin's incarceration (Hagan and Dinovitzer 1999, 148–54; see also Hagan and Coleman 2001, 363–65). This recognition of imprisonment's repercussive effects quickly gained currency, as evidenced by the publication of five edited volumes on the subject in rapid succession (Mauer and Chesney-Lind 2002; Harris and Miller 2003; Travis and Waul 2003; Pattillo, Weiman, and Western

2004; Mele and Miller 2005). The interdisciplinary scholars and activists contributing to these books provide a rich and nuanced assembly of investigations into the socioeconomic and cultural outcomes of large-scale confinement through consideration of issues such as welfare assistance, employment, housing, disenfranchisement, public health, and the breakdown of social control in neighborhoods.

Keenly attuned to the poverty, joblessness, single motherhood, and other burdens shouldered by those most affected by the nation's punitive penal policies, many researchers tend to position incarceration as the catalyst of such woes—that is, being sentenced to spend time in jail or prison is claimed to be the disruptive force that results in unemployment, family disintegration, social ostracism, and the like. In the words of Donald Braman (2004, 221), who conducted three years of ethnographic research with fifty families of prisoners in the Washington, D.C., area, "by draining the resources of families, by frustrating the norm of reciprocity that inheres in family life, and by stigmatizing poor and minority families, our current regime of criminal sanctions has created a set of second-order problems that furthers social detachment." Although solid cases for this premise can be made (particularly when examining the civil restrictions applied to and labor-market difficulties faced by ex-convicts—see Pager 2003; Mele 2005), the omission of serious investigations into whether shame, stigma, hardship, and penury were preexisting conditions (and thus the "collateral damage" of a source other than the prison) and whether incarceration somehow mitigated or altered such conditions (perhaps rendering them not so "damaging" after all) is a limitation of much contemporary work. This "damage assessment" perspective obstructs examinations of people's relationships to the prison in their full range and complexity by reducing inquiries to negative-positive accounting. In this respect, there is a tendency for those researching prisoners' families to lag behind their crime-and-deviance counterparts, who for decades have acknowledged that, in Walter Miller's (1958, 8) evaluation, "getting into trouble" can be "multi-functional" or even "prestige-conferring." Indeed, as Garland (1990, 280) advises:

We need to realize that in the penal realm—as in all social experience—specific events or developments usually have a plurality of causes which interact to shape their final form, a plurality of effects which may be seen as functional or non-functional depending upon one's criteria, and a plurality of meanings which will vary with the actors and audiences involved—though some meanings (or, for that matter, causes and effects) may be more powerful than others.

The null hypothesis that incarceration is unconditionally negative results from the stigmatization of the prison as a "deeply discred-
ited" and tainted institution, to paraphrase Erving Goffman (1963, 3).
Now a massively distended repository for the poor and the darker
skinned, the penitentiary has lost its status as a social institution
like others meriting objective analysis and has become for many crit-
ics an aberration to be reflexively castigated. Yet, in order to arrive at
measured conclusions about the role of punitive confinement in the
lives of millions of people, the prison must be returned to its position
as a social institution that can be analyzed like any other "people-
processing"—and not *ex definitionis* "people-damaging"—institution,
such as hospitals, schools, or military barracks (Hasenfeld 1972), in
all its gradations and contradictions. Indeed, Richard Sparks, Anthony
Bottoms, and Will Hay (1996, 29) note that "[a]s prisoners, prison officers, and governors [wardens] know, prisons are in fact much more perplexing places, intellectually, practically, and morally, than is generally admitted." If this tenet holds true for the denizens of correctional
facilities, it follows that their loved ones, particularly those who spend
long hours visiting behind bars, will experience similar ambiguity.

When conducting my fieldwork and analysis, I was continuously
struck by the seemingly incongruous behaviors and sentiments of
women as they at once denounced *and* commended the criminal justice system for its intercession in their personal lives, and both rebelled
against and joined with the correctional authorities charged with monitoring, restraining, and sanctioning their partners. To make sense of
these findings, I turned to the concept of "sociological ambivalence"
elaborated by Robert Merton and Elinor Barber (1976, 5–6), which,
in contrast with psychological theories, guides analysis "to the social
structure, not to the personality":

[A] basically sociological orientation toward the study of ambivalence . . . focuses
on the ways in which ambivalence comes to be built into the structure of social
statuses and roles. It directs us to examine the processes in the social structure that
affect the probability of ambivalence turning up in particular kinds of role-relations.
And finally, it directs us to the social consequences of ambivalence for the workings
of social structures.

Accordingly, my aim in this book is to study women's statuses and
roles in their complex and shifting relationships with the social institution of the prison, so as to unearth and explicate the sociological ambivalence that arises in these relationships and its multifaceted social

consequences for both women and their partners, without the imposition of moralizing frameworks mandating a monotonal evaluation of "good versus bad." In doing so, I demonstrate that, as the penitentiary invades women's domestic and social spheres via the punitive regulations applied to their partners, wives and girlfriends in turn adapt their romantic expectations to carceral realities and recast their relationships as benefiting precisely from the strictures that contain and control their mates. In particular, women who have experienced high levels of dissatisfaction with men "on the outside" (whether the incarcerated partner when he was free or nonincarcerated men more generally) learn to valorize the prison regime as a means of shaping males' behavior that suppresses dangerous or difficult conduct, such as violence or drug use, and elicits rewarding interpersonal exchange. Counterintuitively, women laud their incarcerated partners for a range of stereotypically feminine qualities—intensive communication, attentiveness to the relationship, expression of emotion—and attribute the men's development of these skills to the brute fact of their penal confinement. As will be revealed in later chapters, the seemingly paradoxical sentiment that "if he hadn't gone to prison, we wouldn't be together" is far from uncommon among women visiting incarcerated men.

Secondary Prisonization: "Being Both Ways"

To analyze this study's findings, I returned to a classic study of the carceral microcosm, sociologist Donald Clemmer's *The Prison Community,* originally published in 1940. Based on Clemmer's estimated thirty thousand conversations with twenty-five hundred inmates during his tenure as a member of the mental health staff of a penitentiary in Illinois, *The Prison Community* painstakingly details the organization and daily routines of the correctional facility, as well as the social groupings, relations, roles, and controls created or enacted within its walls.[5] In his preface to the second edition, Clemmer (1958, xi) reminds readers that the book "was intended as a compendium to cover the formal and informal organization of a conventional prison. . . . [I]t can serve as a case study of a prison of the 1930's for students a century ahead." The conclusion of the text presents Clemmer's key conceptual innovation, developed from his observations of the assimilation processes of

---

5. Clemmer's study harkens back to an era when progressive states, among them Illinois and California, employed sociologists alongside social workers and psychologists as part of the correctional staff (see Jacobs 1977).

inmates to the institution: "[A]s we use the term Americanization to describe a greater or lesser degree of the immigrant's integration into the American scheme of life, we may use the term *prisonization* to indicate the taking on in greater or less degree of the folkways, mores, customs, and general culture of the penitentiary" (1958, 299).

While each convict becomes prisonized to a varying extent, Clemmer contends that there are *"universal factors of prisonization"*: "Acceptance of an inferior rôle, accumulation of facts concerning the organization of the prison, the development of somewhat new habits of eating, dressing, working, sleeping, the adoption of local language, the recognition that nothing is owed to the environment for the supplying of needs, and the eventual desire for a good job are aspects of prisonization which are operative for all inmates" (1958, 300). How an individual responds to these and other elements of the prison culture depends on a range of variables related to his life both before and during incarceration. Clemmer creates a schema (reconstructed in table 1) enumerating such variables in instances of high and low degrees of prisonization. He follows this with seven case studies showing how a series of circumstances and adaptations results in stronger or weaker ties to the convict culture, and concludes by conjecturing that prisonization is positively correlated to recidivism and recommending that the former therefore be considered in parole decisions.

Clemmer's identification of the processes and indicators of prisonization provides an initial analytical framework for capturing the gamut of transformative and conservative effects of the correctional facility that avoids the moralizing discourse of the "happy family" versus the "malevolent penitentiary." In his argument, variables such as the duration of an individual's contact with the correctional facility, ability to maintain relationships with nonincarcerated people, degree of absorption into a "prison primary group," and level of resistance to the penitentiary culture's dogmas and codes influence the extent to which that person eventually will exhibit the "universal factors of prisonization." In the chapters that follow, I extend and adapt this framework by documenting how these same variables produce related factors of prisonization among "free" people who interact with the correctional system due to their connections to those behind bars, with the result that carceral contact profoundly transforms women's intimate and social lives through its regulation of their conduct, physical appearances, agendas, sexual relations and fantasies, and speech both at and away from the correctional facility. As wives and girlfriends yield their bodies and homes to penal management in efforts to "do time" with their

Table 1. Variables affecting degree of prisonization

Lower degree of prisonization	Higher degree of prisonization
A short sentence, thus a brief subjection to the universal factors of prisonization.	A sentence of many years, thus a long subjection to the universal factors of prisonization.
A fairly stable personality made stable by an adequacy of positive and "socialized" relationships during pre-penal life.	A somewhat unstable personality made unstable by an inadequacy of "socialized" relations before commitment, but possessing, none the less, a capacity for strong convictions and a particular kind of loyalty.
The continuance of positive relationships with persons outside the walls.	A dearth of positive relations with persons outside the walls.
Refusal or inability to integrate into a prison primary group or semiprimary group, while yet maintaining a symbiotic balance in relations with other men.	A readiness and a capacity for integration into a prison primary group.
Refusal to accept blindly the dogmas and codes of the population, and a willingness, under certain situations, to aid officials, thus making for identification with the free community.	A blind, or almost blind, acceptance of the dogmas and mores of the primary group and the general penal population.
A chance placement with a cellmate and workmates who do not possess leadership qualities and who are also not completely integrated into the prison culture.	A chance placement with other persons of similar orientation.
Refraining from abnormal sex behavior and excessive gambling, and a ready willingness to engage seriously in work and recreative activities.	A readiness to participate in gambling and abnormal sex behavior.

Source: Clemmer 1958, 301–2.
Note: My attempts to paraphrase this schema resulted in a loss of Clemmer's nuances, thus I quote him. By "abnormal sex behavior" Clemmer primarily means sex between men and, to a lesser extent, masturbation.

loved ones, they become primary participants in the interpenetration of the "inside" and "outside" worlds, schooling themselves and those around them on how to adapt innumerable facets of everyday life to the dictates of the prison regime.

Through my analysis of these processes, I propose that women with incarcerated partners undergo *secondary prisonization,* a less absolute but still powerful form of Clemmer's construct, derivative of and dependent on the primary prisonization of their partners. Through their peculiar status as "quasi inmates," these women dwell in the juxtaposition of two ostensibly separate worlds, a situation indirectly addressed by Clemmer (1958, 109–10) in his discussion of convicts who distance themselves from their surroundings: "[A] portion of the men become only partially assimilated and may be said to be on the border, or in the shadows of, two cultures, and not acculturized to either. . . . [T]heir behavior seems confused and illogical to those other inmates who have become assimilated and cling tenaciously to the precepts of one culture or the other. . . . 'You can't be both ways,' the inmates say over and over again." Yet to be secondarily prisonized *is* to be "both ways," at once captive and free, and thus is a status marked by profound ambivalence.

In this book I build my arguments through a series of concentric circles, with each chapter increasing the scope to encompass a wider range of interaction and thereby showing expanding levels of secondary prisonization. Chapter 2 concentrates on a single hallway at San Quentin—known as "the Tube"—in which visitors wait to enter the correctional facility. Drawing on Clemmer's prisonization and the "pains of imprisonment" schema of Gresham Sykes (1958), I dissect the physical architecture of the corridor and the social architecture of the relations it harbors, illuminating how prison authorities instruct visitors in the behaviors and appearances required by their denigrated status. Although these interactions primarily take place directly outside the gates of the penitentiary, they reverberate broadly, as women adjust their schedules, wardrobes, and demeanors to meet correctional mandates and thereby lay the groundwork for more extensive forms of secondary prisonization.

Chapter 3 examines the various ways women stay in touch with their partners from beyond the perimeter of the prison: exchanging letters, sending packages, receiving phone calls, and engaging in shared fantasies. Here I highlight how the reach of the penitentiary extends into the home, as women experience secondary prisonization at a distance through the elaborate regulations governing their communication with their mates. I also introduce women's abiding ambivalence regarding the penal control that distorts their personal lives but also serves as a means of forging a prized intimacy unique to carceral circumstances. Incarcerated men learn to invest themselves in the emotional aspects of relationship maintenance and become highly communicative and expressive during their confinement. For their part, women take pleasure in this transformation and respond by nurturing their partners with extra food, supplemental clothing, and other auxiliary items. Yet tales of prisoners "using" women for material goods haunt these exchanges, miring couples in struggles to assert power, exact desired behaviors, and establish primacy in the relationship. Ultimately, the penitentiary itself benefits, as women exercise leverage in their dealings with men by withholding or subsidizing incentives and thereby shaping their partners' "good" behavior.

Chapter 4 accompanies women into the prison itself and provides accounts of three supposedly "private" activities emblematic of conjugal intimacy enacted within its walls: sharing meals, getting married, and spending the night together. Here secondary prisonization reaches its zenith as the boundaries between "home" and "penitentiary" dissolve, the correctional facility becomes an alternative site for the performance of domesticity, and women integrate so fully into the prison culture that they profess pleasure about—and at times even a preference for—their experiences within the carceral border. Continuing arguments seeded in Chapter 3, I underscore how the poverty and unstable or unsafe housing characterizing many women's lives, combined with their partners' domestic violence or substance use when the men are not incarcerated, position the prison as a peculiar refuge in which couples can enact idealized versions of romance and cohabitation.

Chapter 5 contextualizes women's relationships with their partners by examining their accounts of previous relationships and of why they now "stand by their man." Deepening the analyses of previous chapters, I show how incarceration can heighten romantic attachment by radically altering men's emotional responsiveness, positioning them as victims of a racist and unjust society, and interrupting—or at least relocating—their destructive behaviors. Through a close analysis of case histories and interviews, I illustrate how financial and social resources hinder or promote the secondary prisonization of women: wives and girlfriends with higher incomes and educations are better able to maintain their footing in the "outside" world through friendships, leisure and professional activities, and domestic settings that pull them away from the penitentiary and situate it as an exceptional environment. Conversely, women with scarce resources gradually see the prison absorb their daily lives, as the majority of their kinship and social networks become inmates, former inmates, or visitors, and as the hours they spend behind bars contrast favorably with those spent navigating the perils of housing projects, destitute neighborhoods, or the streets.

Here, the criminal justice system emerges as the most consistent and powerful public institution available to low-income women, transforming incarceration into a readily accessible tool provided to them by the state as they attempt to reframe and manage relationships with men in significant need of mental-health services, employment assistance, and substance-use treatment. The notable dearth of social-welfare programs offered to poor women, and the singular lack of intervention by any institution other than the criminal justice authorities in their lives, underscores how the disintegrative repercussions elaborated by the collateral-consequences perspective and the integrative functions of the prison-as-peculiar-social-service coexist, and indeed operate distinctively in different domains of a woman's life, depending on her socioeconomic standing and relationship circumstances. For example, someone with a drug-addicted husband might keenly miss his companionship but find herself more financially secure during his incarceration, when she is better able to control expenditures of her money. Alternatively, a woman with an income-generating but abusive partner could experience a simultaneous increase in penury and safety.

Chapter 6 concludes the book with the application of the concept of secondary prisonization to future research, particularly examinations of plea bargaining, parole, the politicization and disenchantment of prisoners' families, and the impact of mass incarceration in an international context. A discussion of the poor in the United States compared to the impoverished in other Western countries emphasizes that the utilization of penal confinement as an unusual "resource" for managing tension-fraught gender relations arises specifically in the context of a post–welfare state characterized by an absence of alternatives. Indeed, as is clear throughout this book, women do not choose incarceration over other existing services, nor do they promote it as a particularly successful means of bettering their lives in the long term. Rather, women plainly realize that correctional facilities cause their own forms of harm and are inferior substitutes for the family-centered, therapeutic, and economic programs that they and their partners desire. It is the wretchedness of the life conditions of America's destitute and working poor that causes women to turn to what is ostensibly an option of last resort as a primary "social agency," as they seek to live safely and with a modicum of stability while maintaining a romantic partnership.

A Note on Methodology

A full account of this study's setting and methods is provided in appendix 1, but a few points about the field site and scope of the analysis bear mentioning here. First, San Quentin contains a wide variety of prisoners because it hosts California's Death Row and execution chamber, encompasses minimum-security and medium-security areas, and also serves as a "reception center" where newly sentenced prisoners undergo a medical exam, receive a security classification, and await the completion and consolidation of their paperwork before being sent to the facility where they will serve their sentence. This in turn means that a wide variety of women come to the prison, from long-term visitors of Death Row (also referred to as "condemned") and life-sentence inmates (or "lifers"),[6] to those coming to a correctional facility for the first time to see a recently arrived convict in the Reception Center, to people heading to the low-security areas where their loved one is serving a short sentence for a parole violation. When recruiting participants for interviews, the only eligibility criterion I used was that the woman considered an incarcerated man to be her partner, whether that meant they were legally wed, in a committed relationship, or casually dating.[7] My sample therefore includes women whose partners were serving various lengths of time: four of the partners were on Death Row, eight had life sentences, two had sentences of over twenty years, two were serving between six and ten years, seven faced between one and four years, twenty-five were serving one year or under (mostly for parole violations), and two were awaiting sentencing (see appendix 1 for more information about the participants' and partners' demographic and social characteristics).

Second, it is important to stress that I primarily recruited my interview participants when they came to the prison as visitors. Although there was variation in the degree of commitment to their relationships, and some women could not or did not visit often or regularly, this book concentrates on women who maintain a direct connection to their incarcerated partners, as opposed to women who voluntarily or involuntarily lose touch once their man goes behind bars. This distinction is critical to my analysis in that contact with the correctional facility is precisely what shapes the processes and effects of secondary prisonization. On a related note, as described above, I chose to conduct my fieldwork at San Quentin in large part due to the strong rapport I had already developed over several years with the visitors there, which I believe significantly enhanced the quality of my interviews and granted me access in my field observations that would have been difficult if not

6. Actual sentences falling under the "life" category vary, ranging along a scale of minimum time to serve (e.g., "seven to life" or "twenty-five to life") and including sentences of life without the possibility of parole.

7. In order to enter San Quentin, visitors must be eighteen years of age or older, or they must be accompanied by a parent or legal guardian who presents the child's birth certificate, which permitted me to ensure that all participants were considered legal adults by the state of California.

impossible to obtain at an unfamiliar site where I was unknown. I did not select San Quentin as a penitentiary that is positively or negatively remarkable, and the focus of my investigation is women's interactions with the prison as a social institution, not their interactions specifically with San Quentin. Disguising the identity of this facility is infeasible since no other prison in California holds Death Row inmates, but readers should keep in mind that while policies and procedures fluctuate from prison to prison, those implemented at San Quentin are not noticeably more punitive or lax than those employed at other U.S. penitentiaries.

Finally, as of this writing (August 2006), I continue to be involved in research projects on women visiting men at San Quentin that have repeatedly informed and confirmed the analyses presented in this book (see Comfort et al. 2005). I also remain in contact with some of my previous interview participants. Although there have been transformations both in women's relationships with their partners and in a few institutional policies, I have refrained from giving details of these alterations throughout the text in order to preserve the synchronicity of the fieldwork period. A discussion of salient changes in policy is provided in appendix 1. After reflection and discussion with the participants with whom I am still in contact, I have decided not to supply updates on their circumstances in this book both as a means of protecting their privacy and because this study is meant to be a snapshot of a moment in time at San Quentin: the individual romances of the participants may have changed over the years, but there are other women visiting now who articulate similar sentiments and who face comparable challenges as my participants did six years ago.

TWO

"On-Line" at San Quentin

People come into the institution and think the staff wants to take away their dignity. We don't want to take away people's dignity, but this *is* a secure institution so we *are* going to have to take your shoes and run them through the x-ray machine. FORMER VISITING LIEUTENANT (THE CORRECTIONAL OFFICIAL IN CHARGE OF VISITOR PROCESSING AND ALL VISITING AREAS) AT SAN QUENTIN STATE PRISON

One thing my husband told me about coming up here is, "Always expect the worst." A VISITOR WAITING IN THE TUBE

People who temporarily enter prisons in order to visit their intimates and kin detained therein constitute a peculiar category of "quasi inmate." Not convicted felons, but not beyond the suspicion of the authorities, their penetration of a guarded, secure space catalyzes a tug-of-war between contradictory processes of identification and attributed group membership.[1] Correctional officers, responsible for the maintenance of order through the reduction of incarcerated bodies to depersonalized, manageable units (Kauffman 1988; Conover 2000; Crawley 2004), attempt to transform prison visitors into an obedient corps of unindividuated, nonthreatening entities that can be organized according to the prison's rules. On the other end of the rope, visitors—cognizant of their status as legally "free" people—resist this imposed prisoner label, clamor for respectful,

1. Following Rogers Brubaker and Fred Cooper (2000), I avoid the use of "identity" as a preformed entity or substance since the issue here is precisely to examine how various forms of group membership and institutional processes of categorization influence social conduct and representation.

nonpunitive treatment, and fiercely struggle to import the "outside world" into the facility via their personally stylized appearances and comportment. The ongoing clash between forcibly assigned quasi-penal properties and defended civil attributes unfolds in the border region of the prison where outsiders first enter the institution and come under the gaze of its authorities. The space surrounding this area therefore becomes the site of contested personhood, an intermediary zone where visitors continually define and defend their social and physical integrity against the degradation of self (Garfinkel 1968) required by the prison as a routine condition for visiting. In this chapter I draw on direct observations of one such area—the desolate, drab hallway at San Quentin State Prison known as the Tube—to examine the secondary prisonization of women at their point of first bodily contact with the penal institution.

A Concrete-Walled Dividing Line: The Tube

Unlike many U.S. correctional facilities, which dot rural counties far from major urban centers (Shichor 1992), San Quentin State Prison is eighteen miles from both San Francisco and Oakland, sixty miles from San Jose, and a mere nine miles from Richmond.[2] The prison is located just off the first exit on the Marin County side of the Richmond–San Rafael Bridge, and a Golden Gate Transit bus stops at this exit every half hour on weekdays and once an hour on weekends as part of its trek between the San Rafael Transit Center and the El Cerrito Bay Area Rapid Transit (BART) station. Those passengers going to the prison walk under the highway overpass and make their way past the charming bungalows and beachfront property along San Quentin Village's Main Street. At the end of the street, a thick yellow line is painted on the ground, just at the edge of the U.S. Post Office on the visitors' right-hand side and the entrance to the prison parking lot on their left. Ahead of them is the East Gate of the facility and an imposing sign announcing CALIFORNIA STATE PRISON: SAN QUENTIN against which giggling tourists occasionally pose for photographs. Turning left and crossing into the parking lot, people confront another sign: NOTICE: BY

---

2. The prime location of San Quentin and the deteriorating conditions of its antiquated buildings have led to debates over the benefits of razing the prison, relocating its inhabitants, and selling the land. Prisoner advocates oppose the closing of San Quentin because its proximity to urban centers makes it the most accessible prison in California for lawyers, family members, and volunteers. At the time of this writing, the debate over this issue continues without resolution (Podger and Fimrite 2001; Ritter 2001; Martin 2005).

Figure 2.1 The Tube and its environs

ENTERING THIS PROPERTY YOU HAVE CONSENTED TO A SEARCH OF PERSON, PROP-
ERTY AND VEHICLE. The warning is followed by numerous prohibitions—
including possession of explosives, alcohol, or drugs; giving articles to
or receiving them from inmates without permission—and is repeated
in Spanish. Just past this sign lies a gray metal door propped open by
a large, soiled, plastic trash can, and above the doorway hangs a third
weather-beaten sign: VISITORS ENTRANCE. Walking through this doorway,
people go into a stark, approximately eighty-foot by six-foot corridor,
a dingy, forlorn, emotionally charged territory in which hundreds of
women and children spend hours of their lives each week: the Tube.

No one could tell me when the moniker "the Tube" came into use,
but correctional staff and visitors alike use it to refer to this concrete-
walled dividing line between general state property and the actual
prison grounds. With a door on either end opening onto the parking lot
and one in the center leading to the visitor-processing area, it is the fun-
nel through which all visitors, including attorneys, enter San Quentin.[3]
Overall, the atmosphere of the Tube evokes the observation of Gresham
Sykes (1958, 8) that "the physical conditions of life in prison would seem

---

3. Staff, volunteers, and administrative guests do not enter via the Tube. Instead, they have
their identification checked by the correctional officer working at the East Gate or West Gate,
who then directs them as needed within the institution, depending on their activity therein.

Figure 2.2 Visitors' entrance to the Tube, with the
prison in the background

to reflect a sort of half-hearted or indecisive punishment, the imposition
of deprivation by indifference or forgetfulness rather than by intent."
The Tube is an unheated structure lit by naked white fluorescent lights.
Because the hydraulic hinges on the two exterior doors are frequently
broken, the doors must be propped open by garbage cans to prevent
them from continually slamming shut; having them simultaneously
ajar transforms the Tube into a mini–wind tunnel through which chilly
gusts blow throughout the day. The outer wall of the Tube has large windows running its length at shoulder height, and through the scratched
glass one can see boats sailing on the bay and stately houses dotting the
lush Tiburon Peninsula opposite the prison. The inner wall holds four
bulletin boards that are bare aside from scattered informational flyers
from the visiting center, religious propaganda posted by visitors, and
memos from the prison about changes in visiting policies or upcoming
holiday schedules. From the time I began working at the prison in 1995,
the area was in a blatant state of disrepair: sections of the ceiling were

ripped out or dangling, exposing the innards of the electrical system, and paint was peeling off the walls. In the late spring of 2000, however, San Quentin had a crew of prisoners summarily fix the structural problems and coat the grimy corridor with fresh white paint.

Logistically, the Tube serves as a means of buffering correctional officers from a flood of oncoming visitors: the processing-area door is locked from the inside, and officers admit one person or one group—all who come to see a single prisoner are admitted together—at a time by pressing a button that temporarily unlocks the door while emitting a high-pitched whine. In addition, the initial containment of people in an excluded zone and the formal and impersonal means of permitting their entry accentuate the tenuous legitimacy of the visitors when on the prison grounds and signal expectations of their deference to authority before they even pass through the door, aptly demonstrating Daphne Spain's (1992, 8) claim that "[p]risons are the clearest example of space being used to reinforce a hierarchy and to assert power." Once inside the processing area, people undergo a series of identity and security checks characteristic of those implemented by what Zygmunt Bauman (1995, 107) calls "factories of order . . . sites of purposeful activity calculated to result in a product conceived in advance . . . restoring certainty, eliminating randomness, making the conduct of the inmates regular and predictable—certain—once more." The visitor first presents a pass she filled out in the Tube and her driver's license or other identification to one of the two officers working at a computer, who locates the prisoner's California Department of Corrections identification number in the database to verify that he is eligible to receive visitors and that the person or people visiting him have been approved to enter the institution.[4] She then hands over her shoes, coat, and other belongings to be sent on a conveyor belt through an x-ray machine, and she walks through a metal

---

4. The only way someone can be approved to visit a prisoner at San Quentin is for the prisoner to send her the required clearance forms. This procedure is designed to protect prisoners' privacy against unknown "fan" visitors who follow publicized crime stories or from surprise visits by rival gang members or other unwanted guests. Potential visitors then return the completed forms to the visiting staff, who run computerized background checks; people with "on-going criminal proceedings" (those who have outstanding warrants, are on parole or probation, are involved in court proceedings, or are taking part in a court-mandated program including drug-treatment and anger-management programs) are prohibited from visiting a prisoner. Former inmates must have written permission from the warden to visit a prisoner, and people discharged from parole must have proof of discharge in addition to written permission from the warden. If someone is denied approval, the prison staff notifies her of this fact in order to protect her privacy; if she is approved to visit, the prisoner is told that he should inform the person that she can visit him. The approval process requires approximately thirty working days (interview with former San Quentin visiting lieutenant, May 10, 2001).

NOTICE

BY ENTERING THIS PROPERTY YOU HAVE CONSENTED TO A SEARCH OF PERSON, PROPERTY AND VEHICLE.

IT IS A FELONY

TO BRING UPON THIS PROPERTY; EXPLOSIVES, INTOXICATING LIQUORS, BEER, WINE, NARCOTICS, BENZADRINE, MARIJUANA OR DANGEROUS DRUGS.

IT IS PROHIBITED

TO GIVE TO OR RECEIVE FROM AN INMATE ANY ARTICLE WITHOUT PRIOR PERMISSION.

AVISO

AL ENTRAR A ESTA INSTITUCION USTED ESTA DE ACUERDO A QUE SE LE REGISTRE A USTED Y A SU VEHICOLO.

ES UN, CRIMEN

BEBIDAS INTOXICANTES, CERVEZA, VINO, NARCOTICOS, BENZEDRINA, MARIJUANA TRATAR DE INTRODUCIR A ESTA INSTITUCION; ARMAS DE FUEGO, EXPLOSIVOS, Y DROGAS PELIGROSAS.

Figure 2.3 Sign outside of the Tube warning of the possibility of "a search of person, property, and vehicle"

detector while the officers assess her clothing and determine whether she conforms to the visitors' dress code. She retrieves her possessions on the other side of the x-ray machine, puts on her shoes, reassembles herself, and collects her ID and her pass, which has been stamped to indicate that she has been "processed" and can move to the next checkpoint. The slightest hitch with documentation, appearance, or behavior can result in a visit's delay at best or its refusal at worst. Visitors with a remediable problem (such as unacceptable clothing) are told they must fix, remove, or replace the offending item before they are readmitted to the processing area, but visitors with more serious problems—such as no record in the computer of institutional approval or lack of official birth certificates for children under eighteen—are told they will not be permitted to visit until the issue is resolved, and they are sent away.

Because the Tube is not surveilled by correctional officers, it provides the final "free" space in which visitors ready themselves for the scrutiny they undergo in the processing area, a space in which they muster the "presentation of self" (Goffman 1959) that occurs once they step onto the prison grounds. It is a liminal space, the boundary between "outside" and "inside," where visitors convert from legally free people into imprisoned bodies for the duration of their stay in the facility. Four days a week in this barren corridor, prisoners' relatives, lovers, and friends perform the mundane actions that cumulatively signify and materialize their denigrated status: prohibited belongings are deposited in lockers, forbidden treasures are secreted in undergarments, necklines are raised and hemlines lowered, gum is spat out, sodas are drained, tempers are bridled, children are hushed. To perform these actions, to wait in the Tube for permission to enter the prison: this is to be "on-line" at San Quentin.

In this chapter, I dissect the Tube as a zone of friction in which visitors prepare for, submit to, and chafe against the control prison officials attempt to exert over their bodies and behaviors as a requisite for admittance to the facility. Following Arnold Van Gennep's (1909; see also Gluckman 1962) analysis of rites of passage, the Tube can be viewed as an area of "suspension" bridging the conditions of "segregation" and "aggregation" found on opposing sides of the penitentiary walls. While hovering between their outside lives and the inner world of the institution, people congregate essential properties and suppress or mask taboo ones to comply with the requirements for their passage from one region to the other, repeating the process each time they move through the intermediary space in accordance with the direction they are heading. An analysis of the various techniques and "ceremonies of degradation" (Garfinkel 1968) used by correctional officials to control prisoners' intimates and kin when they come to the facility illuminates the curious status of visitors as quasi inmates, people at once legally free and palpably bound.

Secondary Prisonization and the Hybrid Status of Prisoners' Intimates and Kin

In his article "People Processing Organizations," Yeheskel Hasenfeld (1972, 257) stipulates that such an organization does not explicitly set out to alter people's behavior: "Rather, it produces changes by identifying and defining the person's attributes, social situation, and public identity, which in turn typically results in both societal and self-reactions." When further comparing people-processing and "people-changing" institutions, Hasenfeld postulates that the former are distinguished by their relatively short-term contact with clients and by the deployment of their activities on the boundaries of the organization, in that their goal is to determine a classification that will be utilized by exterior agencies to effect behavior change in the individual. By contrast, people-changing institutions sustain long-term contact with their wards (students, patients, prisoners) and locate their activities within the center of the organization "particularly as the intensity of the change efforts increases" (Hasenfeld 1972, 257–58).

The application of this model to the experience of coming to see an inmate highlights the peculiar relationship between prison visitors and the correctional authority. In a single visit, a person undergoes processing through a short-term encounter in a peripheral space, then immediately carries her assigned classification to an interior zone where she spends a longer—but still relatively brief—period of time modifying her behavior according to the rules governing her locally imposed status. After her stay she reverses her path, leaving the center and crossing back through the boundary area (this time without enduring any processing activities), officially shedding her temporarily attributed identity. To reenter the prison she will be required to undertake the entire routine from the beginning.[5]

This scenario exposes the ambiguity of Hasenfeld's identification of short-term contact as a distinguishing feature of people-processing organizations, in that each individual session may be concise but a regular visitor will have extensive contact over time with one institution because she is processed frequently. When the experience of being processed is particularly intense or humiliating, one can posit that recurrent exposure to this ordeal will itself become a transformative course, especially if each occurrence is followed by immersion in a distinctively abrasive and depersonalizing environment constructed to modify and control behavior. Indeed, for prison visitors who come to the institution repeatedly, the people-processing and people-changing operations of the correctional facility merge so that individuals are al-

5. People are not allowed to leave the visiting area until the prisoner with whom they have been meeting has been strip-searched and found to be free of contraband. Thus, they are not "released" from their status of prison visitor until it has been verified that they have performed this role in accordance with institutional regulations.

tered both by the initial identity-ascribing procedures to which they are forced to continually submit and by the treatment they receive once they have been classified and enter the official grounds. As Clemmer (1958, 299) notes:

Every man who enters the penitentiary undergoes prisonization to some extent. The first and most obvious integrative step concerns his status. He becomes at once an anonymous figure in a subordinate group. A number replaces a name. He wears the clothes of the other members of the subordinate group. He is questioned and admonished. He soon learns that the warden is all-powerful. He soon learns the ranks, titles, and authority of various officials. And whether he uses the prison slang and argot or not, he comes to know its meanings.

I argue that the prison authorities, ostensibly charged with processing and temporarily containing visitors, establish instead a singular relationship with this population that generates changes in self-images and behaviors through rituals of debasement and the persistent denial of prestige, that is, through the application of what Sykes (1958, 63–84) terms "the pains of imprisonment": the "deprivation of liberty," "deprivation of goods and services," "deprivation of heterosexual relationships," "deprivation of autonomy," and "deprivation of security." What distinguishes this relationship from that formed between officers and prisoners is its temporal scale (visitors are not confined to the facility twenty-four hours a day, seven days a week for many months or years) and the legal status of visitors (who forfeit some rights to enter the prison but are not officially "convicts"). Yet a close analysis of the strictures applied to visitors while on the prison grounds illuminates the parallels between them and their incarcerated loved ones. Indeed, a dissection of prison visiting using the concepts of "prisonization" (Clemmer 1958, 298–320) and the "pains of imprisonment" (Sykes 1958, 64–83) reveals that inmates' associates and kin are subjected to weakened versions of the elaborate regulations, concentrated surveillance, and corporeal confinement governing the lives of ensnared felons and thus are secondarily prisonized by their interactions with the penal institution.

Going Nowhere: Waiting and Lining Up for Visits

You're stuck in the Tube with a million people and everybody's upset cuz there's only one slob in the processing, children are crying, and you know, you just want to get in there, you got to go back to work tomorrow—I mean, there's so much pressure and it's easy to get frustrated and upset with other people [and you get to the point where] it's like, *"Why can't that bitch control her child?"*

A LONGTIME SAN QUENTIN VISITOR

Officially, it is "a privilege," that is, not a legal right, "for inmates to have personal visits while confined in CDC [California Department of Corrections] institutions and facilities"—although visits are ostensibly encouraged as "an avenue to develop and maintain healthy family and community relationships" (California Department of Corrections 1999, 1). San Quentin has four primary forms of visiting. Prisoners in the general population—who are referred to as Mainline prisoners and who are housed in either North Block (higher security), H-Unit (lower security), or on the Ranch (minimum security)—have "contact visits" held in cafeteria-style rooms where people can sit side by side. "Noncontact visits" are allocated to prisoners who are in the Reception Center, in the Adjustment Center (solitary confinement), or who are denied contact visits for security or disciplinary reasons. During noncontact visits the prisoners and visitors are separated by Plexiglas and talk through a speaker system or telephones (hence these visits are also referred to as "phone visits"). Visits for Death Row prisoners take place in individual caged areas called "cubicles" that narrowly accommodate three people, enabling each prisoner and his visitors to touch each other but prohibiting the prisoner from having contact with other inmates or outsiders. The fourth type of visit is "family visits," when eligible family members and eligible prisoners spend two nights together locked in a small complex within the prison.[6] Noncontact, Death Row, and family visits all must be scheduled in advance and occur at specific times, while contact visitors may show up at the time of their choosing within designated hours on a visiting day.

The Tube is informally divided into three areas corresponding to the types of visits, each occupying roughly one-third of its length. In the first segment, between the Main Street door and the processing-area door, wooden planks secured to the wall form benches on both sides of the corridor. This space is assigned to people waiting for noncontact visits and Death Row visits. The next segment, from the processing-area door to the top of an eight-step staircase, is where people with contact visits must stand in line. There are no benches in this portion of the hallway, and the line forms to the left of the door as one stands facing it, alongside a large window between the processing area and

6. The processes of and eligibility criteria for family visits are described at length in chapter 4.

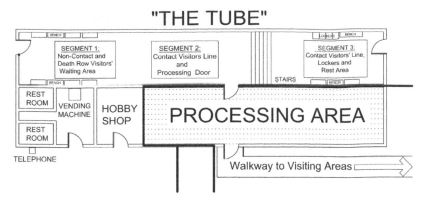

Figure 2.4 Spatial division of the Tube

the Tube that is nearly obscured by outdated memos about visiting procedures and policy alterations taped to the glass, as well as by a change machine in the processing area that blocks a third of the view. On the right-hand side of the door frame an unmarked holder containing the passes visitors are required to complete for entry is suspended five feet from the floor, and below the holder sits a small rickety table typically strewn with half-finished beverages, gnawed ballpoint pens, and visiting passes adorned with children's scrawls. The Tube's final segment runs from the foot of the staircase to the lower door, which opens onto another brief staircase leading to the parking lot. This area has the same wooden-slat benches as the first segment plus a bank of sixty small blue metal lockers in which people can secure their belongings for fifty cents. This space, which is removed from the hub of the processing-area door, is the portion women use to fix their makeup before depositing their handbags in lockers, to change babies' diapers, or to sit and rest on their way in to or out of the prison. On busy days, the line of contact visitors spills down the staircase and through this segment, sometimes winding down the outside steps and into the parking lot.

At any prison, much like at an inner-city emergency room serving a low-income clientele (Abraham 1993, 93–110), the sense of urgency felt by the population trying to get in is unlikely to be matched by the response time of the facility's officials. Although some San Quentin visitors choose to forfeit a portion of visiting time and come later in the day in order to avoid extensive waits and long lines in the Tube, the majority arrive during the peak periods—the two hours before a designated area opens for visitation—in an effort to spend as long as possible with their loved ones. As a result, the average visitor passes a significant quantity of time within the corridor's walls before she enters the confines of the prison. On Thursdays and Fridays contact visiting begins at 11:30 in the morning and lasts until 6:30 in the evening, and on Saturdays and Sundays it starts at 7:30 a.m. and finishes at 2:30 p.m. Queenie and Betty, both of whom visit their husbands two or three days a week, arrive at the Tube between 8:30 and 9 on weekdays and between 5:30 and 6 on weekends in order to secure the first places in line. They make an odd couple, waiting out their previsit vigils together in this bleak atmosphere. Queenie, a sixty-year-old African American who seems closer in age to her forty-year-old spouse, is the mother of fourteen children and has cared for forty-six foster children; her late husband was a Black Panther, and Queenie still limps slightly from a leg injury she explains was caused by a car bomb planted in retaliation for her own political activities. Betty, a white woman in her mid-fifties who met her husband through a Bible-study class for prisoners, wears the sweet, wistful expression of a daydreaming child, occasionally stroking her blonde tresses and singing out pronouncements like "I just really like sugar-plum fairies!" What the two women have in common is that they both are devoted to men with life sentences whom they met and married while the men were incarcerated. Both of them also believe it is worthwhile spending several hours waiting in the Tube before their visits so that they can be at the front of the line and obtain one of the few seats in the visiting room by the windows. According to Queenie:

There're three window seats in the whole visiting room. And both of us [she and her husband] are slightly claustrophobic. It's worth it to me to get up there at nine o'clock, eight thirty, just to know that I'm first on-line and I will get the window seat. . . . I've always felt like, if you're gonna do something, do it. I don't wanna stand on-line, be twenty-fifth on-line, fifteenth on-line, standing there waiting for everybody to get—you know? I'm gonna wait [at] one end or I'm gonna wait [at] this end![7]

The line that Queenie leads begins at the processing door and flows through the middle segment of the Tube, continuing as needed down the stairs into the third segment by the lockers and through the lower door. Since the middle segment has no benches, the first fifteen to

7. In the quest to be first "on-line," head-to-head rivalries can form. Queenie once laughingly explained to me that another visitor had tried to usurp her lead place by arriving thirty minutes earlier than Queenie's customary hour. For the next several visiting days the women vied for first place, each coming earlier and earlier, until the other woman "broke" and returned to showing up at a more typical hour, at which point Queenie also reverted to her usual—and now uncontested—schedule.

twenty visitors in line are required to stand. On weekdays, an average of twenty people who have contact visits form a line between 9:30 and 11:30, while batches of ten to fifteen people who have noncontact or Death Row visits arrive around forty-five minutes in advance of their appointments, which are scheduled at staggered one-hour intervals between 7 and 12:30. On weekends and holidays the corridor teems with women, children, and a scattering of men (usually accompanied by their wives, daughters, or mothers, unless they are clergymen), with the line of bodies often streaming down the stairs and into the parking lot during the hour before visiting begins.[8] Each day, there are typically between five and ten uninitiated visitors grappling for the first time with San Quentin's environment and procedures; the rest of the people awaiting their turn to walk through the prison's door are all too familiar with the grimy concrete and the restless throng in which they must take their places while "doing time" in the Tube.

The presence of Queenie, Betty, and other "regulars" fosters an orderly pattern of lining up for entry based on the principle of "first come, first served" routinely noted by observers of waiting lines (e.g., Schwartz 1975, 93–96) that is punctuated by "time-outs" to relieve the tedium and corporal stress of standing for hours. Women waiting to enter San Quentin follow a simple system for indicating their place in line before processing starts: when a visitor enters the Tube, she fills out the obligatory visiting pass, folds it in half, writes the position of her arrival on it (fourth, ninth, thirteenth), and then slips it under a slender pipe that runs along the wall against which the contact-visitor line forms.[9] This scheme, customarily taught to newcomers by the regulars, enables women to maintain their places while using the restroom, sitting on the benches, smoking cigarettes in the parking lot, or chatting outside of the Tube. However, the system's workability is tenuous, as it relies on a tacit agreement among visitors as to the permissible length of breaks and the counterbalancing amount of time physically devoted to the waiting line required to "demonstrate that [an individual's] right to priority is confirmed by an unquestionable willingness to undergo further suffering" (Mann 1969, 344). Indeed, suspicions that some visitors are usurping other people's numbers, posting passes for friends who arrive later, or posting their passes and then leaving the prison grounds to run er-

8. The California Department of Corrections schedules five holiday visiting days each year: New Year's Day, the Fourth of July, Labor Day, Thanksgiving, and Christmas.

9. This practice is similar to that of Australian soccer fans, who "stake a claim" to hold their place in line by "leaving some item of personal property" to mark their spot while enjoying a temporary reprieve (Mann 1969, 344).

Figure 2.5 Interior of the Tube, with lockers on the right and the processing-area door on the left at the top of the stairs

rands or buy food lead to angry confrontations that occasionally result in verbal complaints made to the processing officers when women enter the facility. The authorities then respond by issuing a memo—multiple copies of which are taped to the windows in the Tube—forbidding the place-holding scheme and legitimating only a lining-up system based on physical presence. Although most visitors ignore these memos and continue securing their numbered passes to the wall, the rules escalate tensions by validating the claims of the minority faction who oppose this practice. The most vocal and formidable personage from this camp during my fieldwork was Carla. Her vociferous eruption one Friday morning illustrates the tendency of people to vent their extreme frustration with the long, degrading lines by further humiliating their peers, rather than by challenging the remote and powerful prison authorities:

———

Carla arrived around 11 this morning and found numerous passes tucked behind the pipe and just a few visitors scattered in the corridor. A statuesque and intimidating woman, she glared at those of us clustered around the processing door.

"Where are all these people?" she demanded harshly. Queenie quietly responded that folks were around, either in the bathroom or smoking, and then calmly walked out of the Tube herself to go mail a letter to her husband.

Carla half-replied to Queenie's back, half-shouted to the general public: "I wanna know where these motherfuckers are! There's a sign right here that says R-E-A-D, and if motherfuckers would read then they'd know they ain't s'posed to put they passes up on the wall and not be here!"

An older woman with painfully swollen legs who was using a cane hoisted herself off the noncontact-visitor bench and shuffled over to the processing-area door, eyes downcast and murmuring worriedly, "Oh, I should stand in line."

"No, ma'am," Carla barked, her slicing voice at odds with her words. "I'm not disrespectin' nobody. If somebody's elderly or has trouble standin', I understand, but these other motherfuckers should be here!" Despite this acknowledgment, Carla did not make further efforts to persuade the old woman to return to her seat, and the lady in fact remained standing in line until she was finally processed over an hour later.

Each time I had seen her previously Carla had made explicit her hatred of the prison and everything connected to it: the guards, the rules, the visitors, the tedious hours of waiting.[10] *On this day, her rage barreled forth, accusing and assaulting everyone in her path; once she finished berating people for posting their passes, she launched an attack on those who jammed up the line for the processing-area metal detector:*

"It takes people all that time to go through the metal detector—it ain't like you motherfuckers are going to go straight through! You should be gettin' ready now to go through that metal detector, take off all that jewelry and them pins outta your hair! It should take one minute for each motherfucker to get processed—if you haven't learned after all these visits what to wear and

10. One day Carla was striding about in the Tube, peering through the processing-area window and muttering, "I need to restrain my anger!" She looked at the other women in line: "You know, they tried to end my visits forever!" "Girl, why?" someone asked. "I put a hole in the wall!" she exclaimed proudly, as people gasped in surprise. "I was *angry!*"

*how to get through the metal detector on the first try you are really a stupid
motherfucker!"*

*The atmosphere in the Tube was excruciatingly tense; the unfortunate new
visitors were petrified and desperately tried to decipher Carla's harangues,
huddling together with hairpins and jewelry clutched in their fists. The regular
visitors were either withdrawing into themselves and trying to block out the
situation (Sophia, who was standing next to me a few feet away from Carla,
seemed to be in a trance, murmuring dreamily, "There's so much emotion in
here") or beginning to seethe with their own rage. As the minutes ticked by,
people started compulsively checking their watches and shifting onto the balls
of their feet to stare into the processing area. Eleven thirty came and went
with no sign of the officers being ready to begin the day's entries; 11:33, 11:37,
11:42 passed, and Carla found new fuel for her fury: "We're unorganized, so
the guards think they can be unorganized! We go in there and don't know what
the fuck we're doing, can't even get through the motherfucking metal detector,
so they think, 'Why should we be on time and know what we're doing?' "*

*When she wasn't yelling Carla was practically panting, breathing heavily
with an obvious effort to contain herself and her fury. The sharp heels of her
stiletto shoes clacked on the concrete as she paced the hallway. I was frozen to
my spot along with the other visitors, barely daring to sneak sideways glances
at her; when I finally braved a head-on look I noticed that her makeup, always heavy and striking, today was completed by thick, perfectly delineated
eyebrows drawn over her outraged eyes.*

—————

As this excerpt from my notes indicates, the unpredictability of
the precise moment when processing begins causes significant strain
for visitors. Barry Schwartz (1975, 38) observes, "Punitive sanctioning
through the imposition of waiting is met in its most extreme forms
when a person is not only kept waiting but is also kept ignorant as to
how long he must wait," which then thrusts the individual "into an
interactionally precarious state wherein he might confront, recognize,
and flounder in his own vulnerability or unworthiness." Regardless of
the official schedule, the commencement of visiting varies by up to
twenty minutes for each group admitted to the prison, and pressure
in the Tube regularly mounts and eases in association with these entrance times. Peaks of apprehension occur every half an hour, correlat-
ing with the times when the noncontact or Death Row visits are announced. Typically, a correctional officer calls for these visits over the
loudspeaker ten to fifteen minutes before the scheduled appointment

time (e.g., 8:45 for visits at 9); the visitors then leave the benches and move to the front of the line, entering the processing-area door one at a time as the buzzer sounds. Some days, however, the announcement will come twenty to twenty-five minutes before the designated time, and other days it will be delayed until the appointed hour or even later. The logic of calling for processing in advance of the appointment is to enable a visitor to be seated in the phone booth or cubicle at the time the visit is scheduled to begin, thereby allotting her the full time of the visit. The tendency for processing to impinge on the precious visiting minutes and the randomness of when the announcement is made cause much anxiety in the Tube, and during the half hour preceding each appointment time trepidation grows as visitors eye their watches, strain their ears for the first crackle of the loudspeaker, and murmur hopes that the officers will call them on time.

On Thursdays and Fridays the contact visitors witness several rounds of noncontact and Death Row appointments before their own waiting reaches its crest. Around 11:10 people going to the North Block and H-Unit areas begin their final preparations for entering the institution, using the dingy, poorly maintained restroom around the corner from the Tube (which visitors claim is preferable to the facilities available in the prison) and readying themselves for processing by locating their passes and driver's licenses, securing their bags in lockers, unlacing their shoes, and removing their belts. By 11:20 Queenie is peering through the window in the processing-area door, through which she can see one officer's desk directly and observe the reflection of the second one in a mirror angled to provide officers with a view of the door. She delivers reports of "who's on" (which officers are working) and what they are doing: "She's got a fork in her mouth and is looking through papers. And he's stuffing his face and talking on the phone!" Knowing which officers are on duty assumes paramount importance for the women because this determines how swiftly visitors will be processed. Certain officers are renowned for strictly interpreting the dress code and for sending virtually everyone to change her attire, nearly doubling the time necessary to process the full line of visitors. Groans also meet Queenie's announcement of a new or substitute officer, since this person is likely to move slowly through the unfamiliar routine and to err on the side of caution when enforcing the rules.

Unlike for noncontact and Death Row visitors, no announcement is made when contact-visitor processing begins: the first signal is the abrupt whine of the door buzzer sometime around 11:30, possibly as late as 11:45. From 11:25 onward, therefore, Queenie teeters on the tiny step in front of the processing-area door, her hand gripping the handle expectantly. The regulars have mastered the special technique required to open the door—a firm wrench of the handle immediately as the buzzer sounds, then a hearty push on the door—and their finesse facilitates a swift and reassuring commencement of processing. Yet many people have difficulty opening the door, sometimes because they are elderly, disabled, or holding a baby and cannot muster the strength needed, sometimes because they do not know how to react to the buzzer and think the door will open automatically, and often because the correctional officers do not activate the buzzer long enough for someone to turn the door handle and push. This last problem causes consternation in the Tube since it is hard to discern whether the officers genuinely cannot calculate how long someone needs to enter the door, or whether, as many women suspect, the officers deliberately abbreviate the time they sound the buzzer in order to "play with" the visitors.[11] This combination of an uncertain and unannounced commencement point and an obscure, awkward entry procedure plunges individuals into a "practice [that] leaves the client in a psychologically as well as ritually unsatisfactory state" and thus "by causing [the] client to become tense or nervous the server undermines the self-confidence necessary for him to maintain proper composure" (Schwartz 1975, 39).

The times of highest tension in the Tube occur when processing is under way for noncontact, Death Row, and contact visitors simultaneously (between 11:30 and 12:30 on Thursdays and Fridays and throughout the morning on Saturdays and Sundays). Correctional officers have no way of viewing the lines in the Tube unless they leave their desks and open the processing-area door, and they therefore begin calling noncontact or Death Row visitors according to the appointment time without knowing how many people are waiting for contact visits. Frequently, therefore, someone at the end of the contact-visitor line will just reach the door when an announcement is made for noncontact visits, and she will then need to wait an additional fifteen or twenty minutes while the noncontact visitors are admitted to the facility. On busy mornings, noncontact-visitor and Death Row processing may suspend contact-visitor processing multiple times, meaning that someone arriving at 11 for 11:30 visiting might be delayed by both the 12 and the 12:30 appointments, not entering the prison until 12:45 or later.

11. Women feel their suspicions are confirmed when the officers sound the buzzer in short quick bursts to the tune of "shave-and-a-haircut" while the visitors are trying to enter the door. However, it is not clear whether the officers intend to agitate the women or rather are trying to share a lighthearted gesture with them.

Even more unpredictable than the morning waiting lines is the period when entering visitors must wait for "count" to finish. Prisoners in San Quentin are physically counted multiple times throughout the day in order to verify that all bodies are present and no one has escaped. Each day there is an institutional count at 4 p.m., in preparation for which all "movement" (the transfer of inmates from one area to another, such as from a cell to the visiting room) ceases at 3. This means that contact visitors must enter the institution before 2:30 so that everyone can be at his or her final destination within the next half hour.[12] Anyone not present before the deadline must wait until the count "clears" (that is, until the officials are certain all prisoners are on-site); swift counts finish within thirty minutes, but typically the 4 p.m. count clears between 4:45 and 5:15. Even for women who know about count, meeting its exigencies is stressful: from 2 to 2:30, women race into the Tube directly from work or from their children's schools, swearing at the sluggish traffic or the late buses, perspiring and panting as they frantically dash to the processing door. However, many women, especially new visitors or those who have only visited on weekends, do not know about count and stroll into the Tube from 2:30 onward, only to be instructed by the correctional officers that they will be admitted "after the four o'clock count." The imprecision of this starting time is agonizing for people as they stand impotently in the concrete corridor and watch the clock edge closer to 6:30, when visiting ends for the day.

———

By 4:15 there were six women in the Tube, and as always at that hour, the entire focus was on when count would clear. People were starting to mill around the entrance and line up, and Lupé, the leader of the line, placed her hand vigilantly on the processing-area doorknob, keeping it there even while she spoke with us. As with contact visiting in the morning, they don't make an announcement when postcount processing begins, so the first woman in line always hovers anxiously around the door, eager to push her way inside as soon as she hears the shriek of the buzzer.

"What's the longest it's taken for count to clear?" one new visitor asked. The regulars all groaned.

12. Because weekend visiting ends at 2:30, the 4 p.m. count does not interfere with processing on Saturdays and Sundays.

"You don't wanna know," Grace replied heavily. *"You* really *don't wanna know."*

There's no reliable way to discern how far along count is, although sometimes it's possible to dimly hear the clanging bell that's rung when all is clear. Around 4:55 today, our collective audio hallucinations began. "I think that's the bell!" Linda pronounced, unzipping her heavy coat in anticipation of going through the metal detector.

"Yeah, I hear it too!" Lupé cried excitedly. Silence fell in the Tube as we all listened attentively, nodding our heads. Our premature optimism disintegrated when, ten minutes later, nothing had happened. Darkness descended outside, and I noticed that I could see my breath under the harsh fluorescent lights. A few people began muttering insults about the guards. "How hard is it to count?*" one remarked sourly.*

"Some people cain't count!" cackled Dee. "That's why we ain't got no president!" [13] *Everyone burst into laughter, and Dee—sensing she was on a roll—continued: "These people got* master's, *all the degrees you can get, an' they cain't figure this out!" She shook her head, bemused. "We should just have four more years of Clinton! I like Clinton! You don't want your president to be all uptight! You want your president to be relaxed." She cocked her head at us, mischievously, "So what if he 'got some' on the side? He's relaxed." The other women chuckled appreciatively.*

"Ooh, look!" Lupé called out. "The mens is back!" We craned our necks to look through the entry-door window and saw the handful of prisoners who work in the processing area troop back to their posts. It was commonly agreed that this was a good sign: surely count must have cleared if there was inmate movement. Still, no officers were visible in the vicinity. At 5:15 we heard a nearby phone start ringing, probably the watch commander giving the guards the OK to start letting in visitors. The phone rang and rang and rang, its forlorn trill the only sound as the women—their patience now exhausted, their spirits now deflated—glared at the wall and fidgeted angrily. Ten rings. Fifteen. Twenty. "Answer the phone," *commanded Grace, her voice steely and low.* "Just pick it up and *answer it."*

This blend of certain uncertainty and enforced time wasting also plagues noncontact and Death Row visitors during the endurance test they must undergo before even arriving at San Quentin: calling

13. This conversation occurred shortly after the contested Bush-Gore presidential election in November 2000 and the ensuing recount of the Florida votes.

for an appointment. Appointments are not required for contact visits, but the logistics of assembling people in booths or cubicles for fixed chunks of time make them a necessity for noncontact and Death Row visits. To schedule an appointment, people must call a dedicated number at the prison at 8 a.m. on the appropriate day.[14] Those who work or have other commitments at 8, or who do not have a phone, are obliged to make alternative arrangements, usually relying on family or friends to phone for them. Scores of women complain bitterly about this process, which typically involves twenty-to-forty minutes of intense effort to reach a human voice. Laura, a thirty-eight-year-old white U.S. postal worker engaged to a man on Death Row, explained:

[Sometimes] we get a recording that the visiting call line is open from 8 a.m. to 10 a.m., and, at 8:05, you'll get the recording that tells you all the visits are full . . . [After repeated busy signals, when the phone starts ringing] sometimes it'll ring two, three minutes, I've timed it! I think it rang two minutes, two minutes and thirty-nine seconds, and then all of a sudden [it] converts to the busy signal. Or it will ring, and then a recording will come on and say, um, your party's not answering and this line doesn't take a message. The hardest part is just the constant, when it's busy-busy-busy-busy.

Laura's friend Bernice, a forty-four-year-old African American nurse's assistant also engaged to a condemned inmate, described the teamwork this process fosters among Death Row visitors:

[We] all work together, me and Laura and a few other ladies. We start on ourself first, and once we get ourself in, then we start jumping on the next person, and then the next person. That's the only way it works. Laura does it for me when she is able to get to the phone and I can't, because I work eight to eight, nights, eight at night you know to eight in the morning. . . . So, most of the time lately Laura's been getting me in, because she's had better luck. I mean we sit there with two telephones each, sometimes I have two, I have two cell phones going and a telephone, and she has two telephones going, trying to get in.

I experienced these difficulties firsthand when Sophia, a thirty-seven-year-old white nanny whose husband is serving a life sentence, asked me to call for her appointment because she needed to work early

14. At the beginning of my fieldwork period people called three days in advance of their visits. As of August 2000, the regulations changed to require scheduling of noncontact visits one week in advance.

one morning and could not access a phone.[15] According to her instructions, I made my first call to the prison at 7:55 a.m. and immediately received a busy signal. During the next thirty-nine minutes I received a busy signal and hit the redial button 190 times; four times the call was not completed and I heard silence on the line; one time my call was misdirected within the San Quentin phone system; and one time I reached a recording that informed me "the number you have dialed is not in service." On the 197th try the phone rang, and after twenty-seven rings the attending officer responded, at which point I was tremendously anxious that all of the appointments would be full. Fortunately, this was not the case, and I successfully completed the phone call at 8:34.[16]

Unlike being "on hold" for an operator while tuning out Muzak, listening for busy signals and redialing absorbs the caller's attention and hands, prohibiting her from attending to other tasks, drinking her morning coffee, or focusing on the television or radio. Noncontact visitors are permitted to schedule two one-hour appointments a week, one on a weekday and one on a weekend, so regular visitors must forfeit up to an hour of their week to secure two hours of visiting time. Death Row visitors are also limited to two visits per week, but each of their visits lasts two hours, so they spend approximately one hour on the phone for every four hours of visitation. This assumes that the caller actually obtains a visit each time she phones, since due to limited numbers of booths and cubicles not everyone can be accommodated each day; once all of the appointments are scheduled, there is no waiting list and no priority is given for future appointments to those who were unable to arrange a visit on a certain day.

The three types of waits imposed on visitors of San Quentin—the morning waiting line, the count period, and the redial purgatory of appointment scheduling—converge to signify the devaluation of prisoners' intimates and kin in the eyes of the authorities. Indeed, "the distribution of waiting time coincides with the distribution of power" since "waiting limits productive uses of time and in so doing generates distinct social and personal costs" (Schwartz 1975, 5). For this reason, "queuing is confined largely to the less-privileged groups in society"

15. Sophia and her husband normally enjoyed contact visits, but at this juncture he was in solitary confinement and therefore was restricted to noncontact visits.
16. I tape-recorded this entire process in a manner that allowed me to hear all that happened on the phone line. For the first fifteen minutes I made observational comments about my thoughts and levels of nervousness, but by the 100th redial I was punching the buttons in grim silence, only tersely noting the time at periodic intervals.

(Mann 1969, 353), whose time is considered inferior to and more expendable than that of the higher-ups running the show. Tellingly, personal association with a prisoner de facto erases any other privileges connected to economic or cultural capital when it comes to visitor processing: although most people lining up to enter San Quentin are low-income African Americans or Hispanics, the well-to-do white women coming to see their loved ones endure the exact same conditions of waiting as everyone else. Only attorneys enjoy a modicum of priority and are allowed to ring a buzzer by the processing-area door that alerts officers to their presence, yet even they are subjected to extensive delays when officers fail to respond promptly.

The lengthy and inefficient waits required for visiting a prisoner do not just belittle the worth of his family's and friends' time—they deprecate the importance of the visit itself, the preciousness of moments spent with those who are otherwise physically barred from one's presence, as argued by Lynn, a thirty-eight-year-old white fund-raiser whose fiancé is serving twenty-five years to life:

[F]or instance, visiting hours are seven thirty to two thirty. But they don't start processing you until seven thirty. And that's a frustration to me in that: "No, I would like to be face-to-face by seven thirty. Why can't you start processing at seven fifteen?" What is the problem with the mentality behind starting processing fifteen minutes prior to visiting time? . . . [Once processing begins] then they take their time, and they have to know that every minute—or maybe they don't. Maybe it's just a matter of not really comprehending, *every minute* is so valuable.

For many women, it is this disparagement of the sanctity of visiting time that wounds most deeply. Those who arrive hours in advance at the prison gates accept long waits as a logical precondition, having "wised up" in Clemmer's (1958, 300) sense to the prison dictates that this is part of the "agreement" that must be made when free people wish to enter the institutional walls. Some even endorse the authorities' devaluation of their time, asserting, "I don't mind waiting, I have nothing better to do," while others recast their lost hours as investment in their relationships.[17] However, women strongly resent their lack of autonomy over *what* time they sacrifice, and while tempers may be relatively placid when processing is not expected to be under way and people know they are wasting "free" time, tensions soar as soon

17. Following Schwartz (1975, 42), "because suspension of activity in deference to another entails forfeiture of alternative activities and associated rewards, deferential waiting comes sharply into view as a functional equivalent to sacrifice."

as women understand that the wait is impinging on potential visiting moments. Indeed, Lynn's anger over the starting time for processing evokes Sykes's (1958, 74) observation that "the many regulations and orders of the . . . official regime often arouse the prisoner's hostility because they don't 'make sense' from the prisoner's point of view," and while fifteen extra minutes may seem a small favor to ask, "the incomprehensible order or rule is a basic feature of life in prison."

"It Reminds Me of a Slave-Holding Tank:" Architecture and Design in the Tube

Today, shortly after ten o'clock, a heavyset woman, winded from the climb up the small staircase, took a seat with her young daughter by the noncontact visitors. A short while later an officer stuck his head into the Tube and looked at the benches, saying, "You all here for noncontact visits?"

The woman hesitated, then replied tiredly, "Oh, I'm just lazy, I'm here for Mainline."

"Well, ma'am, you need to stand in line then, I'm afraid. Otherwise it causes problems, right?" the officer said politely, looking at the other visitors for confirmation. The cluster of people ducked their heads uneasily and avoided his gaze.

The woman heaved herself to her feet, nudging her daughter off the bench as well: "Come on, Boo, we gotta stand." As the officer withdrew into the processing area, the woman sighed loudly and lumbered over to the contact-visitors' line. The person standing behind her placed a hand on her shoulder and offered kindly, "Don't worry, you can sit. I know you're here," but the visitor ahead of both of them shook her head disapprovingly, clucking, "Well, I wouldn't want to have to be told twice." The heavyset woman remained standing for the next ninety minutes, repositioning her weight uncomfortably and occasionally leaning on the windowsill for support, eventually shooing her wriggling daughter back to the benches to rest.

––––––

The architecture and design of the Tube—coldly functional, inhospitable, and lacking basic amenities—mirrors Sykes's (1958, 7) description of the interior of a prison: "The most striking feature is, perhaps, its drabness. It has that 'institutional' look shared by police stations, hospitals, orphan asylums, and similar public buildings—a Kafka-like atmosphere compounded of naked electric lights, echoing corridors, walls encrusted with the paint of decades." (See also Irwin 1985, 59–61.) The above extract from my field notes suggests that the Tube also can be considered a "disabling environment" (Hann 1983), one that contains structural barriers that block or impede participation in an activity. That women must covet the "privilege" of sitting for an hour or more on a hard wooden bench signals the low status hampering them throughout their dealings with correctional authorities. Multiple physical stressors compound this message of inferiority, communicating lowliness through corporeal discomfort. Seated or standing, adults in the Tube shift, pace, fidget, and rock, while their children squirm, holler, whine, and cry. Pregnant women perch awkwardly on the narrow benches, supporting their bellies in their hands because they cannot recline far enough to relieve their backs of the weight of their wombs. Elderly people, many of them using canes, lower themselves precariously onto the wooden slabs. Mothers of infants clumsily assemble feeding bottles and apply fresh diapers in the absence of clean water, sanitary surfaces, or changing tables. Mothers of toddlers clasp their antsy children in their arms, unwilling to let them play on the filthy floor; and mothers of school-age kids, unable to leave their place in line, yell impotently as their offspring gallop down the hallway and into the parking lot. The concrete corridor's acoustics amplify and echo every outburst, squeal, tantrum, and reprimand, and visitors brace themselves against this cacophony while shivering with cold, slumping with fatigue, and dodging the wasps that periodically emerge from their nests in the ceiling.

The Tube's conditions signal officials' disregard for the waiting populace. Queenie offers this somber analogy between her predicament and that of her ancestors: "[The Tube] reminds me of a slave-holding tank. Every time I walk in there and look out the windows at the water, all I can think is a place to hold slaves till the ship comes in." In his study of welfare waiting rooms, Charles Goodsell (1984, 473) notes the small but significant elements present in a few select agencies that inform clients that their well-being is of concern to the staff. In addition to providing physical commodities such as "ample seating" and "application-completion tables, raised to a comfortable height for writing . . . [that are] equipped with working ballpoint pens attached by chains," attentive bureaus advertise pertinent information, ensuring that "[o]ffice hours are clearly posted" and "[r]acks of forms and program brochures stand in prominent view and are kept filled." Such services are entirely absent in the Tube. The dearth of amenities such as adequate seating, a functioning water fountain, and a clean restroom

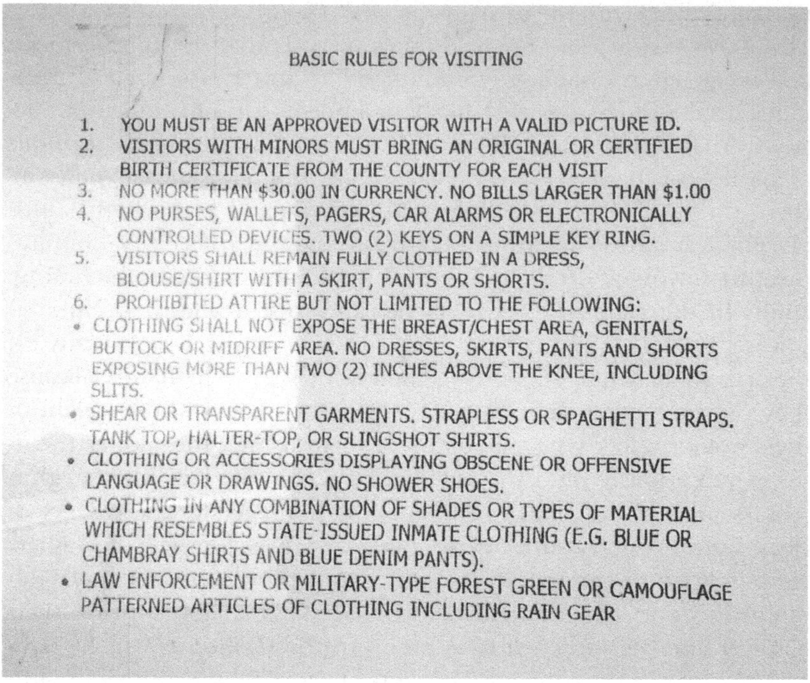

BASIC RULES FOR VISITING

1. YOU MUST BE AN APPROVED VISITOR WITH A VALID PICTURE ID.
2. VISITORS WITH MINORS MUST BRING AN ORIGINAL OR CERTIFIED BIRTH CERTIFICATE FROM THE COUNTY FOR EACH VISIT
3. NO MORE THAN $30.00 IN CURRENCY. NO BILLS LARGER THAN $1.00
4. NO PURSES, WALLETS, PAGERS, CAR ALARMS OR ELECTRONICALLY CONTROLLED DEVICES. TWO (2) KEYS ON A SIMPLE KEY RING.
5. VISITORS SHALL REMAIN FULLY CLOTHED IN A DRESS, BLOUSE/SHIRT WITH A SKIRT, PANTS OR SHORTS.
6. PROHIBITED ATTIRE BUT NOT LIMITED TO THE FOLLOWING:
   - CLOTHING SHALL NOT EXPOSE THE BREAST/CHEST AREA, GENITALS, BUTTOCK OR MIDRIFF AREA. NO DRESSES, SKIRTS, PANTS AND SHORTS EXPOSING MORE THAN TWO (2) INCHES ABOVE THE KNEE, INCLUDING SLITS.
   - SHEAR OR TRANSPARENT GARMENTS. STRAPLESS OR SPAGHETTI STRAPS. TANK TOP, HALTER-TOP, OR SLINGSHOT SHIRTS.
   - CLOTHING OR ACCESSORIES DISPLAYING OBSCENE OR OFFENSIVE LANGUAGE OR DRAWINGS. NO SHOWER SHOES.
   - CLOTHING IN ANY COMBINATION OF SHADES OR TYPES OF MATERIAL WHICH RESEMBLES STATE-ISSUED INMATE CLOTHING (E.G. BLUE OR CHAMBRAY SHIRTS AND BLUE DENIM PANTS).
   - LAW ENFORCEMENT OR MILITARY-TYPE FOREST GREEN OR CAMOUFLAGE PATTERNED ARTICLES OF CLOTHING INCLUDING RAIN GEAR

Figure 2.6 Basic Rules for Visiting sign

with a baby-changing facility in the area is conspicuous. So too is the lack of essential facts and tips for visitors. Despite the plethora of memos, flyers, and signs decorating the corridor, no directions are displayed telling visitors how to enter the prison. There is a Basic Rules for Visiting sign hung at the far end of the hallway near the Main Street door briefly listing various stipulations in small, bland typescript:

1. You must be an approved visitor with a valid picture ID
2. Visitors with minors must bring an original or certified birth certificate from the county for each visit
3. No more than $30.00 in currency. No bills larger than $1.00
4. No purses, wallets, pagers, car alarms or electronically controlled devices. Two (2) keys on a simple key ring
5. Visitors shall remain fully clothed in a dress, blouse/shirt with a skirt, pants or shorts.

Among uninitiated visitors, these poorly worded rules increase confusion rather than provide answers. Whose birth certificate exactly is required when visiting with a minor? Are coins allowed as well as one-dollar bills? If purses and wallets are forbidden, are diapers, baby formula, tampons, or prescribed medication permitted? The handwritten admonishments posted around and on the processing-area door provide no further enlightenment: NO BLUE, NO EXCEPTIONS! NO HAIRPIECES, NO WIGS, NO EXCEPTIONS! Nowhere among this mosaic of stipulations can new visitors find the instructions they need to fill out a visiting pass, wait on the benches for noncontact or Death Row visits until the appointment time is announced, wait in line for contact visits, or turn the processing-door handle when the buzzer sounds.

Even for long-term and regular visitors, the Tube is often a zone of uncertainty. On any given day, people arriving at San Quentin might discover handwritten signs taped to the windows and walls advertising an immediate alteration of policy; these changes apply to dress-code regulations, processing protocol, access to certain areas of the institution, or other aspects of the visiting regimen. One example was the posting on August 17, 2000, of a memo dated July 31, 2000, that announced a change in procedure effective August 17. The memo stated that "to better accommodate the needs of the public and those of the inmate population" the scheduling of appointment visits would occur seven days in advance of the visit instead of three days beforehand. Disgruntled visitors immediately identified the inherent problem with the new policy: many people routinely came to the prison between 7:30 and 9:30 in the morning and therefore were not able to make the requisite phone call at 8 for the following week's visit. "How'm I s'posed to be on the phone when I'm up here visitin'?" one woman demanded angrily, while another shook her head plaintively, "I be on the bus between eight and ten gettin' up here, so how'm I supposed to be callin' then?" As noted by Celina, a twenty-three-year-old African American who made a three-hour round-trip commute on public transportation twice each week during her partner's six-month sentence, the memo's claim "to better accommodate" the needs of the visitors was questionable: "Accommodate *who?* Accommodate people with cars, with cell phones, people in the workforce." In addition, the lack of advance notice regarding the policy change further aggrieved women, since they had already missed their opportunity to phone for the next week's visit. Constrained by work schedules and childcare arrangements, many people were not able to come on an alternate day and therefore had to forfeit the following week's reunion and not see their loved one for fourteen days.

While short-notice alterations cause considerable confusion and anxiety, other adjustments may be made without notification, as I observed one Saturday:

———

When I arrived at 8:45 the Tube was fairly busy, and within the hour it became much more so. Today the guards were using some new "Station A" and "Station B" system to process visitors, and it was not going well at all. There was no information up in the Tube, and the loudspeaker just kept blaring unintelligibly (apparently calling "Station A!" and "Station B!"). Everyone was totally baffled, asking each other, "What's Station A?" "What station is North Block?" and other questions. The conversation generated by the confusion caused even more commotion because it became so noisy you couldn't hear the loudspeaker, so people really didn't know what was going on. Folks kept stumbling in at the wrong time, and the officers kept shooing them out. Women who were long-time visitors and usually knew what they were doing were suddenly perplexed, and everybody was growing fearful of doing the wrong thing and becoming reluctant to go in because they didn't want to annoy the guards, who apparently were growing more and more irritated. Calling visits in this way also heightened tensions among the visitors, because there was so much more room for error: people were snapping at each other and jostling each other around since there was suddenly this new division among visitors. So everyone was off balance and uneasy from the start.

Finally at noon a female officer—whom I had heard women refer to as "Broom-Hilda" [18] *due to her "witchy" attitude and fondness for sending people to change clothes—came out into the Tube to kill some wasps about which a woman had complained. She was actually very pleasant, although I could sense the military roughness that she must display to the women: she was corpulent, with penciled-in eyebrows, wore her hair swept severely back into a bun, and exuded a definite no-nonsense attitude. She "borrowed" someone's newspaper and ferociously battered two wasps to death, telling us that she had just single-handedly rid her house of three wasps' nests. Then she looked around the Tube and hollered, "Now where are those signs?" Marching back into the processing area, she returned a few minutes later with two large, hand-written, cardboard signs reading "Station A: Mainline and H-Unit" and "Station B: Non-Contact Visits and Ranch."*

18. Broom-Hilda is the name of a witch in an eponymous comic strip series by Russell Myers.

Figure 2.7 Handwritten sign announcing visiting changes

"Now I see why everyone was so confused!" she exclaimed. "I thought these signs were up!"

———

Abrupt policy changes have a similar effect on regular visitors as the lack of information has on new visitors, feeding a sense of commingled bewilderment, helplessness, and fear. As Sarah, a thirty-one-year-old white account manager for a high-tech firm who has been visiting her lifer husband for two years, remarks: "That's probably what is the biggest challenge for me, is the fact that nothing stays the same there [at San Quentin]. They're constantly changing the rules . . . there's no consistency, there's no stability, nothing stays the same, and that sort of living in the unknown is *really* difficult." Although a moderate delay or glitch in the line of communication from the institutional authorities to the visitors would be a natural feature of a large bureaucracy (Lipsky 1980), disorientation seems to be "deliberately fostered by the prison officials in that explanations are often withheld as a matter of calculated policy. Providing explanations carries an implication that those who are ruled have a right to know—and this in turn suggests that if the explanations are not satisfactory, the rule or order will be changed" (Sykes 1958, 74–75). Indeed, excluding people from knowledge about institutional decisions that affect them "gives staff a special basis of distance from and control over inmates" (Goffman 1961, 9). As with the imposition of agonizingly long and uncertain waits, sudden and arcane policy alterations deny visitors autonomy by blocking their ability to comprehend and thus to predict, contest, or remedy the conditions affecting them at the prison. Similarly, by failing to provide sufficient amenities to cover visitors' physical and hygienic needs and by withholding elementary advice and using designs of "secrecy" to engender feelings of apprehension and powerlessness (see Spain 1992, 18–21), officials mark those forced to wait in the corridor as disgraced beings.

―――――

A delayed entry, a missed visit, a foreign procedure, a perplexing sign: these events and details accrue in the lives of visitors at San Quentin, imposing on them a sense of dishonor even before they are permitted into the institution. During their wait in the preparatory space of the Tube, visitors are subjected to mortifying practices that communicate the group's diminished worth and generate feelings of stigma, confusion, trepidation, and humiliation. Deprived of physical comfort and basic information, obliged to comply with impractical and unpredictable regimens, visitors learn—much like their partners, sons, fathers, or friends—that from the moment they enter this bleak corridor their identities are that of "anonymous figure[s] in a subordinate group" (Clemmer [1958, 299), namely, quasi-incarcerated beings who will be treated as such while on the facility's grounds.

"We're So over a Barrel!"
Processing and the Struggle for Personhood

There were two visitors in line. The first was an older woman, probably in her early seventies, with a cloud of white hair hovering around her crinkled face.

She was wearing an oversized purple shirt unbuttoned over a heavy, white T-shirt and loose black pants. When the buzzer sounded the woman faltered with the cumbersome door and the second visitor, a middle-aged woman dressed in a high-buttoned blouse and floor-length skirt with her hair pinned in a chignon, assisted her with a strong shove. A minute later we heard raised voices, and the second woman cocked her head to see through the processing window, staring intently at the commotion: "Oh, they're so terrible! That poor woman in there is saying that she can't wear a bra because of a medical condition, but they're telling her she can't come in without a bra. As if she's going to try to be sexy! What a dishonorable thing to do to someone!" The woman watched a few minutes more, spitting with anger: "I wish we didn't feel we're so over a barrel with these people! We have to do everything they say!"

A moment later, the older woman came out of processing. I was perplexed: she was carrying the wooden tray in which belongings are sent through the x-ray machine. A bra, some jewelry, and her shoes were scattered in the tray, and the woman was in her stocking feet. She wandered to the end of the Tube, looking a bit dazed, so I went after her. "Can I help you, ma'am?" She quietly asked me where the bathroom was, and I took her around the corner, warning her to watch out for glass shards as we crossed over the asphalt and sidewalk. "This is the worst place I've ever been to," she remarked, with a touch of venom. "Thank you, dear." She went into the dilapidated bathroom, returning to the Tube a few minutes later and then disappearing into the processing area once more.

Once they leave the Tube and enter the processing area, visitors commence their official registration as temporary occupants of San Quentin State Prison. To do so, they must submit to "[a]dmission procedures [that] might better be called 'trimming' or 'programming' because in thus being squared away the new arrival allows himself to be shaped and coded into an object that can be fed into the administrative machinery of the establishment, to be worked on smoothly by routine operations" (Goffman 1961, 16). Item by item, correctional officers scrutinize people's documents, attire, and belongings to determine whether to permit them direct access to the facility or whether to require a clarification or modification of some sort. Prison officials state that they design the criteria for visitor approval in the interest of institutional safety by attempting to verify that everyone coming into the prison is legally authorized to visit, unarmed, not transporting contraband (defined as any item not explicitly permitted in the prison), and dressed in a nonprovocative manner that can be easily distinguished from prisoners and correctional staff.[19] Each regulation corresponds to a prison-security concern, and compliance with the ensemble of rules thus results in "docile bodies" (Foucault 1977, 135–69), inhibited and humbled versions of the visitors' selves suited to the prison environment and its requisites.

"My Penitentiary Wardrobe": The Regulation of Apparel and Belongings

In an environment of strict social constraint, high value is placed on symbols of bodily control (see Douglas 1970). Clothing, "a key technique in the performance of identities," is a "recurring target" (Skidmore 1999, 515, 514) for corporeal regulation, particularly the management of sexual expression. At San Quentin, dress-code violations are the most common problem visitors encounter during processing. On average, each day one-quarter of all visitors are ordered to change some aspect of their attire before they are permitted into the facility; on busy days or days when particularly strict officers are on duty, this number easily rises to one-third or more. A primary reason the dress code causes abundant difficulties is that visitors are not advised of it in advance: when prisoners are told to notify their family and friends of the institution's approval of their visiting privileges, the inmates are not consistently given information about the dress code or visiting hours to pass along to their loved ones.[20] As a result, most people arrive at the prison outfitted in the clothes of everyday life—blue jeans, sleeveless or white T-shirts, thigh-high skirts—and are refused entry based on their apparel.

The fact that the dress code proscribes many ordinary garments, styles, fabrics, and colors makes adherence to it problematic, especially for people on low budgets who cannot afford to augment their wardrobes (and the wardrobes of their children over two feet tall, who must also comply with the rules). Among the forbidden items are those

19. Interview with former San Quentin visiting lieutenant, May 10, 2001.

20. The lack of information given to prisoners about visiting (and, sometimes, prisoners' lack of comprehension of any visiting information they are given) is a major problem for people who are trying to visit San Quentin. People often arrive at the prison without having filled out visiting forms or without having made an appointment for a noncontact visit because the prisoner did not know or communicate that this was necessary. Visitors also frequently come to San Quentin at the wrong time or during a period when they are prohibited from entering the prison due to the lack of information provided to them.

detailed in the earlier-mentioned Basic Rules for Visiting sign in the Tube:

Prohibited attire but [*sic*] not limited to the following:

- Clothing shall not expose the breast/chest area, genitals, buttock or midriff area. No dresses, skirts, pants, and shorts exposing more than two (2) inches above the knee, including slits.
- Shear [*sic*] or transparent garments, strapless or spaghetti straps, tank top, halter-top, or slingshot shirts.
- Clothing or accessories displaying obscene or offensive language or drawings. No shower shoes.
- Clothing in any combination of shades or types of material which resembles state-issued inmate clothing (e.g. blue or chambray shirts and blue denim pants).
- Law enforcement or military-type forest green or camouflage patterned articles of clothing including rain gear.

In addition to being awkwardly phrased, the derogatory wording of this list infantilizes visitors by reproaching them as if they were children who needed to be taught the basic rules of civilized life ("Don't expose your genitals!"). The clear targeting of women's sexual expression indicates the assumption of a hypersexualized body and the need for a systematic enforcement of "moral" attire.[21] Also, this list does not warn visitors of all of the dress-code pitfalls: no bright yellow (the color of prisoners' rain gear), no bright orange (the color of high-security prisoners' jumpsuits), no white T-shirts (worn by many prisoners), no overalls (the shoulder snaps trigger the metal detector), no hats, gloves, or scarves (considered security risks), and no shirts displaying any of the shoulder area or sweatpants with writing across the derrière (considered sexually provocative). Yet it would be impossible to warn visitors of *all* of the rules because—like "Station A and Station B"—they are subject to erratic changes without notice. During my observations, several new rules were announced (usually by a handwritten sign taped to the processing door), rigorously implemented for several weeks, and then abandoned for no identifiable reason, a sequence that delegiti-

---

21. Such regulation evokes parallels with nineteenth-century Anglo portrayals of African women as animalistic and lascivious temptresses possessing overdeveloped sexual organs that could hardly be covered or restrained (see Fausto-Sterling 1995). As Susan Bordo (1993, 9–11) notes, these images exert considerable influence over contemporary Western culture.

mated the policies in visitors' eyes and reminded one of Sykes's (1958, 73) comment that "it is precisely the triviality of much of the officials' control which often proves to be most galling."

The regulation of garments during visitor processing even encompasses undergarments, and virtually every woman on her first visit is sent away to remove the wire from her underwire bra so that she can pass through the metal detector without triggering the alarm. This causes embarrassment and consternation among visitors, both because of the intimate nature of the offending item (often brought to women's attention by a male correctional officer) and because rectification of the problem involves either wearing a communal soft-cup bra offered by the visiting center or ruining one's own bra by cutting the fabric so that the wires can be detached.[22] Once they have eviscerated one bra, visitors add it to their San Quentin-designated wardrobe: "I got my regular bras, an' I got my penitentiary bras!" one woman joked.

After a visitor has undergone processing several times, she learns that not only does the official dress code change frequently and unpredictably but it is irregularly and haphazardly applied. Women complain bitterly about certain officers, deemed to be stringent to the point of harassment, who order people to raise their arms above their head to determine if their shirts rise unacceptably high, consider "transparent" any apparel that allows the outline of an undergarment to be seen, or deny entry to toddlers wearing blue denim. These officers earn their tough reputations in contrast to their more relaxed colleagues who wave visitors through who are not in flagrant violation of the dress code, overlooking dubious attire or minor infractions.[23] The range in leniency means that people may have a single outfit accepted one day and rejected another, as Fern, a forty-three-year-old white substance-abuse counselor for a correctional facility whose parole-violator fiancé is serving six months, observes: "You wear the same outfit for five or six visits, and all of a sudden it's not appropriate. And so you have to

22. When someone is stopped by the metal detector due to her bra, the correctional staff sends her to the restroom on the other side of the Tube with a thumbtack to pierce the bra's fabric and remove the wire. However, thumbtacks are too blunt and hard to maneuver when ripping the strong underseam of a bra. After gouging my finger while assisting one woman—who caught me off guard when she wordlessly handed me the thumbtack, hiked her black T-shirt above her rose-tattooed breast, and expectantly presented the seam of her lacy bra to me—I started keeping a small pair of sharp-nosed scissors in my backpack for women to use.

23. These two styles of processing correspond to the "two competing models of prison officer work" noted by Alison Liebling (2000, 346), the "rule following/compliance model" and the "negotiation model."

go change. . . . And all that time that you're taking to change, most of that's coming off your visit." Because there are two processing stations (one on each side of the processing area) in operation most of the day, this spectrum of enforcement also means that visitors being processed simultaneously may experience significantly different treatment. The erratic interpretation of the dress code undermines women's ability to assemble outfits that they know they can count on to make it through processing, which in turn disrupts their feelings of mastery over the projection of a persona compatible with their self-image. As Alison Guy and Maura Banim (2000, 324) explain in their study of women's interactions with their clothes:

Women saw themselves as actively engaging with their clothes to create images that were consistent with aspects of their identity. Asserting control seemed to be about reconciling three dimensions through an image; appearing in control of oneself; appearing appropriately dressed for the situation; the clothes performing as expected. The success of the achieved images was often measured by how (more or less) powerful women felt in the situations that they had dressed for.

Being compelled by correctional staff to modify their attire affronts women, many of whom carefully selected or specifically purchased their garments for their visit. This is a particularly resonant matter for poor women, who may invest significant portions of their scarce resources in cultivating and displaying a fashionable "look" that imbues them with a sense of command denied to them in other aspects of their lives (see LeBlanc 2003; Gonnerman 2004).[24] As in professional settings where lower-class workers are forced to comply with dress codes set by their elite bosses (Bourgois 1995, 158), the processing area serves as a crucible in which "physical appearance becomes a fierce arena for enforcing or contesting power." The decision that they are "inappropriate" incenses or humiliates visitors, especially if they are chastised for being too sexually enticing.[25] The combination of not being permitted to dress alluringly for a romantic partner and of having a correctional

24. People's increased desire to maintain authority over the self by creating and exhibiting specific clothing styles in the face of external turmoil is noted by Beatrix Campbell (1993, 271) in her study of riots in Britain. See also Stanley Cohen's (2002, 163) discussion of the importance of fashion among the Mods.

25. This distress corresponds to Guy and Banim's (2000, 319) finding that a "particular area of concern" for women when constructing their wardrobes "was that clothing should not identify them with crude sexual signaling," that is, attract unwelcome sexual comment.

officer criticize one's sexual expression leaves women feeling diminished, shamed, and often frustrated to the point of tears. At the visiting center, they discover a selection of donated secondhand clothes in outdated or unflattering styles, colors, and fabrics from which they must choose a garment approximately their size. Most visitors take pride in their personal appearance, feeling disheartened and self-conscious when instructed to don "'poor' clothes that become associated with personal deficit" (Guy and Banim 2000, 320). The recognition by other visitors and by prisoners of these clothes as visiting-center outfits compounds the demoralization of wearing them, reinforcing women's sense that they must discard their own identity and assume a prescribed carceral character in order to gain access to the prison.[26] As Goffman (1961, 20) explicates:

The individual ordinarily expects to exert some control over the guise in which he appears before others. For this he needs cosmetic and clothing supplies, tools for applying, arranging, and repairing them, and an accessible, secure place to store these supplies and tools—in short, the individual will need an "identity kit" for the management of his personal front. . . . On admission to a total institution, however, the individual is likely to be stripped of his usual appearance and of the equipment and services by which he maintains it, thus suffering a personal defacement. . . . [T]he institutional issue provided as a substitute for what has been taken away is typically of a "coarse" variety, ill-suited, often old, and the same for large categories of inmates.

In addition to the enforced modification of their appearances, visitors must forfeit other "tools" of their "identity kits" in order to enter San Quentin. There are strict limits on what items people can bring into the prison: no makeup, sunglasses, cigarettes, gum, sanitary supplies, electronic gadgets, pens, papers, or nonprescription medications are allowed.[27] Visitors are only permitted to have an identity card, two keys, up to thirty dollars in coins and one-dollar bills, an unopened pack of Kleenex tissue, a comb or brush, and ten photographs, all of which may be contained in a small clear plastic purse or bag. Umbrel-

26. Some women perceive the wearing of communal charity clothes as so demeaning that they prefer to drive five miles to Ross Dress for Less (a popular chain store that offers closeout merchandise at significantly reduced prices) where they purchase new garments for their visit instead of accepting loaned apparel.

27. Prescription medication must be left with officers in the processing area, and a visitor will be escorted to her medication if she requires it. Nitroglycerin tablets and inhalers are permitted in the visiting areas (California Department of Corrections 1999). Visitors who need sanitary napkins or tampons must purchase these items directly from a correctional officer in the visiting area.

las are prohibited, and on stormy days visitors make their ways along the long walk to and from the visiting areas unprotected from the elements. People with children are allowed to bring six disposable diapers, a factory-sealed pack of baby wipes, two prepared bottles, two jars of factory-sealed baby food, one transparent pacifier, and one baby blanket into the prison, but are forbidden to transport strollers, baby seats, toys, or containers of formula onto the grounds. The barring of strollers and baby seats presents distinct difficulties for women, first because the lockers are not large enough to store these items if someone arrived with them on public transportation, and secondly because the visitor (with the help of the prisoner she is visiting if they are permitted contact) must then hold her baby for the entire duration of her visit.[28]

Visitors possessing a prohibited item can return it to their vehicle, secure it in a locker for the price of fifty cents, or leave it on a bench in the Tube with the hope that it will still be there after the visit. Because most people have already placed their shoes in the tray to be sent through the x-ray machine when they are advised that they must discharge an article, they commonly return to the Tube in bare or stocking feet, tip-toeing around the patches of spilled soda and food wrappers as they make their way to the lockers or even to the parking lot:

––––––

Today I observed a mother with an infant, a toddler, and another child parade to and from the lockers three times, prancing high on her red-varnished toes through the filthy corridor. Her first trip was to put her container of baby formula in a locker: "The things they make you do! Baby can't have no formula. I always think I got everything taken care of, but I guess I don't!" Realizing she needed two quarters, she returned to the processing area to retrieve a coin from her purse, then came out and deposited it, taking

28. In the mid-1990s, the wife of San Quentin's warden at the time arranged for the purchase of a supply of strollers that are kept by the door through which women exit the processing area. Visitors may use these strollers to transport children along the walkway between the processing area and the Mainline and noncontact visiting areas, although they are not allowed into the visiting areas themselves, nor are they allowed on the buses that take people to H-Unit and the Ranch. A few cribs are available for use in each visiting room, but many women say they avoid using them due to concerns about cleanliness (visitors are not allowed to bring in sheets for the cribs). Restrictions on baby accessories and children's toys also seriously encumber people during family visits, when visitors spend three days and two nights locked in the facility with their incarcerated relative.

the locker key with her. A few minutes later she appeared once more with a ten-dollar bill, this time having left her brood behind; unwilling to reopen the locker, which would have required the insertion of two more quarters, she carefully slipped the bill through the crack in the locker door and made her way back, shaking her head bemusedly and side-stepping a puddle of Coke.

———

The embargo on most personal items obviously causes practical problems for visitors, yet the psychological impact of being denuded of property is profound since "persons invest self feelings in their possessions" (Goffman 1961, 18). One morning I observed a vivid manifestation of the suffering wrought by stripping individuals of their belongings:

———

Among the visitors today were an older man and an elderly woman, probably in her mid-to-late eighties. They were unfamiliar with visiting procedures, and I helped the man figure out that they needed to be in the Mainline waiting line. Since the woman looked very frail, I offered to have her sit with me on the noncontact benches until he reached the front of the line. He helped her get settled and then took his place at the bottom of the stairs. It soon became evident that the woman was indeed quite aged and a touch senile; she kept nervously remarking to me, "I don't see that man I came with! I hope he's still there! I hope he hasn't left me! Where is he?" Even when I would promise her that I saw him in line or point him out for her, she wasn't reassured and would soon start worrying again.

As we sat there together, the woman sporadically patted her thighs and the space on the bench just by her hips. "I feel lost without my purse!" she cried plaintively. "I keep looking for it!" Over time she became increasingly anxious, "I can't see him! I can't see the guy I came with. Maybe he left! I sure hope he doesn't leave me here! I don't have my purse!" She clearly felt very vulnerable and discombobulated, deprived of both her companion and her belongings, and I tried to distract her by asking her whom she was going to visit. "That's my sonny boy in there. It's been a long time since I've seen my sonny boy." She told me that her legs hurt from walking just from the car to the Tube and that she was tired already, so she hoped she wouldn't have to walk far once she entered the prison. Fidgeting nervously, she craned her neck to look down the line as her hands wandered over her thighs and onto the bench. "Where's my purse? Where's that man?" she wailed mournfully, her rheumy eyes brimming with alarm and bewilderment.[29]

"In modern Western culture," asserts Sykes (1958, 69), "material possessions are so large a part of the individual's conception of himself that to be stripped of them is to be attacked at the deepest layers of personality." In the instance of prison visitors, the "pain" of this particular denial—the deprivation of personal goods (1958, 67–70)—has a twofold effect. Most obviously, it reinforces people's feelings of impotence and subservience in their relationship with the correctional facility, regardless of their cultural or economic capital in the "outside world." Sophia, a college graduate, observed: "I'm articulate and educated and I carry myself with class and all that. However . . . I understand that I'm in a state penitentiary, and I understand that by the law it is a privilege, not a right, that I visit my husband. And with that in mind there are certain guidelines that I have to follow. I have to dress a certain way, I have to conduct myself in a certain manner. And I'm willing to do that." Yet the regulation of visitors' physical appearance also transcends the prison boundaries, seeping into women's shopping expeditions and their closets as they—especially those on strict budgets who cannot afford a wide variety of attire—accumulate their personal belongings in accordance with the institution's rules. Butta, a thirty-two-year-old African American "Welfare-to-Workfare"[30] participant whose husband just began serving a twenty-year sentence, grumbled:

My biggest problem is when you go in there they got this dress code. If it's a certain kinda material you can't wear it. They don't want you to wear nothin' see-through. I mean, they jus' like, *changing your whole wardrobe!* I mean, what if everything you had in your closet was see-through, or, had splits in 'em more than two inches [referring to the designed slits in skirts, which under the dress code cannot reveal more than two inches of flesh above the knee]? I mean, that's the biggest problem. So, so what I've been doin', when I go shoppin', I try to buy

29. After a wait of over an hour, this pair finally entered the prison and exited abruptly a few moments later. The man was clearly agitated, and I did not feel comfortable interrupting them to ask what had happened. I saw them drive out of the parking lot several minutes later.

30. In 1996, President Clinton signed the Personal Responsibility and Work Opportunity Reconciliation Act, also known as "welfare reform." This act established a five-year lifetime limit on receiving welfare benefits and placed strict requirements on states to move welfare recipients into the workforce (see Sidel 1998, 201–27).

conservative stuff where I know that they cain't say anything, so I can just go through there. Because I know if, say one day I've just been through the wringer. I don' wanna turn around an' be cussin' 'em out, sayin', "Well, you know, forget you!"

As Butta's comments reveal, the facility's management of visitors' bodies and behaviors does not stop at the institution's gate. It permeates women's domestic and social spheres in unintended and uncharted ways, affecting such personal traits as one's purchase of possessions and development of fashion style.[31] Yet in the face of this "widening net" of punitive control (see Cohen 1985, 40–86), options are available to visitors that are denied to inmates, primary among them the choice not to enter the prison: when told to replace her trendy shirt with a modest blouse, Paige, the twenty-nine-year-old white unemployed fiancée of a parole violator serving six months, retorted hotly to the correctional officer, "No! I'm not a prisoner. *I'm free.* I'm free to wear my own clothes, and I'm free to walk out of here."[32] This choice naturally carries the penalty of not seeing the inmate, and those who decide against this forfeiture are hemmed in to a narrow range of permitted looks and behaviors from which to concoct an "approvable" self. Although mandating and monitoring the presentation of a "front" (Goffman 1959, 22–30) befits the authorized penetration of a highly controlled environment, a comparison of the processing of correctional staff, volunteers, and guests with the hypersupervision and subjugation of visitors reveals the powerful influence of "courtesy stigma" (Goffman 1963) brought to bear on prisoners' associates and kin.

Neither Fully Captive nor Fully Free

When a visitor tells me "I'm not an inmate, you can't treat me like an inmate," I tell her, "Ma'am, I *do* treat you like I treat an inmate—*with the utmost respect.*"
FORMER VISITING LIEUTENANT AT SAN QUENTIN STATE PRISON

31. The custom of requiring certain clothes for prison visiting, and the resultant replacement of low-income women's individual wardrobes with "approved" garments, contrasts markedly with the absence of a dress code for prison visitors in Brazil, where the practical constraints of poverty are recognized more readily; not only the prisoners but even the guards do not wear uniforms due to individual and institutional financial hardship. During a field visit to Rio de Janeiro's notorious Bangú prison complex in October 2001, I observed female visitors *and* guards wearing skintight jeans and halter tops—dressed exactly like women in the favelas and along the beach boardwalks.
32. Paige did walk out—and then had me assist her four-year-old daughter in photographing her posing sexily next to the large SAN QUENTIN STATE PRISON sign at the East Gate: "We're going to send the pictures to Daddy and show him we were here! Hi, honey!" she waved. "We were here, but we couldn't get in! This is what you missed!"

The enforcement of security provisions is an accepted, and indeed expected, component of the running of correctional institutions. To some extent, each person entering San Quentin submits to stipulations governing the facility: officers wear uniforms, administrative workers and volunteers adhere to a dress code, and everyone undergoes background checks and presents sanctioned identification papers. Yet the forms of degradation presented in this chapter—extensive, unpredictable waiting periods, relegation to an inhospitable and confusing environment, and stringent monitoring of appearance and possessions—uniquely apply to people who arrive at the gates due to a personal connection with a prisoner rather than a work-related purpose within the institution. Correctional staff drive their vehicles directly into the prison grounds, showing their ID to the officer at the outer gate, then parking in designated lots and proceeding to their posts. Volunteers and administrative guests register at the East Gate, where the on-duty officer checks their security clearances, eyeballs their attire for gross dress-code violations (about which they have been warned in advance), and verifies that they are not transporting any electronic items or weapons in the purses, bags, or briefcases they are allowed to bring into the facility. Only a portion of volunteers and guests are scanned with a metal detector (depending on where in the institution they are heading and what level of security clearance they have been granted), and unless there is a specific problem, most people typically move through the prison gates within ten minutes of their arrival.

Concerns about the contamination of a protected space logically would pertain to the admission of any outsider, including correctional officers, who are known to have been embroiled in drug smuggling, violence, and other forms of corruption within prison walls (Coffman 2000; Johnson 2000; Reuters 2000; Sward and Wallace 1998). The assignation of extra "security" measures solely to families, lovers, and friends, however, suggests the extension of the convict body to the visitor body, which then becomes a permissible subject for punishment and the extraction of retribution. Indeed, while the regulations pertaining to staff, volunteers, and guests appear as common sense in the governance of a prison (background checks, prohibition of weapons), the conditions of neglect and indignity imposed on visitors do not resonate as a bureaucratic necessity but rather as punishments orchestrated to sternly communicate "the loss of . . . status which defines the individual as someone to be trusted or as morally acceptable" (Sykes 1958, 67). The gulf between the treatment of the "professional outsider" and the "prisonized visitor" is sharply apparent to women who met their partner while working or volunteering in a correctional facility and who therefore experienced both forms of processing. Sophia first met her husband while working as a coordinator for a prison Alcoholics Anonymous group:

MC: Tell me about the transition from being a volunteer to being a visitor.

SOPHIA: [*forcefully*] What a shock. What a wake-up call. It's night and day, the way you're treated by staff. It's a rude awakening. As a volunteer person you're in some respects given the sense of [*breezily*] "Oh, you're one of us," as far as staff [is concerned]. They were in support of us coming in and bringing programs and service to the inmate population. And suddenly, I went from being a person who was credible and positive and helpful to being scrutinized and regulated and treated like a third-class citizen, just like the inmates are treated.

The transition from volunteer to visitor was similarly jarring for Sarah, who had been involved in a prison education program:

In terms of passing the guards and security it's so lax as a volunteer. I mean, I would wear things that would trigger the metal detector, like overalls with metal clasps, you know, there was very little oversight, they trusted you. . . . I had had so many freedoms coming in as a volunteer. They didn't care what I wore. They never checked that I was bringing anything in. I used to bring in candy and fruit and books and magazines and—this [coming in as a visitor] was *totally different*. You know, I couldn't bring anything in, I couldn't bring in papers, we [she and her husband] couldn't do work together. . . . Plus, just getting through the process of transitioning into being a visitor—and not only the procedure for getting in every time I go see him and what that experience is like, but the way that you're treated and all of the unknowns and the crap and the unfairness of visiting.

Darla, a fifty-year-old white woman, was employed by the California Department of Corrections in a clerical position when she met her husband,[33] who is serving a life sentence:

I had a hard time when I first went back [as a visitor] because of me working there, and they *knew* me. And of course, I was a "traitor," as they called me, and first they

---

33. Darla visits her husband at a California state prison other than San Quentin. Because she is still a state employee (although no longer a correctional employee) and has extra concerns about maintaining her confidentiality, I am not identifying this prison. Although my fieldwork focused on San Quentin, interviews with women who visit men at other prisons, as well as literature on partners of prisoners (e.g., Girshick 1996; Fishman 1990; Bandele 1999), suggests strong commonalities among people's experiences at a variety of correctional facilities.

wouldn't let me go in and visit, but I had an OK from the warden because once you're not working for that department they can't do anything about it. And we did everything legal and above the law, you know, cuz I quit before I ever went back and seen him and everything, but they still treat you very, very nastily.

A personal allegiance with a prisoner therefore negates the confidence and integrity otherwise accorded to an individual, sullying a woman with the stigma of the offender and identifying her as potentially threatening and deserving of recrimination. As a polluted and inferior body, her processing by the correctional authorities entails a series of deprivations, degradations, and other insults, connecting her experience of the prison regime to that endured by her incarcerated loved one and blurring the distinction between who is an "inmate" and who is not. In Sophia's words, "[The correctional officers] view prisoners as well as their family members as on the whole being uneducated, being criminal, and trying to get over on you and not to be trusted and always, always there's an air of suspicion and there's a superiority and a power that permeates everything in the way the staff treats inmates and visitors in general."[34] Or, as Stephanie, a twenty-five-year-old African American security guard and college student married to a man serving four years, explained:

They [the correctional officers] try to make it as hard for them [visitors] as possible and, with them like changing, you know, the dress codes, where you can't hardly wear anything, they're searchin' you, you have to go through a metal detector, an' sometimes people are humiliated, you know, *that* is treating the family members as if they're incarcerated too, if you really look at it. Because, I mean, okay, you have to watch what you say, you have to treat them [the authorities] with respect, and if you don't, your family member who is incarcerated can lose their visiting privileges!

Yet, as noted above, visitors in a sense willfully subject themselves to these forces of secondary prisonization because—contrary to convicted felons—their presence at the penitentiary is voluntary and seemingly discouraged rather than obliged. Also, an ironic dissimilarity distinguishes those dwelling behind bars from those who are fleetingly contained therein: while the former are expected to demonstrate

---

34. These complaints resonate with those expressed by women visiting prisoners in other U.S. prisons (Fishman 1988) as well as in institutions in England (Blake 1990) and France (Béranger 2000; Maksymowicz 2000).

"change" through compliance and altered individual attributes in order to earn their release *from* the facility, such transformations are demanded of the latter before they are permitted to *enter* the guarded space. All of these elements reinforce the curious position that visitors occupy in their relations with the prison: neither fully captive nor fully free, they juggle self-modification and self-preservation in their efforts to pierce the carceral border, gaining short-term rights of entry while unwittingly preparing a foundation for the institution's long-term distortion of their personal, domestic, and social worlds.

THREE

"We Share Everything We Can the Best Way We Can"

The wife, the partner, the friend, the girlfriend, they do more than endure the prison: they share it. In their head, in their heart, in their flesh, in their womanly life. DUSZKA MAKSYMOWICZ, *FEMME DE PARLOIR* (MY TRANSLATION)

Having a relationship—and particularly a marriage—with an imprisoned man challenges contemporary Western conventions about the essential ingredients of romantic involvement. When "typical" couples in modern societies describe their relationships, "[e]xclusive, bounded activities, such as travel and meals and evenings together, [are] often momentous events in the narratives. The home appears as an especially powerful symbol of marital boundaries and is a focus of intense description" (Collins and Gregor 1995, 80). Although the maintenance of amorous bonds under conditions that prohibit or temporarily suspend the enjoyment of private time and shared domesticity is not so uncommon—affecting, among others, military officers and their families (Stone and Alt 1990; Rotter and Boveja 1999; Hedges and Minaya 2005), immigrant laborers supporting families from afar (Groves and Chang 1999; Ehrenreich and Hochschild 2003), couples dwelling on traditional kibbutzim (Spiro 1979), and career professionals whose global-networking paths seldom cross those of their spouses (Bunker et al. 1992; Holmes 2004)—the punitive management, interdiction, and surveillance characterizing prison relationships mark these liaisons as extreme cases of the situational and authoritative control of intimate life. Following the previous chapter's discussion of the daunting impediments to gaining access to the prison visiting areas, the foremost questions that arise are: Why do women choose to continue their relationships once their partners are imprisoned? Why do they not instead opt to form new partnerships with "free" men? What satisfaction can women possibly gain from these relationships that compensates for the grief of forced separation and prison visiting? Chapters 3 and 4 dissect the specific interactions that occur between couples during periods of a man's incarceration to show the workings of prison relationships and the interpersonal production of rewards for "standing by your man."

This investigation furthers the analysis of secondary prisonization along two theoretical lines. First, it demonstrates how women—motivated by love, compassion, and the fear that problems behind bars will cause injury, mental illness, or a delayed release date for their partners—vigorously apply themselves to the tasks of mitigating the "deprivations" (Sykes 1958, 63–84) that characterize penal internment. Their strategies for doing so include writing and receiving letters, sending packages, accepting phone calls, visiting their partners, and participating in fantasy play, even when these activities require forfeiting their own privacy, depleting their scarce resources, and jeopardizing their emotional well-being. Through this approach of "doing time together" couples create feelings of closeness and collectivity despite the ostensible segregation and isolation of imprisonment, and thus they perceive their efforts as being in opposition to the castigatory functions of the correctional institution. However, this willful dualization of the convict body that suffers the punishments of detention reinforces the secondary prisonization of nonincarcerated women by repeatedly subjecting them to extensive penal scrutiny and control. Ironically, it also assists men in serving their sentences with minimal disruptions and minimal demands of the authorities and thereby generates the "docile bodies" (Foucault 1977, 135–69) desired by the prison.

The second theoretical point connects to Clemmer's (1958, 312) assertion that "the inmate who has become prisonized to advanced degrees would be a poorer risk on parole than others who had not" largely because of such an individual's grafting on to a "prison primary group" in his social interactions. As women provide abundant emotional support during their partners' incarcerations in efforts to affirm men's connections to the outside world, the prisoners, confined to a dreary and difficult existence, typically value this outpouring and invest significant energy in showing appreciation and need for it. Couples thus become enmeshed in a pattern of exchange that accentuates and enhances the romantic devotion and yearning in their relationships, transforming the men's incarceration into an extended period of what Laura Fishman (1990, 162) terms "renewed courtship" that may contrast greatly, and even favorably, with the tenor of home life and daily interactions away from the prison. Paradoxically, then, the maintenance of connections across and within carceral borders prisonizes intimate ties, in many cases positioning the correctional facility as a regulative device that—despite the enormous sacrifices, indignities, and control it demands—becomes integral to the functioning of relationships.

"Everything That a Husband and Wife Should Share": Techniques of Communication

Every day it's like I do *somethin'*, every day I do somethin' that has somethin' to do with him. If it's gettin' ready for when he come home, or gettin' somethin' for him while he in here or writin' a letter or gettin' a card, or somethin', I'll fill up every day.

BRANDI

When couples cohabitate or have unimpeded and frequent interaction, their various mechanisms of communication are often obscured by their proximity and their habituation to each other's presence. The enforced separation and extensive control of mates makes these methods explicit, providing a converse example of Georg Simmel's (1950) "stranger" (he who is physically close but socially distant) that can be used to probe the meanings of near and far, intimacy and remoteness. Penal researchers, as well as journalists and "in-house" writers, have abundantly documented the ingenuity of convicts in adapting, stretching, and thwarting the powerful regulation of seemingly every aspect of their lives while incarcerated (see, for example, Cohen and Taylor 1974; Rideau and Wikberg 1992; Demello 1993; Martin and Sussman 1993; Frazier 1995; Conover 2000). Female partners apply a similarly high level of energy and innovation to means of staying in touch, thereby maximizing the range of permitted methods of communication and shouldering a portion of the burden of "doing time." The following four sections illuminate the secondary prisonization of women and the concomitant prisonization of their social and familial bonds as they employ the four methods possible for communicating with their loved ones over distances: letters, packages, phone calls, and a form of fantasy play I call "presence creation."[1]

Letters

Among my research participants, letter writing and receiving was the most common way of staying in touch: 98 percent stated that they or their partner or both wrote at least periodically during the incarceration period, and over half identified exchanging letters as a highly gratifying activity central to their experiences of courtship and relationship development.[2] In contrast to packages, phone calls, and visiting, correspondence is relatively inexpensive (requiring only stationery, a pen or pencil, and postage) and can be performed daily in accordance with one's own time schedule, in the (semi-)privacy of one's cell or home, and without the immediate engagement of correctional officials. There is, however, strict monitoring at a secondary level: as Title 15 of the California Code of Regulations, "Crime Prevention and Corrections" states, "All nonconfidential inmate mail is subject to being read in its entirety or in part by designated employees of the facility before it is mailed for or delivered to an inmate" (State of California 2003, section 3138[a]). Because only correspondence with government officials, legal-service organizations, and attorneys is deemed confidential, mail sent by or to prisoners is systematically opened and inspected, a process that retards the distribution of incoming mail by two-to-six weeks. Although long acknowledged as degrading for residents of "total institutions" (Goffman 1961, 31), the censorship of mail also affects the outside writer who knows that each tender word or intimate thought that she or her loved one writes will be exposed and judged. The policy under which prisoners' outgoing mail is "marked indicating that it originated from a California state correctional facility" (State of California 2003, section 3147[2])—stamped with the name of the institution in bold, capital letters on the envelope—compounds this stigmatization.[3]

Twenty percent of the interview participants said that they or their partners or both wrote to each other almost every day, and another

1. Chapter 4 examines face-to-face interaction during visiting.
2. Gina, a twenty-two-year-old African American receptionist and the only person not to correspond with her husband during his eighteen-month sentence, said that the couple had written during a previous stint in prison but no longer found it rewarding. High levels of letter writing are also documented by Braman (2004, 47–48).
3. This policy, theoretically to prevent prisoners from writing to someone without disclosing their convicted felon status, is common at correctional institutions (Hairston 1999).

Figure 3.1 A letter sent from San Quentin

22 percent sent or received multiple items a week. These missives ranged in length anywhere from a few sentences on a postcard to digests in excess of twenty pages and sometimes included self-authored poems or short stories in addition to personal news, reflections, and the occasional photograph.[4] Thirty-six percent of women specifically remarked that their partner wrote more prolifically than they did (anywhere from two to five times as often), a phenomenon that overwhelmed them both positively and negatively, as Josephine, a thirty-five-year-old African American assembly and warehouse worker whose husband is completing a fourteen-month sentence, explained:

MC: Do you write to each other?
JOSEPHINE: Oh my Lord! [*laughing heartily*] Let's not talk about writin'! This man writes me a letter, I will get at least a letter a day. *Yes!* [*slowly, incredulously*] One time he wrote me a twenty-one-page letter. Yes! Yes, he did. [*chuckles*] I'm not the writin' type. But, because of him, I was writin'. . . . So, you know, I've been writin' him, he just wants the pen on the paper, so I do it all, I've just done it all. And now he's gettin' out [*richly, with comic expression*], thank you Jesus!
MC: [*chuckling*] Then you can stop all that!
JOSEPHINE: I'm tellin' you, [*emphatically*] I do not like to write. Not at all. I have never wrote anybody in my life, other than—*no.* If I cain't talk to you—I know that's not good, cuz they say it's good to write, but huh! *I'm not the one!*

It is striking that couples turn to high levels of correspondence as a primary means of staying in touch during a man's incarceration given

4. Correspondents are not allowed to send anything other than a standard letter or card plus a limited number of photographs.

that 16 percent of the participants did not graduate from high school, 28 percent had no education beyond a high school diploma or General Educational Development (GED) credential, and only 36 percent held white-collar jobs. Among the men, at least 22 percent did not graduate from high school and 42 percent had completed their education with a GED or high school diploma.[5] Lack of education is a blunt fact among the carceral population: nationwide, 19 percent of adult inmates are completely illiterate and 40 percent are functionally illiterate (indicating an inability to accomplish directed tasks in writing) (Kirsch et al. 2002),[6] and in the California prison system the average inmate reads at a seventh-grade level (California Department of Corrections and Rehabilitation 2005).[7] Although education levels did not bear any relationship to the frequency of correspondence among the research participants, poor writing skills and illiteracy constitute serious and costly hindrances for prisoners wishing to keep in touch, necessitating the enlistment of the services of an inmate "scribe" in order to produce a suitable document. The demand for such manuscripts leads to an informal industry, as described by a long-term San Quentin prisoner:

I have written letters for people who cannot write. Usually I will do something like that as an act of charity. But if the letter is too long or extensive in its nature then I may charge a small fee. Normally someone will tell you what they want to say then you write it in your words. Sometimes after you have written a letter for someone who can write but is not a good speller he will copy it in his own handwriting so as to not give himself away. . . . Often people will buy greeting cards with sayings or poems. There are a number of guys in here who make greeting cards. (Personal correspondence, April 9, 2002)

As this man notes, a prisoner may strategically try to "not give himself away" and hide his lack of education from his partner. Only one participant—Tee, a forty-two-year-old white nurse's assistant

---

5. Eleven participants did not know what level of education their partners had attained. It is probable that this 22 percent of the men had at most a high school diploma.

6. According to the same study, 4 percent of adults in the U.S. general population are illiterate and 21 percent are functionally illiterate (Kirsch et al. 2002).

7. According to course instructors (personal communication, April 11, 2002), the students in San Quentin's Free to Succeed literacy program initially test on average between a fifth- and sixth-grade reading level—even if they have a GED or high-school diploma—and 17 percent of the institution's prisoners are completely illiterate.

whose husband is serving a life sentence—seemed aware of her husband's illiteracy and spoke openly about the strain this places on their correspondence:

TEE: He'd have other people write letters for him. Yeah, he'd just dictate to 'em and they'd write 'em. But it's still hard for us to communicate because of his not being able to read and write that well. Cuz in order to get anybody to write a letter for you, you gotta pay 'im. *Nothing's* free in the prison system. *No-thing.* To get somebody to write a letter, he has to get a book of stamps, or whatever [to give as payment], so it's kinda hard. Right now, while he's in the Hole [solitary confinement], that's really hard. But he takes like a poetry book and just writes down, you know, word-for-word stuff and sends it to me. It's like we can't really communicate well. That's why our visits are so important because we can't communicate that well in writing.

MC: Do you write to him?

TEE: Yeah, I send him cards, with simple things that he can read easy. But our main communication is when I visit, that's why I'm so regular to come every chance, every visiting day practically. Because it's like, that's the only way our marriage can survive.

That, despite such problems, men persist in sending frequent and often voluminous letters signals the powerful practical and symbolic importance of these missives in a prison relationship. The exchange of mail between prisoners and their partners serves five main purposes. Most obviously, and most conventionally, it provides *a means of communicating with someone over a distance,* in this case someone who may be geographically far away but who also is barred from partaking in more regular or intimate interaction. Due to the institutional constraints of censorship and the delayed delivery of incoming mail, however, letters often serve less as couriers of concrete information (since women who are financially able to visit and accept phone calls find it more efficient to discuss everyday life directly with their mates) and more as instruments used to enrich relationships by combating prisoners' sense of isolation and thus the "pains of imprisonment" wrought by the "[s]terile aesthetic spaces [that] permeate prison environments. In this deadened aesthetic sphere, ideas, images and imagination are critical to maintaining sanity" (Phillips 2001, 370). Blessing, a thirty-eight-year-old African American representative for a communications firm who has been partnered for thirteen years with a Death Row prisoner she met and married at San Quentin, uses correspondence to fight the prisonization of her husband by injecting such critical elements into his barren life:

BLESSING: From day one, he has *always* received at least one or two pieces of mail a day. Whether it be a card, a postcard, or a letter, he's receiving something.

MC: Wow! And why do you feel that's important?

BLESSING: Because [*long pause, reflecting*] they need to communicate more than just with the people that's inside there. It's just like you yourself, I mean, would you just want to communicate with one or two people that's around in your house and that's it? You need that *outreach,* you need somebody that's outside those walls, and somebody that's caring for you and loving you, and you need to know about what's going on, because all they have are these walls around them. And some of them don't have TVs, some of them don't have radios, so to give him everything I possibly can—I cut out pictures, I send in pictures that you take, you share scenery or something, that you might take a picture of the city, because they don't see it unless it's on television or in a magazine, that's another thing, you send magazines in to them.[8] If you go to school like myself, to an adult-type school, and whatever I learn I'm going to send to him for him to learn as well. So, just everything I can possibly share! That I think a wife and a husband should share.

The process of epistolary exchange can become all-consuming, highly ritualized, and even sanctified for women: in their homes, numerous participants displayed scrapbooks or filing cabinets filled with meticulously organized correspondence, sometimes complete with longhand or photocopied reproductions of their own letters as well as those received from their partners. Such arrangements serve the practical purpose of helping women keep track of their correspondence, as Bernice and Laura revealed:

MC: How often do you write?

BERNICE: Oh, I write almost every day.

LAURA: Almost every day. But it takes two weeks for them to get our mail.

BERNICE: [My fiancé] was telling me, in fact today he said, "I got a letter from you," and I said, "Which one?" and he said, "It's a yellow envelope"—that's how we have to [keep track of the letters sent, by making something distinctive about each one], either this one's gonna be a yellow envelope, a green envelope, the date, the first sentence that I told him, cuz a lot of times, he doesn't get [the mail I send].

LAURA: We have to keep a *diary* of what we write, so we even know what we've sent them, because it takes so long.

8. Prisoners may receive magazines through direct subscriptions from the publisher.

Both Bernice's and Laura's partners have death-penalty sentences, and neither woman knew her intended spouse before his imprisonment: Bernice met her fiancé while visiting her brother (who was on San Quentin's Death Row for eighteen years before being executed at the age of thirty-eight in another state shortly after his California conviction was overturned), and she introduced Laura to one of her brother's friends who is also on Death Row and whom Laura now plans to marry. For those who are intensely involved with partners whom they have no opportunity to see in private, letters are imbued with a second key role: they become *"body substitutes,"* tangible extensions of the person that are the sole physical part of the beloved someone is permitted to embrace in her home and enjoy alone, away from the watchful eyes and ears of the authorities. The poet Asha Bandele, whose memoir *The Prisoner's Wife* (1999, 32) chronicles her courtship with and marriage to a lifer in the New York State prison system, describes this sensuous attachment to her husband's missives: "You have to understand, Rashid's letters are like dates. I have to get myself ready. I have to give them their proper space. Before I read his letters, I take a long, mango-scented bath. I burn white candles around the edge of the tub, and sandalwood incense, serenade my own self with Nina Simone songs."

Allen Shelton (1994, 201, 206) notes that the love letter or "[t]he perfect Valentine is the perfect translation of the individual into a set of objects" that then "not only function as cues for behavior, but as frames for the self." The envelopes decorated by inmates are famously artistic objects, lavishly ornamented with graphics similar to those imprinted on the flesh through prison tattoos (Phillips 2001). Similarly, women transform paper into skin by adorning and scenting their letters, fabricating a corporeal substitute that is permitted into the restricted areas of the correctional facility and that penetrates the prisoner's intimate space:

LAURA: I spray all of his cards and letters with perfume!

BERNICE: Both of us do!

LAURA: Believe me, you can't imagine how much perfume we go through! And it's not cheap!

BERNICE: I only buy it for the paper, I don't wear it.

LAURA: Well, see I wear perfume, and so that's what started that, but I can't buy expensive perfume anymore because the paper absorbs it, and I want him to have a real clear smell.

In admitting that she does not wear perfume, Bernice reveals the degree to which her letters have become replacements for her physical self: she purchases nominally body-enhancing products solely to garnish her writings, to create a sensual entity for her fiancé to relish with an immediacy forbidden to the pair in other interactions. Although women are not strictly "deprived of heterosexual relationships" (Sykes 1958, 70–72) in that they are free to become involved with nonincarcerated men, those who wish to remain committed and monogamous keenly feel the interdiction of sexual contact with their partners. As explained in detail in chapter 4, to be eligible for "family" (or overnight) visits in California, couples must be legally married and the prisoner, among other criteria, must have a date scheduled for his release from custody. This means anyone with a life or death-penalty sentence is automatically prohibited from being with his partner in private. Indeed, for most couples mail is the only authorized sexual forum available during the incarceration period, and even women who describe themselves as "self-conscious" will write graphically steamy texts or enlist a friend to snap erotic photographs to send to their partners as a means of participating in a sexual relationship. In these instances, the relativity of the freedom of correspondence becomes more salient since women know that these materials will be viewed by a correctional officer during the mail-inspection process and possibly later during a cell search, as Duszka Maksymowicz (2000, 69; my translation) laments: "When my words reach you they are already read. . . . When my absent-body offers itself for your caress, it first has been ransacked by the gaze of the reader-voyeur." Laura recounted how these infringements on intimacy became intolerable for her fiancé:

One time I sent him some pictures that were risqué. And he looked at them, and the more he had them the more he thought about, when the guards come in they're gonna look at them. And he couldn't stand it, it was just really bothering him. And you can understand that he didn't want other people looking at me! Not like that, anyway, as he said, "in a way that no other man should be seeing you." And that's understandable. Well, I found out that he had them for a couple of days and then he tore them up and threw them away.

While those who first encounter their partners in prison conduct entire courtships under such conditions, women who were involved with a man prior to his imprisonment and who thus had established histories of physical closeness find the conversion of bodily contact into epistolary expression arduous. Celina, who was restricted to noncontact visits during her partner's six-month sentence, testified:

But, it's like, [*dejected*] man, I didn't realize what it felt like to be in a relationship with someone that has to be incarcerated. You have a relationship that you maintain when you're at [home with your partner], you know, and it's so full of life and stuff like that, but this is like a whole different type of relationship. It is truly *a whole lifestyle* when you get up in here. I mean, when you have someone that's in jail, you have to do little things just to get your love across and like, kiss paper [*giggles*], like with lipstick and whatnot and spray the perfume all over your letters and whatnot, and different pen types, markers, and all that type of stuff, just to show, you know, show "I love you, baby" and all that. You know, it's just weird, the things you do in order to, cuz you can't touch them—well, cuz he's not on Mainline you can't touch them and stuff like that, and you really can't express, you know, *physically* how you feel, so you have to either convey it mentally or you know, verbally, in letters or whatnot.

The amount of energy, creativity, and time women devote to crafting their prison correspondence readily suggests its third function, *the letter as a gift* or "ritual offering that is a sign of involvement in and connectedness to another" (Cheal 1996, 96). While the above quotations clearly show women's efforts to prepare literary offerings for their partners, men's reciprocity in this exchange holds particular significance in that sending dispatches is the only means of interaction available to inmates that does not require the physical or financial participation of women.[9] An epistle therefore ostensibly attains value as a "pure" demonstration of caring and commitment that does not further encumber someone already in the throes of sacrifice—a contributing condition, along with the large proportion of unoccupied hours in a prisoner's schedule, to the abundant numbers of men who write more often than their partners. Yet the propensity of convicts to not only remember but to initiate the celebration of dates that previously eluded them (birthdays, anniversaries, minor holidays) by sending lavishly illustrated and poetically worded cards spurs both pleasure and twinges of suspicion in their partners, since the earnest articulations transmitted from prison often contrast markedly with men's sullenness in the home (or, in the case of those who met their

9. Although women often keep men supplied with stationery and stamps, the majority perceive this as a negligible outlay compared to the hefty financial burdens of packages and phone calls (as discussed below) and visits (documented in chapter 4). On disruptions of complementarity in reciprocity, see Gouldner (1996, 56–57); on asymmetrical gift-giving in male-female relationships, see Komter (1996, 125–30); for a discussion of the intricacies and obligations of the "Pure Gift," see Malinowski (1996).

Figure 3.2 An example of a handcrafted birthday card

loved one during his confinement, with the uncommunicativeness or inattentiveness of a woman's previous partners). Celina commented:

Well, when he's been *out* of jail, he doesn't *talk* as much about hisself and stuff like that, and he doesn't reveal a lot of stuff as much cuz he's so into having to get the dollar, getting work, doin' this and doin' that, and you get so preoccupied with trying to provide for the family, so that we never really get the time to, like, sit down and have time for each other, but [*giggles, seeing the irony*] it's weird that he would have to go to jail for us to be able to get, you know, *sensitive* and stuff like that.

This discrepancy highlights the fourth purpose of epistolary exchange in the carceral relationship, *the showcasing of the "feminization" of the male* and his newfound commitment to providing emotional sustenance. Although immersed in a hypermacho environment (Carter 1996b; Sabo, Kupers, and London 2001), inmates are deprived of stages on which to perform (stereo) typical displays of masculinity for their partners such as sexual prowess or being—however nominally or sporadically—the "provider" or the "head of the household." With few other means of giving or gifting, men thus turn to what is "basically a domestic art, a distant relation of sewing and embroidery. . . . Nobody can deny that to write good personal letters you have to prize the affective life and have a tendency to look inside yourself, both conventionally feminine qualities" (Hofstadter 1996, xvii). Through their missives, men practice the classically feminine forms of "emotional support" cataloged by Sandra Lee Bartky (1990, 102–3): "[t]he work of emotional repair—the tending of wounds—and the bolstering of confidence—the feeding of egos"; "[t]o enter feelingly and without condescension into another's distress"; "to affirm that person's worth"; "affection"; "loving endearments." The prisoner's masculine role is thus diminished and he becomes feminized through his passionate communication that conveys empathy and sentimentality. Jeanette, a thirty-one-year-old African American home-health-care attendant whose husband is serving six months, explained her attachment to her oft-incarcerated spouse: "He's like my friend, I want my friend, it's not nothin', it's not like for the sex, cuz I don't hardly get it! *He always gone!*" Or as Mai, a forty-year-old African American dance teacher who primarily communicates with her "love interest" through letters because he is serving six-to-ten years in an out-of-state federal facility, exulted: "*He is a male me!* He is a male, he is sensitive, loving, he's all of that!"

Confinement undoubtedly spurs men's eagerness to demonstrate their emotive selves through the previously unutilized and often labor-intensive (or pricey, if illiterate and hiring a scribe) task of letter writing. Butta, whose husband sends her two or three amorous letters a day, commented sassily: "That's the best part about him. He's very understanding. But now, in the position he's in, he ain't got no choice *but* to be understanding, right?" Her jibe ties the asserted feminization of the male to the final function of prison correspondence, *retention of the woman's involvement—and hence her emotional, financial, and practical support—in the relationship*. In their writings, men frequently reflect on the error of their ways, atone for past mistakes, and request help in taking steps toward recovery and reform, thereby producing texts that resonate with the purported point of their internment and encourage women to visualize a brighter future. In Ken Plummer's (1995, 34) words, "they turn themselves into *socially organized biographical objects*. They construct—even invent, though that may be too crass a term—tales of the intimate self, which may or may not bear a relationship to a truth." Brandi, a twenty-year-old African American hairstylist waiting for her boyfriend to finish his one-year sentence, enthused:

BRANDI: And [in his letters] he talk about what he want to do, and how he want to change and his goals and stuff.
MC: Do you two talk about that in person too, or does he just write it down?
BRANDI: Yeah, we talk about it in person, but he really get *deeper* into it when he writin'. We might just like talk about it, but he'll really, you know, go *into it* if he writin' it.

A recurrent theme among participants when asked about hopes for the future of their relationships were visions of domestic stability centering on the man's permanent return to the household and successful assumption of the roles of loyal husband and attentive father—although not necessarily the primary financial provider. In the words of Jeanette: "I just want things to work out and me have a chance to be a *beautiful, nice wife,* be there for you [her husband] as much as I can, help you out. I'm not Bank of America, but I can do what I can." Stephanie has similar plans: "And, by then [the time of her husband's release] I just hope that I'm in a field, or career, and then we can just start establishing our family, you know, get stuff together, cuz we wanna have kids, like within the next couple of years. So, get everything together so we can have a good, financially comfortable, happy family." The decision to "stand by your man"[10] prompts women to counteract the cognitive dissonance of choosing a legally stigmatized or dishonored mate by seeking verifications of his "worth" and devotion to the relationship. Stories of redemption therefore play a crucial role in solidifying most partnerships during the detention period by providing verbal assurance that men are making progress toward law-abiding, family-centered lives that complement the domestic stability and harmony the majority of the women covet. Hence the "gifts" of letters become "vehicles and instruments for realities of another order: influence, power, sympathy, status, emotion; and the skilful game of exchange consists of a complex totality of maneuvers, conscious or unconscious, in order to gain security and to fortify one's self against

10. In a work with this title, Kathleen McDermott and Roy King (1992, 51) note that prisoners typically have distorted and "not always realistic" views of their "past, present, and future relationships," which draw "attention to the extraordinary unreality in which any kind of contact [with outsiders] was supposedly maintained." The tendency of inmates to overestimate or fabricate the likelihood of their postrelease assimilation into a quiet and trouble-free lifestyle also is documented by Fishman (1990, 162–8).

risks incurred through alliances and rivalry" (Lévi-Strauss 1996, 19). When narratives of repentance and transformation invoke positive responses from wives, fiancées, or girlfriends, their telling continues, linking couples in a cycle of profession and affirmation that "not only heightens sexual and emotional intensity among couples, but . . . also provides them with a belief in the permanence of their relationships" (Fishman 1990, 168). Keisha, a twenty-year-old African American service-industry worker, was one of the few participants who identified this pattern, bluntly rejecting the messages she receives from her fiancé during his one-year parole-violation sentence for domestic violence:

KEISHA: It seem like he tell me everything I wanna hear, but it's not. You know, you cain't believe letters, that's just a dream . . .

MC: Why do you think you can't believe them?

KEISHA: Cuz I done been through it before. A guy, I wrote him for six months, and he got out and went home to his wife. . . . [My current boyfriend] always tell me, "I'll never do it again!" [pause, dourly] But a person'll say anything while they in jail. They'll tell you everything, "I won't never get in trouble again," [then] they get out [of prison], be cool for three months, and then they back in cuz they done hit you again!

Unlike Keisha, most women suppress any cynicism or misgivings about the contents of their mailboxes and instead ground their convictions about and expectations for the relationship in men's artistically persuasive outpourings: "I told my girlfriends . . . that it was those letters that hooked me. I told them that no woman has ever gotten a love letter until they've gotten a love letter from a man in prison" (Bandele 1999, 30). Feeling optimistic about the future and compassionate toward their mates, partners become willing to shoulder the burdens of the more expensive forms of keeping in touch, packages and phone calls.

Packages

San Quentin prisoners who are not in the Reception Center are permitted to receive one box, weighing thirty pounds, of food, clothing, and tobacco products every three months. To obtain these parcels, a man must send his Quarterly Package Authorization form to an outsider who is willing and able to purchase the desired stock, wrap it appropriately, label it with the authorization form, and mail it to the facility. Fifty-four percent of the interview participants spoke of regularly providing these treats for their partners, usually the full four times a year if economically feasible, and 10 percent said they wanted to send parcels but their loved one was not eligible to receive them. Several women mentioned collaborating with the prisoner's mother in assembling packages, and among those who did not send boxes, the second most common reason for not doing so (following the prohibitive expense) was that the mother-in-law took care of this duty, all of which supports a former San Quentin prisoner's observation that the organization and sending of goodies is distinctly the work of women: "When people get packages, I never heard nobody say 'My father sent me a package.' It's always 'My mother sent me a package.' 'My wife.' 'My girlfriend.' 'My homegirl'" (personal communication, August 20, 1999).

Packages are the only means by which people are allowed to directly give any object other than letters or photos to prisoners, and they are highly coveted since the recipients can supplement their meager institutional allowances with extra clothing and nourishment and hence enjoy higher standards of living than inmates who do not have access to outside resources. Those who are particularly fortunate have loved ones who circumvent the limitations on the number of boxes the man receives by sending him commodities via prisoners without family or friends able to supply them with goods and whose quarterly allocations otherwise lay fallow. These third parties collect a small payment (a tin of tobacco, a few cans of food) for their participation and pass the rest of the merchandise on to the beneficiary of the scheme. Boxes therefore designate privileged inmates, provide "luxury" wares to those living in spartan conditions, and inject materials into the prison barter economy, effects that far exceed the tokenism of the traditional "care package."[11]

Although advantageous for the recipients, three factors combine to make the preparation of packages markedly time-consuming, laborious, and costly for the senders: the intricate specifications of the prison regarding suitable goods, the men's elaborate and precise desires for certain products, and the women's wishes to accommodate their partners' fancies. First, much like the dress code described in the previous chapter, numerous convoluted rules restrict what articles people can send to prisoners (see appendix 4). Perhaps the most taxing is that all merchandise must either be in "factory-sealed" packages or containers (for food and some clothing) or accompanied by a purchase receipt and still-attached store tags (for unpackaged clothes). Implemented as a security measure to prevent the introduction of contraband (which

---

11. For a discussion of the extensive operations of the "underground economy" in prison, see Victor Hassine (1999, 45–55).

allegedly could be sewn into worn-out seams or concealed in food), this rule adds considerable expense to the cost of preparing a package since women are unable to economize with home-baked treats or to send men the garments they left behind in their closets. Participants report spending $70–$300 per package (largely depending on whether they include clothing or cigarettes, which add $100–$150 to the basic cost), with an average expenditure of $150 per quarter. Four such boxes a year could consume 6 percent or more of women's budgets: among the twenty-seven participants who discussed sending boxes regularly, eight had annual pretax incomes (from wages and/or government aid) under $10,000, nine made $10,000 to $20,000, four earned $20,000 to $30,000, and four had incomes in excess of $40,000.[12]

The facility's extensive rules governing acceptable items prohibit certain colors, styles, brands, and forms of clothing and regulate the containers, weights, and types of permissible food. For example, any "athletic footwear" sent to an inmate must conform to the following:

VALUE NOT TO EXCEED $60.00. WHITE OR BLACK ONLY. SMALL COLOR STRIPE, LOGO, OR PATTERN O.K. CAVITIES OR VOIDS, SEALED OR NOT, ARE NOT AUTHORIZED (IE. WINDOWS IN SOLES). NO PUMPS, POCKETS, ZIPPERS, OR VELCRO. NO METAL ARCH SUPPORTS OR FALSE INSOLES. THE BRANDS ARE NOT AUTHORIZED: BRITISH KNIGHTS, BUGLE BOYS AND CALVIN KLEIN. JORDAN'S ARE PERMITTED, HOWEVER THOSE MODELS DISPLAYING AN "XIV" LOGO ARE NOT AUTHORIZED. LIMIT: ONE PAIR. (Mainline Quarterly Package Authorization form, bold emphasis, all-capital lettering, and grammatical errors in original)

Although some of the rules imposed by the prison are for security reasons (for example, no "cavities or voids" in shoes), others make reference to the symbolic messages with which objects become imbued through prison-gang culture (such as brands or colors identifying the wearer's group affiliation). In the absence of abundant material goods, such seemingly small details as slight gradations of color, the presence or absence of a stripe, and the size or shape of a logo assume overwhelming importance both as signifiers of status and as reassurance that a prisoner retains some control over his self-presentation and property (see Phillips 2001). Women shopping for prison packages thus are constrained by *two sets* of guidelines: the stringent interdictions enforced by San Quentin and the often similarly precise demands made by their partners for specific merchandise. Laila, an African American account manager in her early forties, stockpiles bulk quantities of food in her living room for

---

12. Two of these participants declined to state their income levels.

her husband's packages and goes to great lengths to equip him with his preferred possessions as he serves his life sentence: "[My husband] likes gray boxer shorts. Now, ironically, you can't find gray boxer shorts anymore in a single pair. In a single package either. . . . Target has soft cotton boxer shorts. And they have a black and a gray in the package. What I do is I send in three pair, they'll [the correctional officers] rip 'em open, they'll give him the gray and they'll take the black." [13]

Women's longing to nurture their loved ones, particularly through offerings of special treats and comforts, has been repeatedly documented (Murcott 1983; Ungerson 1983; Robinson 1997; Bunting 2001), while anthropologists have noted the symbolic value of receiving food from a trusted source, especially during times of personal vulnerability (e.g., Meigs 1991, 17–29; also, more generally, Leach 1982). For those with scarce chances to physically soothe and nourish their partner, preparing and sending parcels assumes paramount significance:

BERNICE: We get a package slip and [*very excitedly, in a rush*] we like go crazy, "We get to go shopping!" And then it's like, we *run* to the store, we can't wait to buy their stuff and, you know, box it up, and we even run into each other at the post office and we're mailing our packages and it's like, so exciting!

LAURA: For his birthday this year . . . I took the box, put all sorts of stuff on the inside and then took the outside and took felt markers and decorated the whole— and you're talking about a twenty [inches] by twenty by twenty box, big, huge box—decorated the whole thing with like ribbons tied around it, and made, drew a bow on there, and then I did all sorts of markers, little stencil markers my daughter has, all around it, so it looked like a wrapped present! . . .

BERNICE: And like she said, the decorating of the box? They look for it! Cuz my daughter writes, she writes real tiny and she writes little messages, and now he's like, tearing the [items from the] box up to see, and she did it! One time she wrote on the peanut butter in there, you know, "I love you," and stuff like that. But I put all kinds of stuff inside the boxes, and we spray the box! Did you spray your box? I sprayed mine with perfume.

LAURA: No, because I don't want the food to taste like perfume.

BERNICE: Well, he's never complained, and I put it in his shoes, you know, sprayed—

13. When a man receives a package, a correctional officer opens the box in front of the prisoner and takes out each item for inspection before placing it in the inmate's empty pillowcase, which is used as a sack to haul his bounty. Items withheld from packages are supposed to be donated to the visiting center, but Laila voices suspicion that the correctional officers profit from the packages she sends by confiscating the surplus goods for their own use: "Well, the black [underwear] supposedly go to the visiting center . . . [but] I know where they go, they go home with the guard!"

LAURA: You know, I'd probably do that. Am I allowed to take the clothing out of the package?

BERNICE: [*firmly*] No.

LAURA: Okay, see, I can't. See if I could, then I'd probably spray the clothing.

When planning what commodities to purchase and send in packages, women actively work to compensate for the prison's deficiencies and thereby utilize boxes to combat the "deprivation of goods and services" afflicting their loved ones (Sykes 1958, 67–70). The understanding that men receive inadequate supplies of nutritious food, protective clothing, and warm bedding throughout their detention drives many women, like Alice, a twenty-two-year-old African American unemployed mother whose husband is serving three years, to attempt to soften their partners' environment by sending them the comforts of home:

ALICE: Well yesterday I just mailed him his first box. [*very quiet voice, for dramatic effect*] That box cost me *lots* of money.

MC: How much?

ALICE: I had to buy him tennis shoes, which they can't be over a certain amount but it was hard to find them cuz he wears size eleven and a half so it was hard to find him something for cheap. Which I found him some, maybe for like sixty dollars. Then he wanted a sweat suit, underclothes, socks, a thing for his hair, I mean all type of little stuff, and then his grandmother went to the grocery store and bought him like fruit in a can, crab meat in a can, candy—and this supposed to last him three months. So hopefully it will. . . . Under- uh, pajamas, I sent him thermals. . . . He wanted a watch but I didn't send him a watch [*laughs*].

MC: Why not?

ALICE: I said [*sarcastically, alluding to the heavy regimentation of his days*], "What do you need to know the time for?" [*we both burst out laughing*] I said, "You don't *need* to know the time!" I said. "You just worry about getting out!" I said, "Maybe in the next three months I'll send you a watch. But you don't *need* no watch!" But I did send him the shoes cuz he said the boots hurt his feet. But when he first got here, he didn't have no shoes, he had like some thong-slippers that they give 'em, and somebody he knew was here and left, so they gave him some boots and I feel really bad because the boots he had, the shoestrings were *ripped sheets*. I was like, "I *got* to send you some shoes!" That made me feel really, really bad. So, that's why I got him some shoes.

Not all of an inmate's supplemental goods must come from packages: depending on his "privilege group" (determined by behavioral, security,

83

and sentence status), he can spend between $35 and $140 a month on an assortment of food, beverages, smoking supplies, cosmetics, medications, and sundries from the San Quentin canteen (see appendix 4). Like receiving packages, the "weekly canteen, for those who have some money in their prison account, takes on central significance as an avenue of resource accrual and a symbol of status and potential power" (Phillips 2001, 15), thus sending a man money to "put on his books" to use in the canteen is a further way women demonstrate emotional support. The sentiment that one box every three months cannot provide enough food to supplement a meager prison diet (combined with the fact that toiletries cannot be sent in packages, much to the consternation of those who yearn to provide a favorite hair oil or body product) leads many partners to undertake a two-pronged approach to easing a loved one's internment by mailing him boxes *and* money. The amount and frequency of these payments fluctuate, depending on women's financial situations and their perceptions of how much money men require: among the 50 percent of participants who spoke of sending funds, the practices ranged from sending a lump sum of several hundred dollars when someone first arrived at San Quentin, to providing a weekly allowance of twenty or so dollars, to giving three hundred dollars a month.[14] However, not all of the money women send reaches the prisoners: a deduction is taken from those who owe restitution for their crime, child-support payments, or other government debts, as Stephanie, who makes between $15,000 and $20,000 a year as a security guard, discovered:

STEPAHINE: When I send him money, they take a portion of what I send him on his books to go towards the restitution that he owes.

MC: So it's really *you* paying the restitution?

STEPHANIE: Yeah, *I'm* paying the restitution!

MC: What percentage do they take?

STEPHANIE: Usually if I send him, I would say, like fifty-five dollars, they'll only give him forty. And, you know, food in there for them to purchase is extremely high, so, he's not able to get a lot [for that amount].

Although women speak passionately about compensating for the prison's material shortfalls and infuse their contributions to their partners with expressions of love and caring, anxiety about likely hidden motives and struggles for power inevitably haunt these offerings. In ana-

14. Although men can spend a maximum of $140 a month in the canteen, they can also order books, magazine subscriptions, clothing, and electronics, such as televisions or portable stereos, by mail.

lyzing this dimension of giving, a study by Erik Cohen (1986) of foreign men attempting to retain the affections of Thai women whom they met on holiday offers a useful comparative vantage point. For these men, although the initial "sojourn in Thailand usually inspired a feeling of sexual and personal dominance over the apparently submissive Thai girl," once the vacation ends the remote "Thai girlfriend often becomes a single ray of hope in an otherwise subdued and often depressing existence." The "problem becomes one of how to safeguard the relationship, and their girlfriend's attachment or even fidelity, during the long separations between vacations. As a consequence of their attempts to resolve this problem, an astonishingly extensive and lively correspondence develops." Here the men's longing is somewhat offset by the Thai women's interest in their foreign boyfriends as "a source of potential financial and emotional support [that] offers a possible counterbalance to the uncertainties and fortuitousness of daily existence," and they invest accordingly in letter writing as a means to "manipulate relationships to derive whatever benefits they can, by subtle indications of their need for help or by blunt demands" (Cohen 1986, 116, 121–22). In prison romances, these two disadvantages coalesce on the convict's side: he is keen to sustain his connection to his "ray of hope" *and* he is highly reliant on his partner for economic backing. For some couples these issues remain distinct, with a deep-felt love sustaining a partnership that may or may not include financial assistance. For others, however, the needs conflate and result in disingenuous displays of ardor (often in the form of letters and cards, as noted above) aimed at inciting and sustaining the emotional energy necessary for women to tend to their men despite the economic and affective hardships this entails. The specter of "being used" in this manner permeates the participants' discussions of sending packages and money and is often expressed in conjunction with (self-) assurances that an individual had taken steps to avoid this situation.[15] Darla observed:

There's a lot of guys that are in and out of prison constantly, and they marry women just to use them for packages and money, and that's one thing I am thankful my husband has never been. We never got married because we used each other cuz he never asks for anything, and I don't send him money and, you know, I support

15. Rickey, a hustler profiled by Loïc Wacquant (1998, 10, 25) aptly sums up the male attitude participants fear: "[Rickey] takes trouble to maintain 'at all costs' . . . ambiguous relationships that tie him to several women, each of whom believes that she is 'the one and only', even though, when pressed about it, he concedes that 'if a woman lookin' for some guy tha' she depen' on and uh, someone to raise a fam'ly with, it's *not me.* . . . But you know, *I always try to keep me a female with a job* or somethin' whereas, I'm able to git somethin' from her.'"

myself. Matter of fact, he helped *me* out. He sent me six hundred dollars that he had saved up for my son to get a motorcycle. . . . And so it's kind of the opposite. I kind of feel privileged because there is so much of that that does go on.

Jeanette, who was ill-disposed toward her husband on the day of our interview due to rumors that another woman had come to visit him, was more emphatic:

And then when men is incarcerated, that's all they know how to do is manipulate and use women, and mess with people minds to get what they want. . . . I don't know what men do [*sadly, lowering voice to a whisper*] use other women to get money. I don't know. But they ain't usin' me! [*vigorously*] He ain't usin' me, I drew my line! I've already been through past relationships, I know the score *and* the deal!

Although most women denied that their partners pursued their relationships for reasons other than love, the few who did perceive ulterior motives in a man's overtures recast this potential mistreatment in their own favor by emphasizing the inmate's vulnerability and dependence. This reversal adds a more brute dimension to Bartky's (1990, 105) assertion that "the opportunity to attend to the Other" can be "morally empowering . . . through the cultivation and exercise of important moral qualities" since women may use men's reliance on their caregiving to wrest control of a relationship. Joy, a forty-five-year-old white security guard, spoke at length about her feelings of insecurity and dissatisfaction in her relationship with a man serving nine months who had multiple other girlfriends. She acknowledged that his attachment to her during his frequent incarcerations was grounded in economic need: "He told me after he came back in [to prison] this time—well, the one thing that kind of pissed me off is [that he said], 'Nobody knows how to take care of me like you!' [*chuckles sadly*] OK! I'm being used!" Yet when discussing the man's liaison with another woman, Joy gleefully recounted her power to place conditions on her errant beau: "You want packages? You want mail? You want, you know, you just *better not*, if I ever find out that you've been back around her [another girlfriend], hey, sugar mama's gone!" [16]

16. Such remarks highlight the extent of Bartky's (1990, 107) oversight and her missed opportunity for an analysis of "tables-turned" caregiving when she comments that "we must remember that men are able to do without the emotional support of women for long periods of time, in prison, for example, or in the army." In a similar error, Jenny Phillips (2001, 14) argues that "[t]he prisoner is separated from all resources for enacting manhood: women, money, clothing and weapons and access to goods and services," neglecting the fact that the woman may in fact operate as the key supplier of any or all of these commodities.

The utilization of financial support as a means of guiding men's conduct can occur more subtly and in ways that position women as unwitting collaborators in penal control. In Alice's previously cited discussion of sending her husband his package, it is clear that she wants to attend to his needs and protect him from humiliation and pain by delivering him appropriate footwear. But her refusal to include a watch in the first shipment indicates that she plans to withhold certain indulgences as incentives for desired behaviors. Throughout her interview, Alice expressed much concern that her husband, who had never been to prison before this sentence, complete his punishment without incident: "I tell my husband over and over, every visit that I see him I tell him, 'Please don't let it [prison] get to you, just take it one step at a time, you know you'll be home [soon].'" She therefore equips her husband with the provisions necessary for him to maintain his dignity and avoid succumbing to the violence and vulgarity of prison life, but uses the promise of luxury goods to remind him of his obligation to her ("You just worry about getting out! Maybe in the next three months I'll send you a watch"). By implementing such a "reward system" to promote orderly and trouble-free behavior, women facilitate the smooth daily operations of the correctional institution, which benefits from well-tended-to inmates supplied with exteriorly funded enticements for good comportment. Aisha, a forty-six-year-old nutritionist of mixed parentage whose husband is serving a twenty-four-year sentence, summed up this link between her caregiving efforts and the advantages gained by the prison: "When I send a box I send all kinds of tuna, sardines, ah, halal meat in a can if I can find it without a preservative, nuts, all this protein, cuz he doesn't get any protein.[17] And yet I can't send him any vitamins. You know? I can't send him anything aside from food. And that doesn't make any sense to me. I mean, *don't you want a happy, healthy inmate?*"

Phone Calls

At San Quentin, as at the vast majority of U.S. correctional facilities, placing a collect call is the only option a prisoner has of speaking with someone by phone: no incoming calls are permitted, and inmates are not able to use alternative means of payment such as calling cards. As a result, the frequency of phone calls in a carceral relationship depends

17. As a practicing Muslim, Aisha's husband does not eat the nonhalal meat supplied by San Quentin.

on three variables: how often the convict decides or is permitted to contact an outsider, a woman's willingness to accept his call, and her resources for managing the bills. The rate of communication among the 80 percent of participants who said they spoke with their partners by phone fluctuated widely, with 8 percent receiving at least one call a day, 30 percent talking one to four times a week, and the remainder hoping to eke out one or two conversations a month. Most attributed their degree of phone contact to the ability of the prisoner to place a call, a factor that hinges on a man's institutional status (low-security prisoners have more access to phones than their high-security peers), his work schedule (those without jobs have more unoccupied hours during which to place calls), and his inclination to be in touch. The inability to initiate a call themselves and the imprecision characterizing the timing of men's communication particularly frustrates the women, as Sophia described:

Well, let's see, it's Monday, I should be getting a call today, although who knows, I may *not* get a call today! Every five days at this prison [my husband] gets to make a collect call, and they have to sign up for it the night before, and, you never know if they're going to get to call or not because sometimes the staff doesn't want to turn on the phone, or maybe they're locked down because of some emergency or some error or something. So every five days basically I get to talk to him on the phone and [*pause, with a dark laugh*] it's one of the chapters in my book and it's called "It Starts at 6:00." [18] Because from 6:00 at night till 9:10, every twenty-minute interval is when he may call. But I don't know when. And, there's nothing quite like it, you start at 6:00 and you just hang out. You do things. And then it gets to be 6:45. And then it's 7:10. And then you're trying to not think about it. And then it's 9:10 and you're thinking, "Well, *maybe* he is going to get on the phone for five minutes." And so, until 9:30 you, you sit in this state of tension, waiting.

"To be kept waiting—especially to be kept waiting for an unusually long while—is to be the subject of an assertion that one's own time (and, therefore, one's social worth) is less valuable than the time and worth of the one who imposes the wait" (Schwartz 1975, 30). Although directed at inmates, the bureaucratic and punitive delays that disrupt phone calls automatically affect the recipients of those calls and in fact are arguably *more* problematic for outsiders, in that women often

---

18. Sophia was writing an account of her relationship with her husband, whom she married twenty-four years into his life sentence.

(dis)organize their demanding personal agendas to accommodate the prison timetable and then become anxious over conjectured causes of any holdup. Aisha—who is otherwise continually occupied with professional, social, religious, political, and volunteer activities—systematically curtails her evening plans in hopes of hearing the reassuring voice of her husband: "He calls me whenever he can. At least once a week. I usually *always* try to be home by eight thirty, *every night, always*. It's just a habit that I've gotten into cuz that's usually when he calls. What's really awful is when he *doesn't* call. If I go see him, let's say, on Saturday, and I haven't heard from him, and it's Friday, I start to worry a little bit, you know? So getting a phone call, even just once a week, is very comforting."

In addition to this disturbance and uncertainty, any mention of phone calls to prisoners' partners provokes groans of distress over their substantial financial toll. Collect calls under any circumstances cost more than direct-dialed ones, but those originating in penal institutions are even more expensive since it has become standard practice for telecommunications companies to levy hefty surcharges on prisoner-initiated calls and to bill them at rates three times—and in some instances five-to-ten times—the cost of a regular phone call (Hairston 1998, 626; Zoellner 2000; Braman 2004, 131–33). These "service" contracts, which are negotiated by the Department of Corrections authorities on a state-by-state basis, render a commission of up to 65 percent of the revenue from prisoners' calls to the Department of Corrections (McCosh 2001), a practice that, for example, generated $21.2 million for the state of New York in 1997 (Mundow 2001) and $35 million for California in 2001 (Wallack 2002).[19] The penalty of this arrangement falls squarely on the shoulders of prisoners' loved ones: participants said their conversations added from $25 to $300 a month to their bills. Yet women revealed that so great is their desire to talk to their beloved that they rarely, if ever, refuse a phone call due to the expense and, instead, continue to accept phone calls even as their bills inflate to unmanageable dimensions: Basalisa, a fifty-five-year-old Hispanic

19. In June 2002 the *San Francisco Chronicle* (Wallack 2002) reported that "the state [of California] awarded billions of dollars in no-bid deals over the past three years," including a $60 million contract with MCI WorldCom and Verizon to operate the pay phones in the state's prisons. Both telecommunications companies "gave [Governor] Davis substantial campaign contributions [in 2001] at the same time the state was considering awarding the contract to a new bidder." Under pressure from some politicians and activists for prisoners' families, the state apparently "agreed to trim its take to $26 million a year," while WorldCom and Verizon have promised to "slash the rates by 25 percent at adult prisons and 78 percent at state hospitals and juvenile corrections facilities."

computer networker with a partner on Death Row, had a toll block imposed on her line by the phone company when her debt soared, while Josephine's phone was disconnected altogether due to what she called "outrageous" arrears. Meanwhile Celina—who lives on under $5,000 in government disability payments a year for herself and her two young sons—juggles her debts and waits for her partner to return home and pay off her $500-and-growing phone bill: "I had to get credit cards to pay for certain things until he gets home, and when he gets home he'll pay it off and stuff. But, it's like, phone bills, it's just like you find ways to like balance everything out so everything's still working and functioning, and then when he comes home he'll deal with it." Yet the idea of economizing by denying her partner's calls depresses her, since this would eliminate a high point of her otherwise markedly isolated and "*very* boring life":

My whole day would be planned around getting home to [*giggles*] *rush* in to the door and stuff like that [to be there for his call]! And then, sometimes, like, I know when it's him, cuz like on the caller ID it'll say—cuz I don't really have that many people, you know, other than him and family that call me, so I know what calls are which, so it's like, I see the little "unavailable" thing on the ID, I was like [*breathless with anticipation*] "I know that's him! I can talk to—"Hi, baby! It's me!" Or hear that old lady, the recording you know, "We have a collect call from—" and then he'll say something funny or sexy or something on the little, that five-second blip of stuff [when the person states his name for acceptance of the call], so I'll be, like, all excited.

All calls originating from San Quentin are monitored, a fact announced at the beginning of the conversation by the recorded operator greeting: "This is a [phone company] operator. I have a collect call from a prisoner at a California state institution. This call could be monitored or recorded." Despite the clear initial broadcast, the entire exchange is interrupted at varying intervals by an automatic warning system that reiterates: "This is a collect call from a prisoner at a California state institution. This call could be monitored or recorded."[20] Poor phone connections and significant din in the background (the inmate phone booths are located in loud and busy areas—on the ground level of multitiered cell blocks or inside open dormitories—and do not have doors for privacy) further hamper con-

20. Some women said that they received one warning two minutes into their calls, whereas other women reported being interrupted three or four times in fifteen minutes.

versation, and although they receive a two-minute warning, at the end of the fifteen-minute time limit imposed by the prison an abrupt closure of the line terminates the connection.[21] San Quentin ostensibly prohibits men from making more than one call during each phone-access period, but, as Alice explained, in other facilities the combination of censorship and redialing can add considerable expense to women's bills:

At Santa Rita [an Alameda County jail located in Dublin, thirty-six miles southeast of San Francisco], you cuss, or say the wrong thing, or say, "Oh, these police [the correctional officers] are getting on my nerves!"—the phone'll hang up. So he has to call you *back*, and just to accept it is like two-something [over $2]. So, it just keep hanging up if you cuss—it depends what mood they're in, cuz some days you can cuss all day long and they won't hang up, some days cuss—hang you up. They're *charging* you, you know what I'm saying? You've got to watch what you say, cuz they'll hang up on you, then he got to call back, which is *another* two dollars.

Unlike the censorship of letters, which is conducted at the prison and without the direct involvement of either of the concerned parties, the monitoring of phone calls immediately affects a woman while she is in her home. Phone calls therefore are conduits for the "real time" experience of penal control in the domestic sphere. And as with the exigencies for selected items in their packages, inmates rebel against feelings of powerlessness by attempting to impose their own form of regulation on their mates alongside that exercised by the authorities: capitalizing on the unpredictability of when prisoners might phone, some men deliberately call at irregular hours in an effort to restrict a partner's social activities and hold her housebound.[22] Fishman (1988, 60) explicates:

Men often used telephone conversations to exert their authority and dominance by making demands or checking up on their wives. For instance, some demanded that their wives stay more or less confined to their homes, thereby presumably demonstrating love, loyalty and faithfulness. . . . Fifteen wives [50 percent of the

21. Although individual institutions set their own phone policies, these issues characterize the reception of phone calls from other prisons in California (Girshick 1996, 62–63) and other states (Hinds 1982, 8; Bandele 1999).

22. Although only one participant in my study complained of this situation in her own life, in interviews and in the Tube women recounted multiple anecdotes of other people's partners acting in this manner.

sample] reported that they, themselves, felt imprisoned in their own homes—with their husbands in the role of prison guards, checking up on them frequently and unpredictably.

In her study of the wives of men in the U.S. armed forces, Margaret Harrell (2001, 60–61) observes that "an officer's wife becomes an extension of the officer" to the extent that if she attends functions in his place she is addressed with his rank, as if she were him. Meanwhile, "[i]n an environment of decreasing budget dollars, officers' spouses are perceived as an easy solution for addressing the problems faced" by others in the military-base community, so much so that their "volunteerism is valued at millions of dollars each year" (Harrell 2001, 57). As the dynamics surrounding packages and phone calls demonstrate, similar situations of transference and reliance occur in the case of prisoners' partners who themselves contend with punitive sanctions ostensibly reserved for convicted felons while simultaneously subsidizing a rewards system that promotes acceptable comportment and tends to men's "pains of imprisonment" (Sykes 1958, 63–84). During the 1990s, the trend in correctional facilities was to "make the experience of imprisonment more severe by removing gym equipment, televisions, college extension courses and the like" (Simon 2000, 286; see also the prescriptions of "America's Toughest Sheriff," Joe Arpaio [1996]), while implementing policies such as charging inmates for doctor visits, toiletries, or even room and board. The importance of the few remaining privileges—notably phone calls and goods sent by outsiders—increased, as did prisoners' need for financial help to meet their incarceration-related debts. Hence families and loved ones shoulder the economic and labor costs of providing incentives within the prison system, an arrangement with far-reaching repercussions for already impoverished women and children (Davis 1992; McDermott and King 1992; Grinstead et al. 2001; Braman 2004).

Presence Creation

The fourth technique employed by couples to communicate during the man's imprisonment falls outside of the official categories established for staying in touch. I use the term "presence creation" to refer to people's attempts to transcend institutional perimeters by using props, fantasy, and synchronization to incorporate an absent partner into their lives. Among the "forms of togetherness" elaborated by Zygmunt Bauman (1995, 47–48), this strategy best corresponds to *"postulated* togetherness . . . a work of imagination spurred by *homesickness,"* a "togetherness [that] seduces by its promise of intimate encounters guaranteed to be consummated before even attempted."[23] A field note written after an outing with Sarah suggests these melancholic underpinnings:

Sarah and I elbow our way into the crowded café and quickly determine our optimal lunching strategy: she will stand in line and place our orders, while my assignment is to sweep the room and seize a table when one becomes available. I have swift success, and as I guard our eating quarters I watch Sarah's trim frame advance toward the cashier. A college graduate with a six-figure income from her job in the high-tech industry, Sarah recently married a man at San Quentin who is serving a fifteen-years-to-life sentence. A few months after the wedding, the bride moved into an apartment in Marin County whose key feature—unbeknownst to the landlord—was a splendid view of the prison, prominently visible through the large sliding-glass doors in the living room that open onto a spacious balcony from which Sarah now "greets" her husband each morning before she leaves for work and bids him goodnight before retiring—alone—to bed.

The newlywed winds her way to our table, and I help her unload two of the super-sized salads for which this café is renowned. As we finish shuffling around coats, bags, and trays to maximize the space for our meal, Sarah reaches into her purse and pulls out a Polaroid photograph of her and her spouse in front of the familiar faux-Monet background that brands the pictures of all San Quentin couples. She hands me the photo, and while looking at Sarah's face, alight with joy as she nestles against her ruggedly handsome husband's torso, I recall another woman telling me that sometimes she and her partner pay to have their picture taken simply to gain an extra minute of cuddling, since such close contact is otherwise

23. Pedro Almodóvar's film *Hable con Ella* (*Speak with Her*) provides a cinematic representation of presence creation: the love-stricken protagonist tenderly fashions a "joint" existence with his comatose sweetheart by continually talking to her, attending to her bodily needs, frequenting movies and performances she would enjoy, showing her pictures of his home décor, and reading travel guides to her. Another example from the art world is the Weblog "In Network" (www.turbulence.org/Works/innetwork) created by Julia Steinmetz and Michael Mandiberg, which documents the couple's use of cell phones to include each other in mundane activities during a year of living on opposite coasts of the United States.

forbidden during the course of a visit. When I return the photo to Sarah she carefully props it against the saltshaker between the two of us and gazes tenderly at her spouse. "There," she smiles. "Now he can have lunch with us."

———

Informal and personalized, the practices of presence creation evolve over the course of relationships according to the imaginativeness of couples and the time they have to devote to such routines, which often become more intense and intricate as their years together progress. Much like widows striving to simulate commensality (Sidenvall, Nydahl, and Fjellstrom 2000, 416), wives, fiancées, and girlfriends of prisoners frequently use pictures and other representations of their beloved to designate a particular space as occupied by his presence. Although every photograph taken at San Quentin is snapped in a visiting room's designated picture-taking area and thus is perpetually framed by the same background and the men are always dressed in their prison uniforms, women arrange to have themselves regularly photographed with their partners and display multiple examples of these portraits (either in their initial Polaroid form or in a more standard format achieved by making color photocopies of the original and adjusting the sizing) in their homes and wallets.[24] Placed among other depictions of family and friends, these photos integrate the distant man into a woman's personal realm, blurring the dividing line of the prison and establishing the man's status as an intimate. As noted in the discussion of correspondence, letters and other objects also can invoke someone's presence and provide a visceral link between cell and domicile by substituting for the missing person's body. During a nearly one-year period of suspension of contact visits for Death Row inmates, Bernice requested a "prop" from her fiancé to help her "trans-

24. Photographs cost $2 and are paid for in advance by the prisoner, although his visitor often provides the money for this service. A more deluxe alternative to color photocopying was spotlighted in the December 2005 issue of *Harper's* magazine, which featured a sidebar of promotional material from Photos Beyond the Wall, a digital-technology service marketed to prisoners' kin: "Are you tired of seeing you and your family in dozens of photos taken in the visiting room over the years—all with the same old boring backdrops? How would like to see . . . you and your 'Boo' standing by a hot tub, in a plush bedroom . . . or in front of a beautiful gazebo surrounded by flowers—all in photos you can hang on your walls and show to everyone? . . . ESCAPE from the confines of boring visiting-room backgrounds and be released to the free world—right into the photo location of your choice!"

port" him from behind the thick separation glass and into her private sphere:

[I missed smelling him so much] to where I told him, "Send me a package with a shirt that smells like you." He sent me two shirts, and he said, "I stuffed some hand-kerchiefs in the pockets, and they smell like me." So every night before I go to bed I unzip it, because I have it in a big comforter bag that zips, and I throw it in there because I don't want to lose the smell; even though it smells like an institution, it doesn't smell like me remembering his body. So I smell his shirt—[and] his handker-chief smells like him.

Similarly, during the hiatus in contact visiting Laura's fiancé reversed this process and "invited" Laura into his cell by asking her to provide him with the tastes and smells that characterized their meetings so that he could imagine them being together: "[H]e had asked me to send him some popcorn [because we used to eat it during visits] and he says, 'Yeah,' he says, 'I'm gonna put on some of my cologne,' and he says, 'I'm gonna take me some popcorn, and I'm gonna have us a visit!'"[25]

Another means of fictively collapsing the division between the institution and the home is the synchronization of activities, which thereby enables couples to imagine doing things "together." Like other American couples, who "speak of sharing—thoughts, feelings, tasks, values, or life goals—as the greatest virtue in a relationship" (Bellah et al. 1996, 91), women with incarcerated partners place much importance on the exchange of information and the simultaneous engagement in endeavors. Blessing—whom other wives admired for her creativity—manages to actively participate in many of her husband's recreational interests: "I still keep him exposed to everything I possibly can. And all different cultures, whatever I learn, I give to him. We share as much as we can, like, we watch the same movies. San Quentin has a movie station, and I'll go out and rent the movie and watch it with him that way. We'll read the same books, so we share everything we can the best way we can."

This concept of "sharing" may extend as well to women consulting, and even legally including, their partners when making decisions, despite the lack of immediate effect these undertakings have on the men. Aisha, who purchased a small parcel of land in the moun-

25. Following Deborah Lupton (1996, 49), "food is frequently advertised as a means of capturing previous positive experiences and emotions, allowing consumers to revive these positive associations and experience them again each time they eat the product."

tains, stressed the important role she accorded to her husband in this enterprise:

We make decisions mutually. If I have an idea I'll take it to him. I *never* make a decision on my own, especially if it's an important one, without talking it over with him first, cuz I don't ever want him to feel like he's not a part of my life, even if he can't participate out here. We really respect that about each other. I thought that it would be a really good idea, because it would give him something to focus on. You know, it would give him something to look forward to. So when I bought the land I had it put in both of our names, you know, it's deeded to both of us and as soon as it's paid for we'll get the deed. I had him sign all the papers, you know, for the title company, and I take him pictures of it. I go up there, I was just up there in April, I'm going to go again in August and build a campsite. I consulted with him about the campsite. I take pictures from every angle in all different seasons whenever I go to show him, and actually it's really, *really* been a good idea to do that because we talk about it, we talk about what we want to build there, what we want to create there, the spirit with which we want to, you know, live our lives there.

Accounts of presence creation are notably more prominent among women partnered with men serving life or death-penalty sentences, a tendency that might be explained by various factors: a keen yearning to "pretend" a life of domestic sharing exists (when the chances of this occurring are small to nil) in order to sustain emotional energy for the relationship; the concrete reminders of presence (clothes, possessions, mutual friends) left behind by men who enter prison for shorter periods of time that override the need to fabricate artifacts of a mutual existence; or, as elaborated in chapter 5, the generally higher levels of education and income among partners of life and death-penalty inmates, which may free women to engage in highly conceptualized synchronization and fantasy rather than practical, survival-oriented activities. This prevalence also could be explained as a variant of the "self-protection" technique proposed in *Psychological Survival* (1974, 135–40), Stanley Cohen and Laurie Taylor's study of how long-term prisoners cope with confinement. "Self protection" is a strategy that consists in part of "beat[ing] off the unfavorable definitions" of lawbreakers as disgraced beings and refusing to "play the single all-embracing inmate role twenty-four hours a day" by identifying oneself "in terms which have little to do with the convict role." A component of this arsenal of resistance is "mind-building," or the earnest devotion to self-education, a strategy that enables a prisoner to "retain a sense of value and importance in a hostile environment which is loaded with problems." Presence creation—with all its fantasy and intimacy—complements mind-building as a cerebral manner of investing in the alternate identity of lover (rather than prisoner or woman-on-her-own) and of participating in a life that transcends geographic and penal boundaries, tactics that assume high importance among those who endure long stretches of incarceration (whether their own or their partner's) without reprieve.

———

Altogether, the examination of the four mechanisms used to develop and sustain relationships with prisoners demonstrates the significant curtailing of aspects of "free" women's lives through their attempts to alleviate the isolation and deprivation that typify internment. In their efforts to join with and support a loved one, women link their domestic environments to the prison cell, and as a result an array of penalties—stigma, censorship, invasion of privacy, regulation, spatial confinement, and the regimentation of time—reverberates within the home. Hence, even when not physically at San Quentin, women are subjected to secondary prisonization via institutional management and exploitation since the methods for staying in touch with a mate require surrendering the private domicile as an extended site of penal control.[26] Concurrently, inmates and their partners freight their communication with personal struggles for love and power, using letters, packages, phone calls, and presence creation to vie for recognition as the central figure in a committed and interdependent relationship. For some, the heightened passion achieved both in spite of and due to conditions of forced separation causes life *without* the penitentiary to pale in comparison, particularly when that existence is beset by drudgery and hardship. Mimi, a twenty-three-year-old Native American who relies on under $10,000 in welfare payments annually to support herself and her five children, acknowledged that her "loveable and kind" husband blossoms during his frequent incarcerations:

Well, when he goes to jail, I just notice that he, he expresses his love more in jail than he does out in person. . . . It's different because he'll express *everything* while he's in jail, but when he's out it's a totally different thing. He holds in all his

26. Arguably, some of these punishments can be disconnected from the actual residence through the use of P.O. boxes and cell phones (although such devices incur costs that are beyond the means of most prisoners' partners). My point, however, is that women experience these ramifications at a distance, when they are away from the direct surveillance of the prison authorities and ostensibly occupying "private" space.

problems and stuff like that. . . . So, basically we're trying to work it together. He'll tell you one thing while he's in jail, but then when he gets out it's a different thing! [*giggles*] So it's like, we're trying to work on this [so that] what he says in jail *stays* that way [and] when he gets out it be the same.

The diminutive woman, whose father and uncles were also incarcerated, spoke of severe hardship while fending for herself on the streets at age thirteen and during her previous marriage at sixteen to an abusive man. Reflecting on the violence she endured she said quietly, "That's why I love [my current husband] so much, because he'd never put a hand on me." Although Mimi refers to him as "the head of the household," this young man has been home for just over three months total since the couple met three years ago, a situation that gives new meaning to Clemmer's (1958, 312) caution referred to at the beginning of this chapter about the ramifications of settling into "prison primary" relationships, and elicits fresh questions about the prisonization of intimate life.

FOUR

"Papa's House": The Prison as Domestic Satellite

When I pull in to the San Quentin visitors' parking lot at 9 this morning, I note about a hundred other cars already there (since today is Thanksgiving, a holiday, visiting hours began at 7:30 a.m.). There are still plenty of parking spaces available, and I take one on the outer rim of the lot, overlooking the waters of the bay. It's a gray, dreary day, so I grab my heavy coat along with my backpack and head up the ramp toward the Tube. As I walk, I see Melissa and her four children inside the facility's gate, making their way to the main visiting room. This family has been coming to San Quentin at least weekly for four years, and they are well known and popular among the other visitors due to the vivacity and charm of the kids, who range in age from five to eleven years old. Today Melissa is holding the youngest girl on her hip, and as the other three scamper noisily around her heels the oldest daughter notices me and waves cheerfully, "Hi, Megan!" I wave back, and Melissa gives me a smile while the remaining siblings call out greetings as well.

The whole family is obviously in high spirits, and as I watch them I remember a conversation between Melissa and another mother of four (all of whose offspring were conceived in correctional facilities—she met her husband after he had begun serving his life sentence) in which the women commiserated about the difficulties of explaining a father's incarceration to his children. Both women had chosen to be truthful with their kids but agreed that it was hard to decide on the "right" moment to have such discussions. Melissa laughingly said her son, who was four years old at the time, gave her the needed opening

*when he asked, "Why does Daddy wear the same clothes every day?" The
other mom chuckled and recalled her own son's annoyance at age five with
their cramped living quarters and his petulant outburst, "Well, why is Papa's
house so big?" I had been interested to learn from these women that their
children in fact knew their fathers were incarcerated, since in all the time I
had spent playing and talking with the kids they never gave any indication
that they perceived San Quentin as a prison: for them, the massive structure
toward which they skipped each week was indeed, first and foremost, "Papa's
house."*

———

Although visiting is just one means of staying in touch with a prisoner, it is often the focal point for those inmates who receive outsiders,
the people who come to visit, and any family-oriented programming
within a correctional facility. As Nathan McCall (1994, 158), a journalist who had previously served hard time for armed robbery, recounts:
"On visiting days, the whole cellblock seemed to come alive. We played
the radio louder and talked more. Guys waiting for visits paced near
the cellblock entrance. Others climbed onto the horizontal supports
to the bars to look through the windows, which overlooked the visitors' parking lot" (see also Carlson and Cervera 1991a; Jose-Kampfner
1991; Lloyd 1992). Advocates of convenient and humane visitation
conditions at prisons stress the documented correlation between family involvement and lower recidivism rates: "[M]aintaining links is not
simply a way of reducing one of the more deleterious effects of imprisonment but it is also likely to reduce chances of re-offending on the
basis that prisoners who are able at release to renew their domestic ties
are less likely to re-offend than those whose family relationships have
been severed" (Richards et al. 1994, 1).[1] Correctional officials themselves emphasize this link when purporting that visiting programs are
"intended as an avenue [for prisoners] to develop and maintain healthy
family and community relationships" (California Department of Corrections 1999, 1) that will ease prisoners' societal reentry process and
bolster post-incarceration "success."

Yet when carefully dissected, studies of "predictors of reconviction"
reveal "some tantalising but rather confusing hints" (Paylor and Smith

---

1. See also Holt and Miller 1972; Bakker, Morris, and Janus 1978; Flanagan 1981; Jorgensen,
Hernandez, and Warren 1986; Schafer 1991; Ditchfield 1994; NACRO 1994; Breen 1995; Fishman
and Alissi 1997.

1994, 133) about the roles of the family and of visitation programs, which are found to be more ambiguous (Goetting 1982; Schafer 1994) or more problematic (Fishman 1990, 256–76; Nurse 2002, 36–52) than commonly believed or claimed. Indeed, closer inspection cautions against regarding prison visiting as a monolithic practice that automatically confers the benefits of "reunification" on those brought together and highlights the importance of the relationship histories, communication patterns, and coping techniques that bear upon the experience—not to mention the peculiar circumstances of attempting to enact intimate life in a tightly controlled, stigmatized, and highly scrutinized milieu where personal freedoms are sharply curtailed (Carter 1996a; Cardon 2002). As Creasie Finney Hairston (1988, 51) notes, it is the *absence* of social support that is consistently shown to significantly hinder parolees, while the modest array of studies associating reduced recidivism with family connectedness lack the conceptual frameworks necessary to indicate "the effectiveness of these models in achieving their specific objectives, in contributing toward corrections' recidivism-prevention goals, or in maintaining the quantity or quality of family ties either during or after imprisonment," and thus "there is little understanding of why [family-contact programs] do or don't work." Such considerations lead Hairston (1991, 85) to ask a fundamental question about family bonds during imprisonment—"Important to whom and for what?"—and to call for more comprehensive analyses of the personal and social experiences of felons and their kin both within and away from the penitentiary's walls.

In this chapter I analyze three traditionally intimate occurrences—family meals, weddings, and spending the night together—in order to examine the contradictory emotional and institutional processes that complicate and reshape relationships during periods of incarceration and thereby profoundly transform the nature of precisely what visitation is meant to maintain, namely, family life. Continuing the analysis introduced in chapter 3, I propose that as couples re-create and alter ostensibly "personal" practices by lodging them in the correctional setting, "the memories of pre-penal experiences cease to be satisfying or practically useful, [which removes] a barrier to prisonization" (Clemmer 1958, 303). For some women, the growing appreciation of togetherness behind bars, particularly as it contrasts with life in "free" society (whether with or without their partners), leads to a markedly high level of secondary prisonization characterized by "the incorporation of the norms of prison life into one's habits of thinking, feeling, and acting," which may "become chronic and deeply internalized so that, even though surrounding conditions may change, many of the once-functional but ultimately counterproductive patterns remain" (Haney 2003, 38–39; see also Culberton 1975, 128). This characterization resonates with women's colloquial use of the word "institutionalization" when speaking about fears for their partners. Alice, who worries that her husband will become accustomed to San Quentin during his three-year stay, elaborated:

My husband was telling me, like, *it bothers* him to be in here. But other people, he said, it don't bother 'em, he said, some people—*this* is home, and *getting out* is a vacation. You know? And they just go right back. He said it don't bother 'em though, cuz it's just like the streets, and this is more home. Well, sad part is, some people that stay in here for a long period of time get out and be kind of all institutionalized, you know? And that's their life.

One primary way women attempt to combat the institutionalization of their loved ones is by visiting regularly and frequently.[2] According to records provided by a former San Quentin visiting lieutenant, an average of 179 people entered the institution to visit prisoners each Thursday and Friday in a sample month (June 1997), with an average of 396 arriving for this purpose every Saturday and Sunday during the same period. Fifty-two percent of the interview participants said that they saw their partners as often as possible within their personal array of constraints, meaning, for example, that employed women came on all of their days off, while people traveling long distances to the prison tried to budget for a visit every month or two. Seventy percent of the participants frequented the prison between one and four days each week: 24 percent came to see their partners once every seven days, 30 percent made the journey twice a week, 6 percent showed up three times weekly, while a full 10 percent regularly came each of the four allocated days.

Regular visitation shows an intuitive grasp of Goffman's (1961, 15) warning: "Although some roles can be re-established by the inmate if and when he returns to the world, it is plain that other losses are irrevocable and may be painfully experienced as such. It may not be possible to make up, at a later phase of the life cycle, the time not now spent in educational or job advancement, in courting, or in rearing one's chil-

2. This of course is limited to those who are financially able to undertake the costs of visiting a prisoner, such as travel expenditures, cash for snacks and other personal supplies, and, when necessary, money for overnight lodging and incidental expenses, plus income foregone (see Davis 1992; Grinstead et al. 2001; Braman 2004).

dren." Hoping to reduce the "irrevocable losses" incurred by a man's absence from the home, wives, fiancées, and girlfriends attempt to involve their partners in personal and family life by relocating various everyday activities to the prison's visiting room. A curious inversion of the premise that frequent visitation facilitates societal reintegration results: as kinship gatherings, family celebrations, and romance are imported into the carceral environment, the penitentiary becomes a domestic satellite, an alternative site for the performance of "private" life, which, in addition to investing the prisoner more firmly in his outside connections, simultaneously absorbs his relations within the boundaries of "Papa's house." Hence the peculiar predicament facing women fighting the institutionalization of their mates: through their efforts to create strong inclusive bonds with incarcerated partners, they partake in the paradoxical secondary prisonization of their own family lives and thus extend the reach and intensity of the transformative effects of the carceral apparatus.

Bringing Him "Home and Heart and Hearth": Eating Together during Visits

Before I even stepped into the Tube today, I saw Millie, a thirty-four-year-old white woman who works as a retail cashier and to whom I started talking a few weeks ago, shortly after her husband arrived at San Quentin with a six-year sentence. She came bounding out of the Tube to meet me at the entrance, making a gesture like fans do at sports games, pumping her arms around as if she were running and giving me two thumbs up.

"I'm so glad to see you! I'm really sorry I haven't called you back, I've been so busy shopping, getting ready for this visit!"

"Do you have a family visit today?" I asked her, referring to the overnight visits permitted to legally married prisoners. I could already read the answer in her beaming face.

"Yes!" she said with excitement. "And I'm so nervous! I've got all my stuff together. I'm really nervous. My husband and I have to get all reacquainted again." She gulped a breath of air, then set off in an excited rush: "It took me four days of shopping to get all the food together! I had to keep going back, because I wanted everything to be really fresh. Like, I wanted to bring in one of those precooked chickens. But I have to buy cold food, because I'm using food stamps. So I tried to get a chicken the night before, thinking it would be really fresh—but they didn't have any chickens! So no chicken. But you should see the steaks I bought! Big, thick T-bones [she held her fingers

about two and a half inches apart]. *I spent fifteen dollars on two steaks. And then I spent another ten dollars on New York steaks that we'll probably have for breakfast."*

*She looked at me slyly, "My husband said to me, 'If you're not bringing meat, don't show up!'" We both laughed, and Millie continued describing her menu: "We'll probably have bacon and eggs for breakfast today, and the T-bones tonight—*they are this thick!*" She held her fingers apart again to emphasize the steaks' sumptuousness. "I brought Chicken-in-a-Biscuit crackers, Stove-Top potatoes in chicken flavor. And macaroni and cheese—four boxes! The guard even asked me why we had four boxes, 'Do you have kids coming in?' he asked. I said, 'No, we just eat a lot!' He told me that they've had trouble with people bringing in too much food and then smuggling the left-overs to the inmates, but we'll eat all that! My husband and I could easily go through four boxes of macaroni and cheese. Plus, I'd rather have enough and then we'll just throw the extra away. And for snacks, I brought peanut butter, and Top Ramen, you know, just for easy snacks." Pausing, Millie scrunched up her forehead, trying to remember any remaining items on her shopping list. With nothing coming to mind, she glanced impatiently at her wristwatch, shimmied her body nervously, and grinned at me with happy anticipation.*

———

Food may seem a tangential or banal aspect of prison visiting, a low priority compared to the more pressing desires for face-to-face conversation or physical interaction with someone forcibly separated from his loved ones. However, during my interviews and field observations, women repeatedly described their behind-bars eating situations in great detail, elaborating the planning involved in organizing carceral meals, the motives behind purchasing specific types of food, and recollected or expected experiences of communal consumption. Correctional authorities recognize the high value placed by visitors and inmates on food and therefore use the control of commensality as one of three key factors—along with the length of the meeting and the degree of bodily contact allowed—to structure the distribution of visiting privileges along the hierarchy of prisoner security levels. Noncontact visits occupy the lowliest end of this spectrum, as these meetings are limited to approximately one hour, forbid all exchange of touch, and do not entail any opportunities for eating. Slightly more advantageous are the Death Row cubicle visits, which are scheduled for two hours, permit a greeting and good-bye embrace, and allow visitors to purchase food to share with the inmate from the prison's vending machines before the visit begins.[3] Next up on the ladder come the Mainline and H-Unit contact visits, which can last for up to seven hours,[4] take place in large cafeteria-style areas, and sanction a hug and a kiss at the beginning and end of the visit plus holding hands throughout the encounter—within certain limits: "Holding hands on top of the table in plain view is permitted, with no other physical contact. . . . [V]iolation of the rules and regulations may result in termination, restriction, suspension, or denial of visits" (California Department of Corrections 1999). Although no outside food is allowed into these areas, guests may bring in up to $30 a day to purchase a variety of sandwiches, snacks, and beverages from vending machines for themselves and the prisoner throughout the visit. These machines, which are consolidated against one wall of the visiting room, provide a welcome distraction and opportunity to move around in an otherwise stark and physically restricted environment.

People visiting men at the Ranch, the minimum-security area where inmates live in barracks and may work in off-site crews for employers such as the California Transit Authority, enjoy greater leeway.[5] There, meetings occur in an unlocked lodge with an adjoining grassy space rimmed by barbecue grills and shaded picnic tables; although the rules for physical contact are ostensibly the same as those for Mainline and H-Unit, the relaxed atmosphere facilitates furtive caresses and enables prisoners to tussle or play tag with their children. Ranch visitors are allowed to bring in limited amounts of outside food conforming to specific requirements: items must be either in factory-sealed packages or have been bought at fast-food outlets (receipts are required to verify the purchases), and no homemade dishes are permitted, although once at the Ranch people may use the barbecue grills for cooking.

Family visits are the most coveted of all encounters, granted to the immediate relatives and legal spouses of prisoners who have not been convicted of domestic violence or sexual crimes and who have a release date. During family visits, inmates and their guests spend forty-three hours together in one of a cluster of small portable units within a pa-

3. Once visitors are locked inside the cubicle with the prisoner they are not allowed to leave; requesting to exit the cubicle for any reason, including to use the restroom, results in the termination of the visit.

4. If there is adequate space in the visiting room, outsiders may stay until the end of the visiting hours. However, when overcrowding occurs people are "terminated" on a "first-come, first-to-leave" basis.

5. Due to men's work schedules, visiting hours at the Ranch begin at 2:30 Thursday and Friday. The prestige of gainful employment apparently compensates for this abbreviated visiting period, as I never heard women complain about not being able to see prisoners there on weekday mornings.

trolled compound on the prison grounds. San Quentin has two family-visit areas, one for Mainline and H-Unit prisoners and one for those coming from the Ranch. At the former, prisoners must order their food in advance from the institution's cafeteria; at the latter, outsiders are allowed to bring in factory-sealed supplies for "homemade" fare, a prized liberty that generates much excitement, as recorded by my field notes on Millie.

Responsibilities for "feeding the family" are strongly associated with the female gender role (DeVault 1991, 35–57, 95–119; see also Charles and Kerr 1988; Fürst 1997). As Deborah Lupton (1996, 62) notes, "[I]n the general atmosphere of family disintegration . . . producing a 'proper' meal . . . [is] seen as a symbol of family reinforcement." Such desires to succor one's mate become even more salient in tightly controlled relationships with scarce opportunities for shared activities or the exchange of gifts, and thus in prison both the provision and partaking of food develop into central acts for the creation of connectedness and closeness.[6] The belief that men receive inadequate supplies of food and generally no nutritious fare or "treats" during their detention drives women to compensate for this lack when visiting at San Quentin. Wives participating in family visits such as Pat, a thirty-four-year-old homeless and unemployed African American, try to furnish surprises that make the occasion special: "It was like, candlelight, we had little plastic wineglasses you can take in, and they were red. You can't take alcohol in, so you know, we had strawberry and kiwi soda that we poured in the wine glasses. It was candle-lit and steaks for dinner, I mean, you know, we had a nice time."

In a similar effort, many women who are restricted to buying snacks in the prison routinely bring in the maximum amount of money permitted and spend the bulk of it on overpriced victuals for the prisoner. Jasmine, a nineteen-year-old Palestinian American who quit her job as an assembly-line worker following her boyfriend's arrest so that she could move closer to San Quentin during his six-month sentence, described this practice:

JASMINE: Their food in there is *so expensive,* it's like unbelievable! Hot wings are like
   three bucks, a little sandwich like this [*indicating with her hands a square the size*

---

6. The woman's role as provider is accentuated by the regulation prohibiting prisoners from directly handling any money, meaning that the outsider must insert all currency into the vending machines herself and thus purchase each item.

of a piece of Wonder Bread] is three bucks, you know? The only thing that's regular from outside is the sodas. Seventy-five cents.

MC: So how much will you spend on food in a visit?

JASMINE: Um, 'bout twenty-five dollars. And sometimes he won't even be full. So. You know. That's kinda hard cuz their prices don't need to be like that. They're vending machines, you know? So, there's no need for it to be like that. They're just tryin' to get over on people, I think.

For most visitors, the mandatory reliance on the expensive vending machines for their meals is frustrating, since, as Anne Murcott (1983, 81) documents, women often believe that "[w]hat was prepared at home could be trusted. . . . Convenience foods had their place, but . . . the cooked dinner marks the threshold between the public domains of school or work and the private sphere behind the closed front door." Yet visitors still manage to imbue their communal eating of standardized fare with a sense of "home," as Sophia explained:

[During visits] you can buy very disgusting cafeteria food in the vending machines and cook it, together, in the microwave. I mean, at least you can eat together. That's a wonderful part of the visiting, I would say, and it's hard to understand but, as a woman, I want to nurture my husband. The food in there [that is regularly provided to prisoners] is atrocious. . . . The food inside that he gets, yes, horrific! So I try to do everything in my power to bring him nutrition and wholesome and home and heart and hearth and everything that is possibly normal about breaking bread with somebody that you care for, which is a very sacred ritual, for people to share food. That's my only opportunity to really give him anything. I can't bring anything with me, I can't bring my homemade food, so I buy what they have and we break bread.

The desire to augment the standard prison menu is so keen that some women who are not allowed to bring food into the prison resort to smuggling various delicacies to their partners. Aisha confided that her husband, who is a practicing Muslim, "won't eat the meat there, cuz it's not halal. Maybe once a month, they'll get some halal chicken. But, for the most part, he doesn't eat any meat. So I'll take him some, I'll cook him something." Likewise, Sarah once regaled me with the story of her elaborate efforts to share leftovers from Thanksgiving dinner with her husband: after carefully enfolding flattened samples of various dishes in saran wrap, she distributed the packets around her thighs and stomach, holding the items in place with a pair of support pantyhose and cloaking the operation with loose trousers. Once she entered the visiting area, she went to the restroom and dismantled this veritable "moveable feast," hiding everything in her coat pockets. Her next maneuver entailed buying a decoy article from the vending machine, dumping out the uneaten foodstuff from its shallow plastic container, and furtively replacing it with the illicit turkey, stuffing, and side dishes. Successfully managing to heat the meal in the microwave, Sarah carried it (under the convenient cover of a paper towel) to her husband—who then found himself unable to lift a telltale forkful to his mouth due to the persistent vigilance of the correctional officers. "We were sitting there and it seemed like they would never look away, and the food was getting cold and the room was filling up, so I was afraid I was going to get terminated, and I was just feeling miserable," she remembers. Sarah's husband, noticing her distress, asked her what was wrong. *"I just want you to be able to eat your turkey!"* she wailed, almost in tears.

As accounts like these demonstrate, women clearly see eating during visits as occasions to re-create, or import, "home" within the penitentiary walls by employing the practical and symbolic functions of food to nourish their partners' bodies and souls.[7] Yet the concentration of attention on consumption *inside* the prison frequently skews the meanings and practices of eating *outside* the facility, and thus transforms the act it purportedly imitates. For example, although Sophia noted that "I'm a health-food girl, I prefer organic and nonprocessed [food]" and complains about the unwholesome snacks available in the visiting room, she substitutes this fare for her own regular diet during eight of her weekly meals in order to eat with her husband.[8] In addition, the high prices of the vending machines and the considerable cost of bringing in only factory-sealed packages of food[9] mean that Sophia, Jasmine, and numerous other low-income women forfeit the quality or quantity of their own intake both inside and outside of the prison—scrimping on their personal food budgets or skipping meals altogether—so as to be able to afford the satisfaction of their partners' appetites. Even among those with higher incomes, sharing meals with

7. On the use of food in the social reproduction of families, see Charles and Kerr 1988, 17–38; Beardsworth and Keil 1997, 73–99.

8. Sophia typically visits the maximum number of days and hours allowed, four days a week for seven hours.

9. This regulation for the Ranch and overnight visitors includes salt, pepper, condiments, butter, and other items that one typically uses over long periods of time before finishing an individual container, thus new, unopened supplies must be purchased for each visit.

an inmate necessitates the reorganization of eating patterns around visiting hours, precluding dining at more conventional times with family or friends. For people confined to the cafeteria-style areas, the prison environment also disrupts commensality: rather than relaxing comfortably around a table, the prisoner and his guest perch awkwardly side by side in interlocked chairs, hold food in their hands or laps because the knee-high tables are too low to use with ease, and struggle with plastic utensils amid the din of the crowded room.

Yet each of these sacrifices and transformations appears more evident to the analytical observer than the participants, most of whom focus on the pleasurable and sensual aspects of eating in correctional facilities and tout the benefits of blurring the boundaries between prison and home. The latter is especially important for mothers such as LaShawn, a twenty-four-year-old African American bus driver who hesitated to bring her seven-year-old son into standard visiting rooms, preferring areas like the Ranch where "it's just like a picnic" (a statement echoed by Millie in reference to her decision to let her four-year-old daughter visit). As the vignettes presented above document, women use food as a tool to domesticate the carceral environment, and indeed when one surveys the line of visitors tugging their multicolored coolers filled with factory-sealed or fast food behind them, little in their appearance or comportment suggests they are going anywhere more complicated than a light-hearted family gathering.

"The Happiest Day of Our Life": Weddings in Prison

Today was a wedding day: every two months on the first Thursday of the month marriages are performed in the visiting areas for couples who have filled out the requisite paperwork. I had forgotten that today was such a day until I saw an extremely thin dark-haired woman show up in the Tube in a long, white beaded outfit that was one step away from a full-blown wedding dress. She was accompanied by a girl who looked to be about eight years old wearing a dark green velvet and taffeta party dress, an older girl (probably around twelve years old) in a garment that matched the little one's, and the grandmother of the pair. It was unclear to me whether the bride was the mother or the soon-to-be stepmother of the children, but the girls were sweetly excited about the upcoming ceremony, prancing around in their shiny, black Mary Jane shoes, smoothing each other's rustling skirts, and practicing standing alert while clasping their hands demurely in front of them. Also there for a wedding was a very tall, attractive woman whom I recognized as a frequent visitor. At first I didn't realize she was there to be married because she had on a long wool coat that covered her white silk blouse and skirt, although I did notice that her hair was swept back elegantly and sculpted in elaborate curls. Her two sons—who appeared to be about the same age as the bridesmaids— were with her, sitting somberly side by side on the bench.

Processing began as normal with the regular visitors at 11:30, but shortly thereafter an announcement blasted through the loudspeaker: "Attention in the Tube! Attention in the Tube! Anybody here for a wedding, come to the front of the line now! If you're getting married today, come to the front of the line!" The first bride scurried into the processing area, bridesmaids and grandmother in tow. While she had been waiting she told us that she had already brought the dress to San Quentin several weeks beforehand and worn it through the metal detector twice as a "practice run" (carefully returning it to her car afterward and changing into regular clothes for her visit), and indeed the entourage was processed rapidly and without a hitch. The second woman was not as fortunate, returning to the Tube several minutes after entering the processing area due to a slit in her ankle-length skirt that the correctional officers said came too far above her knee. Relatively unperturbed, she swiftly retrieved her backup outfit from her car and donned it in the filthy bathroom, gracefully bypassing the throng of waiting visitors as she reentered the prison and went to join her groom.

———

Under California law, any prisoner has the legal right to marry while incarcerated. It takes several months to file a request to marry and to fill out the requisite paperwork with the assistance of an inmate's "counselor" (a prison employee charged with helping with administrative matters), and among the necessary documents is the fiancée's signed affidavit that she understands her intended spouse is a convicted felon who is serving time in a state correctional facility. Each prison organizes its own schedule for marriages; San Quentin conducts ceremonies six times a year, on the first Thursday of every other month. Typically three or four couples share the same wedding day, but the officiating chaplain performs an individual service for each, attending to them on a first-come, first-conjoined basis. Although relatively few visitors decide to marry someone while he is incarcerated—often preferring to wait until he is released, if possible—the weddings that do occur are highly visible and symbolically valued events with a large social impact, publicly affirming the romance and durability of carceral relationships.

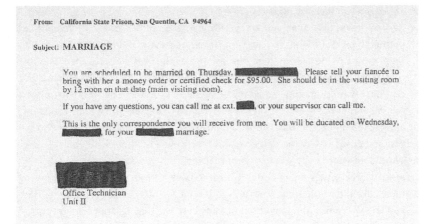

From: California State Prison, San Quentin, CA 94964

Subject: **MARRIAGE**

You are scheduled to be married on Thursday, ▮▮▮▮▮▮▮▮ Please tell your fiancée to bring with her a money order or certified check for $95.00. She should be in the visiting room by 12 noon on that date (main visiting room).

If you have any questions, you can call me at ext. ▮▮▮, or your supervisor can call me.

This is the only correspondence you will receive from me. You will be ducated on Wednesday, ▮▮▮▮▮▮, for your ▮▮▮▮▮▮ marriage.

Office Technician
Unit II

Figure 4.1 Paperwork for a prison wedding

When unembellished by the participants, prison nuptials are austere events, subject to the standard procedures and troubles of regular visits. This was the case for Stephanie, who wed a man held at Corcoran State Prison, a facility 235 miles south of San Francisco:

STEPHANIE: Well that day [*matter-of-factly*], it was like a normal visit, I had to get processed and wait until the shuttle came to pick us up. And then I got there, and they had to get him out. And we had to wait for the pastor to come, and we had to have another inmate, which was his cellmate, sign a marriage certificate. Then we went into a room, it was just a little small room, with nothing inside, just somewhere we could stand, and that's how we got married. . . . I tried to be as special as possible, considering the rules. I had a purple floral dress that was like two sizes too big because it can't be form-fitting. . . . [Then there was a problem because] he had to work on Saturdays, but it wasn't until three thirty. Visitin' was over at two thirty. Well, his ducat [authorization for the visit] said twelve o'clock. But he didn't have to go to work until two thirty, so he was supposed to have his visit until two thirty. But they were like, "No, your ducat says twelve, so your visitin's over at twelve." So after we got married I only had an hour and a half to visit with him, and they made him go back to his cell until it was time for him to work.
MC: So, you went by yourself to get married?
STEPHANIE: Yeah, I drove by myself, and stayed overnight. There was this place, this hotel that's like right down the street pretty much, and they give you like a six-dollar discount if you're visiting Corcoran. [*bursts out laughing*] . . .

MC: How did you feel driving back home?

STEPHANIE: I was like, *man*, you know, this is it, you know, I did that! [*laughs*] I'm married now! But then I was also really upset because I couldn't visit him for that time, they wouldn't let me visit him as long as the visit allowed. I felt like they could've let us have that time, they could've checked later. But they wouldn't do that. I was upset, and I could tell he was upset too because when he hugged me, he wasn't really like, "Okay, I'll see you later," he was just silent. You know, and I asked him about that later and he was like, "You know, I really hated to see you go because we're married now and I can't even be there with you."

MC: And does your family know you got married?

STEPHANIE: Yeah, they know about it. I came back and I tried to hide it from my mom, like hidin' my ring—I wasn't gonna take it off, cuz it's like I'm married, you know? I'm not gonna do that. But I tried to like hide it, I put it in my pocket [*giggles*], and she was like, "I know you're married! I know you went down there and married him!"

Although special circumstances can be arranged for prisoners with no contact privileges, the majority of weddings occur in the regular visiting areas. In accordance with the rule permitting no more than five people to visit an inmate at any one time, there is a limit of four outside guests who may witness the occasion. However, as Blessing explained, couples often capitalize on the lack of privacy surrounding their marriages by including others to enlarge the celebration:

I had invitations go out. . . . And the people I invited [were other visitors and prisoners], because these people become your family, these visitors, these guys that are here, they become like a family to you because you see them! So your feelings grow for them as well. . . . The majority of people [invited] were from here [San Quentin]. Some of them I didn't even know well. But we tend to try to support each other when we get married. Because we know that it's not the same kind of deal. You know, you're leaving your husband here after you get married.

By sending formal invitations to people who most likely would have been present at her marriage anyway, Blessing strives to make a personal virtue out of a penal necessity by recasting a forcedly public spectacle as an elective private affair. Also, by replacing her kinship network with the carceral community—and thus demonstrating the accordance of kin status to social intimates noted by Carol Stack (1974, 29–30)—she manages to preserve her wedding as a "family" event despite the absence of her blood relations ("My family, they don't quite understand, why and how [I decided to marry a Death Row prisoner], and I'm sure that they hurt behind it"). This dependence on the benevolent participation of a collective characterizes penitentiary marriages, for even when a woman's relatives condone her choice of spouse, the five-people-per-prisoner restriction necessitates the substitution of visitors for family members or outside friends on one's wedding day. Queenie's numerous children and foster children were overwhelmingly supportive of her marriage, yet it was impossible for all of them to accompany her to the nuptials. Nonetheless, the ceremony was a large affair, with almost everyone in the visiting room coming to stand with the couple when they were wed, prompting the chaplain to remark, "There's a lot of love here. You have everyone with you." In addition to lending their presence, the other women gave Queenie a range of offerings custom tailored to the penitentiary marriage: one convict's wife brought a disposable camera and snapped photos of Queenie and her friends in the parking lot before they entered the institution; another gave Queenie two $10 rolls of quarters, saying they were for the bride and groom to spend on vending-machine treats that day; a third woman produced a Native American–design necklace made by her inmate husband that she had smuggled out of the facility on a previous visit; and a final loyal friend came to San Quentin at 8 in the morning the day of the marriage, telling Queenie, "I thought you might be nervous and want someone to sit with you [while waiting to go into the prison], so I dropped off the kids and came here to be with you."

Weddings are perhaps the most heavily scripted of personal rituals, propelled by an enormous industry centered on inculcating desires, primarily in women, for a host of specific objects and activities that collectively produce "the perfect day" (Lewis 1998; Shida 1999; Corrado 2002).[10] So powerful are these forces that even women marrying under circumstances seemingly antithetical to romantic pageantry go to great lengths to replicate the dominant model of what constitutes a wedding. Tee married her husband in 1991 at Deuel Vocational Institution (DVI) in Tracy, sixty-five miles southeast of San Francisco, prior to his transfer to San Quentin:

TEE: We had a *very* special wedding that nobody probably has ever had. There happened to be a female guard that knew him really well, and she was affiliated

10. The critique of the so-called wedding-industrial complex (Ingraham 1999, 25–76; see also Currie 1993) for targeting women and saddling them with primary responsibility for a supposedly egalitarian event has particular resonance in prison marriages, since the inmate is excluded from participation in external planning and preparation.

with the same religious organization as us [Jehovah's Witnesses]. So she took the chance to speak for us and say, "I'll be with them and I'll watch them if they can get married out on the garden, in the yard." A real pretty garden with flowers all around and green grass, you know. You could still see the prison in the pictures a little bit but it looked like we had a beautiful garden wedding. And that's what I'd always wanted all my life, was to have a garden wedding. So she was *really* nice, and we had like five inmates, and they all had five visitors, or six visitors, so we had altogether like twenty-five people at our wedding. And I had a *full-length wedding gown*. Full-length wedding gown, veil, *everything*. And I had flowers, a fresh bouquet of flowers. My little niece was my flower girl. It was really a beautiful wedding we had. Everybody, all the guards up there said, "This is the most romantic wedding I ever saw in DVI." [*chuckles*] So. And at that time they allowed us to bring a camera in, to take pictures.

MC: So things have really changed.

TEE: Things have changed a lot. Now it's not-so-nice weddings people have. For one thing, you can't even wear a wedding gown anymore probably, cuz you can't get through the metal detector! But back then they allowed you to wear a regular wedding dress, and they'd just use a wand and wand you. But now they're so strict about everything. I don't think anybody wears, *I've* never seen anybody else wear a full-length wedding gown [*chuckles, proud of herself*]. And a veil and everything.

On the day of her prison-bound marriage, a new bride relies heavily on the expertise acquired by long-term visitors—who take on the role of "wedding veterans" (Westlake-Chester 1995)—regarding the production of ritually satisfying and appropriately "special" ceremonies given the dearth of conventional resources. Sarah, the Silicon Valley account manager, had dreamed of her nuptials since she was a little girl and recounted with much tenderness her friends' concoction of her wedding cake:

SARAH: It was really cute because people get really creative in there. So whenever it's somebody's wedding, a whole bunch of other people will make them a cake. So they'll take something, like a piece of coffee cake—it's all vending machine food—[*excited, appreciative of people's innovation*] and they'll melt cream cheese and they'll frost the inside with cream cheese and then they'll melt like a Hershey bar, and they'll frost it, you know, drizzle it over the top with the melted chocolate.

MC: Where do they melt all these things?

SARAH: Oh, in the microwave. Yeah, and what else have I seen them do? Or they'll take a muffin, and same thing, they'll mix cream cheese with chocolate and frost it, and you know, they'll put little candies all around it, and on top of it, [*happily*] like our cake! You saw the picture of our cake! You know, it was basically a piece of cinnamon coffee cake, and it was frosted, oh, it had chocolate drizzled all over it and then they'd taken cream cheese and they drew an S and B on the top, for Sarah and Ben, and then they put some other little candy or something around it. You know, so they made us a wedding cake.

Sarah's delight belies the stark fact that, by virtue of her association with a prisoner, a woman with an annual income of over $100,000 has a connubial celebration similar to that of Chicago's South Side ghetto residents, whose crushing poverty forces them to "have to make do with degraded imitations and inferior substitutes of the goods, rites, and values sanctified by the encompassing society" (Wacquant 1996, 109). In addition to these severely limited opportunities for pomp and revelry, a fundamental condition of prison marriages is that shortly after being joined in matrimony, the groom himself becomes a scarce resource. Despite this strikingly unconventional feature, some newlyweds, like Blessing, actively pursue a traditional "bridal experience" by partaking in the full range of prescribed activities:

BLESSING: And I had a bridal shower, too. And I had a reception after the wedding.
. . . A girlfriend of mine gave the reception after visiting at her home. And her
dad barbecued and a lot of people came, and it went well into the night! We
had a grand time. I received a lot of gifts. Some gifts I'm still using because of
course they didn't give me gifts that him and I could use, but then they gave me
gifts and I still have a lot of them that I haven't even opened, so it was, it was
nice. Um-hmm, it was really nice. . . . But it makes a big difference I noticed between those who were married and didn't have no real celebration afterwards,
like before they just got married and that was it. Versus women who have had a
celebration *before* and *after*, it makes a big difference.
MC: What kind of difference?
BLESSING: Well, you don't feel lonely probably. And, you're still celebrating like
you should. You know, instead of just "I'm married and I'll go home and that's
it." You're still celebrating like most brides and grooms do except [*laughing*] the
groom's not there! So I think it's a big difference. You know? And most women
here [at San Quentin], I think we started doing these receptions and bridal
showers about five years ago. We try to get each one.

The striking commonality in the accounts of Blessing, Queenie, Tee, and Sarah is their attempt to normalize the holding of a romantic, joyful, and hopeful ritual in a setting whose symbolic organization and practical operation are meant to diametrically oppose and inhibit such emotions. In contrast to outside couples who experience their weddings as "joint enterprises" that can be hypermanaged or flexibly designed (Sniezek 2003), prisoners and their fiancées are exceedingly limited in their opportunities for collaboration and must comply with a date, time, outfit, guest list, chaplain, sermon, menu, reception, and honeymoon dictated by the demands of a bureaucratic authority with no stake in the pair's happiness. The strong backing of other visitors and the energetic deployment of stipulated conventions help to mask the bleak surroundings and circumstances of this happening, which become more apparent in cases such as Stephanie's when there is an absence of social and familial support and a lack of ceremonial display. The key to a gratifying penitentiary wedding therefore is the bride's ability to use external trappings and traditions to obscure the harsh realities of the situation while mobilizing a collective effort to realize the event despite its special constraints. Fulfillment also entails strenuous and sustained "emotion work" (Hochschild 1979) on the part of all involved as people labor both *for* the obligatory cheer suited to a wedding (Mauss 1921) and *against* the resentments and frustrations that well up as the authorities and the environment blight their hopes for this singular and momentous day. Among the women I interviewed and observed who married in the prison, the majority recollected their nuptials with positive, if sometimes bittersweet, sentiment. In the words of Aisha, "It was cool. It was great. It was a really sweet day." Or, as Butta—who married her beloved on the day he was sentenced to twenty years—stated simply, "That was the happiest day of our life."

"Like a Cozy Little Home That I Should Have Outside the Prison Walls": Spending the Night Together

In 1968, under the governorship of Ronald Reagan, the California Department of Corrections established overnight visits—during which up to three members of a prisoner's immediate family can spend three days and two nights locked in a compound with him or her—for a mix of disciplinary and rehabilitation purposes: "Conjugal association in prison is recommended as having the practical consequences of reducing tension and hostility among inmates, providing an incentive for conformity, promoting a more normal lifestyle in preparation for the transition back into free society, increasing the likelihood of post-release success, and fostering marital stability" (Goetting 1982, 63). At San Quentin family visits take place in groups of small portable houses dedicated either to North Block and H-Unit or the Ranch. Each unit is equipped with one or two bedrooms, a bathroom, and a modest kitchen, and benefits from access to the communal outside area, which includes a small playground. The stays are scheduled in forty-three-hour segments throughout the week; up to four families in each spot may have overnight visits simultaneously, and although a mother or sister might occasionally join her relative, wives of inmates constitute the vast majority of participants. The frequency of a couple's visits typically varies between once every thirty to ninety days, depending on the overall number of eligible inmates.

Twenty-four percent of the interview participants qualified for this reprieve from the "deprivation of heterosexual relationships" (Sykes 1958, 70–72) that affects the majority of carceral couples. To meet the criteria for these encounters, couples must be legally married and the prisoner must have a security classification commensurate with contact visits (e.g., not be in solitary confinement); in addition, he cannot have been "convicted of a violent offense involving a minor or family member or any sex offense," nor can he be "sentenced to life without the possibility of parole," "sentenced to life, without a parole date established by the Board of Prison terms," or be "designated a condemned inmate," that is, sentenced to death (State of California 2003, section 3177[1,2]). Prior to 1996 lifers *were* allowed to have family visits, but legislation introduced by California Assemblymember Dean Andal—who justified his bill on punitive and cost-benefit grounds—rescinded this privilege, thereby disqualifying more than half of the roughly twenty-six thousand inmates who previously had been eligible for overnight visits (Davidson 1996).

The belief that it is intolerable to permit prisoners who have committed serious crimes to have opportunities for sexual contact with their partners is a relatively recent development in California. As late as 1989 the California Department of Corrections officially promoted the Family Visitation program: "Good family relationships are believed to enhance the probability of the inmate's successful adjustment to prison, and, later, to his successful reintegration into the community. Therefore, the program is believed to be beneficial to society in general" (Davidson 1996, 8). Although the exclusion of lifers from family visits was effected as a punitive measure in California, Richard Sparks (2002,

576–77) documents how a purportedly rehabilitation-oriented penal system arrived at a similar outcome through the closure of Scotland's Barlinnie Special Unit following the media frenzy over its relaxed visiting regulations:

[T]he unit was simply taken to lack those features which a progressive prison administrator could recognize as tokens of a good prison regime. . . . [I]t had become "dominated by 'visits,'" taken in private (and hence including the possibility of intimacy). It simply cannot be the case—according to the current vocational ideology of prison administration—that such time spent in intensive personal contact with outsiders (nor for that matter alone) can possibly be as good for prisoners as time spent in active engagement with prison officers or psychologists, nor as time spent in the disciplined cultivation of hobbies, crafts and skills.[11]

The revocation of family visits for lifers deeply affected those who previously had been enjoying these periods of closeness with their spouses, as was the case for Tee, who stayed overnight with her husband every few months from 1991 until their visits were eliminated five years later:

And then I think the hardest times came when they took our family visits away. That's when it got real hard. Before, when we had our family visits, we had that little bit of time where you would be together and you would have those two days to be like a real couple. You know, you got a little sense of, "Hey, we're really married! *We're really a couple!* We're really, we're *intimate,*" you know, we got to be intimate and everything. But now, when they took that away, it just, it really made it very difficult, to never have that intimacy. [*heavily*] To me, I felt that it was like a death. Like goin' through a *death* or, you know, because it was just such—we were mourning! We were really in mourning! To know that we would *never* be able to be together intimately. It was so hard. [*pause*] And it's still hard, but it's like, it gets a little easier as time goes by.

11. As Sparks (2002, 574–77) notes, intimate visits were only one of many factors contributing to the closure of the Special Unit, but by far it was the one that most enthralled the media. Both the California and Barlinnie cases contrast markedly with the visiting conditions I observed during my field visit to Rio de Janeiro's Bangú prison complex in October 2001: in a high-security compound housing numerous notorious gang leaders, the Brazilian prisoners were allowed to drag their mattresses, blankets, and television sets into the large visiting room when their family members and girlfriends came to call. The sight of adults kissing, snuggling, and frolicking under blankets while their children scampered about jolted my preestablished idea of prison visiting, but when I explained San Quentin's "one kiss at the beginning and end of the visit," "all hands always plainly in view," and "must be legally married for sex" practices to the warden and prisoners conducting my tour they reacted with incredulity and volubly denounced such prohibitions of sexual contact as shockingly cruel and ridiculously impractical.

According to Sykes (1958, 70), an inmate is "figuratively castrated by his involuntary celibacy" when he is deprived of heterosexual relationships. For a woman, the loss of sexual contact can entail the imposed postponement or abandonment of efforts to conceive a child with a loved one. Indeed, the U.S. Supreme Court ruled in 2002 that inmates do not have a constitutional right to procreate and denied a California prisoner's request to artificially inseminate his wife (Egelko 2001; Chiang 2002). Meanwhile, financially secure wives and girlfriends desperate to conceive children with prisoners in Pennsylvania resorted, with the help of correctional officers, to "sperm-smuggling capers" (Reuters 2000) that cost them thousands of dollars for each frozen sample of their partners' body fluid. At San Quentin during my fieldwork six lifers were placed in solitary confinement due to allegations by other prisoners that the men and their partners repeatedly engaged in illicit sex in the Mainline visiting room. Multiple visitors confirmed to me that these couples routinely snuck into semihidden corners for their hasty carnal encounters, and it was widely known that one of the women in question was in despair as her fortieth birthday approached over the looming possibility of never bearing a child with her husband.[12]

Although partners obviously value family visits as rare opportunities for private sexual contact during the man's incarceration, the three-day, two-night scheduling and the marked contrast with the bustle and exposure of the regular visiting room emphasize the "family" orientation of the encounter, encouraging people to simulate an ordinary living situation rather than fixate on a hurried physical congress. Indeed, through the "quality time" couples may spend together, family visits afford an emotional anchoring fervently expressed by Aisha, who contested the termination of her family visits under the new legislation, since her husband, who is serving twenty-four years, technically does not have a life sentence:

And I *begged* this man [the correctional official] not to do it [stop her family visits]. I begged him, I said, "Look, it's not just about us getting together and having a good ol', you know, ass-slappin' time, okay? This is, it's more important than that.

12. Visitors also report that instances of fondling and intercourse in the visiting areas occur relatively often; the apparent oversight of these acts on the part of the correctional officers infuriates women who are chastised for more innocent embraces, leading to speculation that certain prisoners pay or otherwise reward correctional officers for these liberties. Indeed, the lifers who were placed in solitary confinement were not being punished for their public sexual indulgences, but rather were segregated for their own protection in response to another inmate "dropping a note" (making an anonymous violent threat in writing) saying he was angry about having his children exposed to these dalliances when they came to visit.

It has to do with peace and tranquility and peace of mind and a happy inmate and a happy wife and coping and de-stressing and you know, learning how to pray to- gether and all of the above. Way, way, *way*, much more important than what you might think." [13]

For those who continue to be eligible, the depth of interaction pos- sible during family visits makes them a highlight of a man's time be- hind bars. Women waiting to enter San Quentin for overnight visits typically bubble with nervous excitement, cheerfully comparing stories with each other about the tribulations of organizing food, linens, and clothing for the stay, while in interviews wives warmly recollect their experiences in the compounds, focusing on the recaptured mundane pleasures of being with a loved one. Virtually absent in their accounts is talk of discomforts related to "the deprivation of liberty" (Sykes 1958, 65–67) and being held captive for an extended period in a prison, and in fact such concerns are described as being aberrant or comically dis- ruptive. Pat spoke with amused exasperation about her mother-in-law's intense reaction to temporary correctional confinement:

And, like I say the second one [family visit] was a trip cuz we had his mama there, and my son, and [my mother-in-law] kinda flipped out about bein' locked in. I think she had like a claustrophobia thing come over her, an' they had a little white phone there—if you pick the phone up they gonna automatically think something's wrong. So she's like [*belligerently*], "Well, can't I leave? *I wanna get outta here!* What's this phone for? Lemme pick up the phone!" [*laughing heartily*] She really tripped out! But my son had a great time. You know, we got to swing on the swing, they have little bicycles, they throwin' the football. You know, we really had a nice time, and she felt more comfortable the next day, when there was other couples there, cuz we all got outside and barbecued, and we drunk coffee and talked, and you know, she felt a little better then. . . . Each [prisoner housing] unit has a separate place where they go for home visits. So, yeah. It's really nice, it really is, it's truly nice. It's like your own little two-bedroom *house*! And it's really nice.

The description of the overnight-visit bungalows as being "like your own house" or the assertion that one feels "at home" in the units ap- pears with striking frequency in family-visitors' reports of their prison sojourns. Although such claims clearly affirm wives' appreciation of

13. Aisha and her husband's pleas had no effect: the couple found out that their administra- tive appeal had been denied by the authorities in Sacramento, the seat of the California Depart- ment of Corrections, which blocked any future hope of their resuming family visits.

the privacy granted to them during these visits, they also signal an important cognitive shift in women's perceptions of *what* constitutes their home life and *where* this home life can blossom. For example, Pat—who makes the telling slip of referring to "home" rather than "family" visits—was homeless during her husband's incarceration and had been living precariously for years before his arrest, a factor that contributed to her losing custody of three of her four children.[14] In her case, then, spending a few days in a fixed environment in the company of her kin was a closer approximation of "home" than she normally enjoyed, and this likely contributed to her positive reaction to the "truly nice" living quarters provided by San Quentin. Similarly, Jeanette characterized her residential neighborhood—the infamous public-housing project of Bayview–Hunter's Point in San Francisco—as being replete with "*drama* . . . the drugs and the killin' and the shootin', over stupidity. Over music. Or who's sellin' the most drugs and stuff like that." Although preoccupied during the interview with the rumors that another woman had come to visit her husband, when discussing family visits Jeanette brightened visibly, exclaiming that, since her spouse had been arrested for violating parole shortly after their wedding, "we made our family visits our honeymoon":

JEANETTE: This [San Quentin] is a nice prison. And I enjoy it, I look forward to coming to visit him. . . . I had my two family visits here.

MC: Tell me about those.

JEANETTE: [*rapturous*] They were *beautiful*! Oh my God! They [the correctional officers] give you *much* privacy, they ring the phone every couple a hours. You just answer the phone, look out, wave your hand, let 'em know we still there. I figured that they would come an' knock an' look around, you know, but very much privacy, it's like we're at home. I don't have to do nothin', he [her husband] cooks everything, or we'll cook together [*dreamily*], an' turn the radio on an' dance. [*we both giggle*] Yeah, or watch TV, the TV is nice. . . . It was *wonderful*. The visits, [when] I was there—I slept well. It's peaceful. We got to talk some inner feelings out where you can't talk in front of the room full of visitors.

In the above discussions of eating together and getting married in prison, I specify the ways in which women introduce food, props, and personal traditions into the penitentiary and thereby attempt to do-

14. In an ethnographic study of homeless men, Teresa Gowan (2002) observes that incarceration often precipitates homelessness, while living on the streets frequently catalyzes incarceration. This vicious cycle extends to partners and children of homeless or incarcerated men, whose housing situations may also be contingent on the man's whereabouts or penal status.

mesticate or resocialize the carceral setting by making it more like the familial world. Discourses on overnight visits like Pat's and Jeanette's, however, demonstrate the fabrication of a romanticized "home" environment inside the correctional facility that *surpasses* that which exists away from the prison walls and that—despite the powerful constraints of forced confinement and stringent surveillance—offers women idealized versions of domestic tranquility and emotional closeness not available to them under their regular socioeconomic and conjugal circumstances. Although for some women this discrepancy is temporary and directly caused by the separation from the partner (which then makes for joyous reunions and the strong appreciation of private time), for many a calm and satisfying home life remains unattainable even when the man is *not* incarcerated but simultaneously is not engaged in the household in a manner that fulfills his spouse. Millie explained that for years her husband's drug addiction alienated the pair, driving her into clinical depression and compulsive overeating: "He's not a huggy-touchy kind of person, you know? But, I felt lonely even when he was sitting right next to me. I'd want him to hold my hand and he'd be like, 'Oh *God*, do I have to hold your hand? I don't wanna hold your hand!'" After her first family visit, she reflected:

MILLIE: It [the residence] was like a cozy little home that I should have outside the prison walls. . . . [*wistfully*] We were *so* comfortable in that little cozy apartment with the heater on, you know, and watchin' TV—we actually sat on the same couch, it actually looked just like this [*indicating the couch on which she and I are sitting*]. But it's leather, I mean, we both fit on it comfortably. He leaned here and I leaned there [*showing that she had her head on his shoulder*] and it was so relaxing and cozy.

[. . .]

MC: How has your relationship with your husband changed [since he was incarcerated]?

MILLIE: It's better. [*clears throat, pauses*] The, the main reason why I say it's better is because he's off drugs. We can actually talk—I mean, we'd always get along before, but when he was on drugs, it really wasn't him, it was this false person. . . . It [his incarceration] brought us closer because we now talk about things like feelings that we never talked about before. And I kinda like that; it makes me feel closer to him. Because before we were pretty far apart. . . . In a way, I think it all happened for the best. That sounds kinda weird, but it, it got him off drugs.

The propensity of prisoners and their partners to engage in patterns of intense romantic behavior during a man's incarceration is common, documented both in personal memoirs (Bandele 1999; Maksymowicz 2000) and academic research (Fishman 1990; McDermott and King 1992; Carter 1996a; Klein and Bahr 1996; Braman 2004, 41–64). In addition, women may experience a partner's "imprisonment as family therapy" (Shaw 1987, 34) when confinement interrupts household stressors such as a man's alcoholism, drug addiction, entanglements in the street economy, or domestic violence.[15] Indeed, for women whose volatile partner is detained, time in prison likely corresponds to the stage in Ann Goetting's (1999, 10–11) "cycle of battering" termed "loving contrition," when a man energetically atones for abusive behavior following an explosive event.[16] Millie's commentary reveals that such periods of endearments and tender comportment can differ significantly from a couple's ordinary interactions, leading women to view their penitentiary encounters as opportunities to engage in fantasized, rather than realistic, family relations ("like a cozy little home that I *should* have"). Hence the paradoxical inversion of women's desires to strengthen inclusive bonds with their mates as a means of preventing the men's institutionalization: by facilitating the necessary conditions for rewarding interpersonal contact, the "Papa's discipline" (Carlen 1982) of the correctional apparatus becomes an indispensable element in the performance of intimate life.

Stories like those narrated here illustrate the counterintuitive processes that transpire when wives, fiancées, and girlfriends of inmates strive to bridge the distance between the outside world and a loved one: unable to bring him home, they bring home to him by relocating intimate activities inside the penitentiary walls and concomitant at-

15. Although prisoners convicted of domestic violence are not eligible for family visits, the correlation of risk factors for criminality with those noted among abusive men (Dutton 1992) makes it likely that substantial numbers of inmates imprisoned for other offenses also assaulted their partners and/or children.

16. There are strong parallels between the behaviors described in chapter 3 and Goetting's (1999, 11) description of this cycle:

The man knows he has gone too far, and now he must make it up to his partner lest he lose her. He apologizes, begs forgiveness, pledges his eternal love, and promises never again to resort to such extreme behavior. Turning on that old charm and transforming into that wonderful man with whom she fell in love in the beginning, he reels her back in. He may offer her gifts, invite her to romantic dinners and vacations, promise her anything—whatever it takes to keep her with him under his control. She believes him; they reconcile. Eventually this stage passes, and the couple slides once more into tension building and begins the cycle all over again.

tempts to "civilize" prison existence through mimicry of external life. As the correctional facility develops into a domestic satellite through its hosting of family meals, weddings, and sleepovers, this temporary and fictive domicile can appear—in spite of the enormous sacrifices, degradations, and curtailments exacted by the authorities as requisites for prison visiting—attractive compared to the dire conditions women face in free society. All of which complicates the claims that close family ties decrease recidivism, suggesting instead that the enactment of "private" experiences behind bars prisonizes couples to such a degree that women become reliant on, and even grateful for, carceral control.

Such is the case of Butta, a mother of five who was involved with an emotionally and physically abusive man for eight years. Finding no therapeutic or crisis-intervention services to assist her, Butta eventually escaped her tormentor by having him arrested for domestic violence when she began her current relationship ("I had to do it [end the abuse] on my own, basically. With the help of the police department"). She now is wed to the father of her oldest child, with whom she reunited after she saw a local-television news report publicizing his detention in connection with a high-profile drug bust and car chase. Butta began visiting her lost love in jail and married him on the day he, at her urging, accepted a plea bargain for twenty years instead of facing a forty-to-eighty-year sentence in a trial. Ruminating on her past and present partnerships, she exposes deep ambivalence about her current situation, which at once liberates her from the cage of abuse and embeds her in conjugal loss and loneliness:

MC: What makes this relationship different from your past relationships?
BUTTA: Well, it makes it different because he's not here. He's not here to share in our child's growin' up. You know, bein' there for him for sports, bein' able to walk him to school. Bein' home, you know, where we can have a nice candlelight dinner. It's a big difference. An' those are all the things that I want, but, I guess I can share that with him when I go on a contact, a *family* visit. . . . Sometimes it's, um [*pause, then sadly*], painful. I wish that he was home. But, um [*switching tone, matter-of-fact*], actually it's okay. Because I can, I can move freely, the way I want to move, without someone stayin' on my back. I can move freely, without the hassle. You know, I can have my friends over if I want to, I ain't got to worry about him fussin' about [*with a brutal snarl*], "Well, why they over here?" an' "*What they doin' here? What'ch y'all doin' an' where y'all goin'?*" I don't have nobody tellin' me when to do it, how to do it, why to do it, or how I should do it. If I'm gonna do it, I'm gonna do it. An' he can't object to it. So it's, it's nice. It's not

nice all the time. Like on holidays, it's the most painful because this is when you supposed to be wit' yo' family, wit' yo' loved ones, sharin' the festivities.

Safe but solitary, freed from domestic tyranny but willfully subjected to correctional control, united in matrimony but separated by the penitentiary walls: this is the patchwork construction of a family life spanning the now-porous boundary between domestic and correctional sites, the prisonization of intimate relationships played out in the grip of the "carceral home."

FIVE

"It's a Lot of Good Men behind Walls!"

At the beginning of chapter 3, I raised a series of questions: Why do women decide to continue their relationships once their partners are imprisoned? Why do they not instead opt to form new partnerships with "free" men? What satisfaction do women gain from these relationships that compensates for the grief of forced separation and prison visiting? The investigation in the previous two chapters of the inner workings of carceral relationships and the interactions that take place across and behind bars provides a foundation for answering these queries, demonstrating that through its strictures and requirements the correctional institution can grant women a surprising measure of control and leverage in their dealings with men, structures for enacting the gendered roles of nurturer and caregiver, and substitute sites for domestic and conjugal life that are preferable to or easier to manage than the chaos and stress of the family home. As evoked in the last chapter's discussion of spending the night together, each of these assertions is implicitly rooted in a comparative perspective, that is, women decide to continue their relationships because romance within the penitentiary's grasp is in some way more promising or more rewarding than alternative associations have been or are anticipated to be. In this chapter I therefore broaden the analytical focus to include life away from the prison—both prior to and during involvement with the present partner—to delve further into women's commitment to their relationships and their selection of these particular men. For this purpose I divide the participants into three categories of orientation based on the circumstances under which they met their partners and the factors that contribute to their loyalty to them during their imprisonment: those whose beloved has been incarcerated for the entirety of their relationship, those who "stand by their man" during his episodic encounters with the law, and those who, deliberately or not, rely on carceral intervention to hold together an otherwise untenable or dangerous liaison. It is important to note that these categories are loosely bound and that over time women can move from one orientation to another or have periods when alternate orientations operate distinctively in different domains of their lives.

Due to the scope of my fieldwork, information supplied about family life, former boyfriends or husbands, and other extracarceral details was not easily verified by observation or inquiry. However, in considering the accounts given by participants to explain or contextualize their present circumstances my emphasis falls less on empirical validity or "historical truth" and more on the construction of a "narrative truth" (Spence 1982). Stanley Cohen (2001, 58) makes this distinction in his study of the numerous "states of denial": "Denial theory claims to understand not the structural causes of the behaviour (*the* reasons), but the accounts typically given by deviants themselves (*their* reasons)."[1] My analysis of how women describe and make sense of their romantic involvement with a prisoner thus draws on two bodies of accounts literature, the first being that associated with C. Wright Mills's classic formulation of "Vocabularies of Motive" (1940, 904). The crux of Mills's argument states: "Rather than fixed elements 'in' an individual, motives are the terms with which interpretation of conduct *by social actors* proceeds. This imputation and avowal of motives by actors are social phenomena to be explained. The differing reasons [people] give for their actions are not themselves without reasons."

Gresham Sykes and David Matza (1957, 666–69) famously developed a useful classification of motivational accounts they termed *techniques of neutralization:* "denial of responsibility," "denial of injury," "denial of the victim," "condemnation of the condemners," and "appeal to

---

1. Many common terms in the motivational accounts literature—"denial," "deviant," "delinquent"—may be heard to carry a judgmental or accusatory tone, especially as they have been co-opted in recent years by televised popular psychology and law-and-order commentators. However, I use this vocabulary for analytic purposes—that is, as it connects to classic sociological literature and describes mental processes of filtering and coping as well as lifestyles outside of the mainstream.

higher loyalties." Although these techniques are often called upon after the fact to justify one's actions and "protect the individual from self-blame and the blame of others," Sykes and Matza (1957, 666–67) argue that "there is also reason to believe that [these techniques] precede deviant behavior and make deviant behavior possible," because "disapproval flowing from internalized norms and conforming others in the social environment is neutralized, turned back, or deflected in advance." Although the authors present the techniques as "a theory of delinquency," in the case of partners of prisoners the neutralizations do double duty, accounting for both the man's lawbreaking as well as for the woman's emotional investment in the lawbreaker. Indeed, as illustrated throughout this chapter, partners of inmates "remain committed to the dominant normative system and yet so qualif[y] its imperatives that violations are 'acceptable' if not 'right'" (Sykes and Matza 1957, 667) by situating themselves in the mainstream framework of romantic love and the pursuit of social good while justifying their selection of mate and vindicating an ostensibly undesirable relationship.

The second body of literature utilized in this chapter centers on investigations of the declining rate of marriage among poor and African American women, and notably the work of Kathryn Edin (2000, 112), who asserts that while most low-income single mothers "aspire to marriage, they believe that, in the short term, marriage usually entails more risks than potential rewards."[2] Edin (2000, 114) identifies "five primary reasons why poor parents do not form or reform a legal union with a man": "affordability," or refusal to support an unemployed male; "respectability," or the disinclination to marry an out-of-work, possibly criminally involved man; desire to maintain control of household and child-raising responsibilities; belief that men cannot be trusted to remain sexually faithful; and fear of domestic violence. Continuing the analysis from chapter 4, the personal histories detailed below suggest that for some women—low-income or not—selecting a partner who is frequently or permanently incarcerated becomes *an alternative to nonmarriage,* since a man's penal confinement can help women restructure and "manage" these five areas of concern. Although Edin does not situate her work in the accounts literature, women's invocations of the male shortcomings she identifies when explaining or justifying their carceral relationships show its useful application in this regard.

2. Although Edin and Maria Kefalas address similar points in their joint work (2005, 71–137), in this chapter I rely on a concise version of this argument set forth by Edin in a solo-authored article (2000).

In order to flesh out women's life trajectories and choices, each of the following three sections opens with an in-depth portrait of a participant whose story is representative of others in her category of orientation. Although the women's motivations and actions are multilayered and complex, the subsequent analysis focuses on the most salient accounts offered for entering and sustaining a partnership with an incarcerated man.[3]

"I'd Love to Shout This to the World: Men Out There Are Worthless!"

At age thirty-one, Sarah has graduated from a reputable university, traveled extensively in South America, and profited from the Silicon Valley boom with a six-figure salary as an account manager in a high-tech firm. We first spoke in September 2000, roughly one year after she met Ben, the man who would become her fiancé, while volunteering as a tutor for San Quentin's higher-education program.[4] Ben, a white first-time offender in his early thirties, accidentally killed a man during a fight and subsequently followed the advice of his court-appointed attorney to accept a fifteen-years-to-life sentence as a plea bargain, reasoning that he would atone for his crime by serving the minimum eleven years and then be freed as the public defender had promised. By the time he met Sarah six years later, he and his devoted parents had come to understand the highly charged "no parole" politics surrounding indeterminate life sentences in California and, since plea-bargain sentences are ineligible for appeal, the trio had immersed themselves in campaigning for widespread policy reform in hopes that the outlook for Ben's release would be less bleak by the time of his first parole eligibility hearing.

Sarah recounts that she became "enlightened to alternative press" and politics during college, but it was while working for a design firm in San Fran-

---

3. Each story and its psychological intricacies is riveting enough to fill an entire book on its own, such as poet Asha Bandele's *The Prisoner's Wife: A Memoir* (1999). For popular-culture versions, see Sheila Isenberg, *Women Who Love Men Who Kill* (Simon and Schuster, 1991); Clifford L. Linedecker, *Prison Groupies* (Pinnacle Books, 1993); Jacquelynne Willcox-Bailey, *Dream Lovers: Women Who Marry Men behind Bars* (Wakefield Press, 1999); and Angela Devlin, *Cell Mates/Soul Mates: Stories of Prison Relationships* (Waterside Press, 2002).

4. Due in large part to its proximity to several universities, including the University of California at Berkeley, at the time of this writing San Quentin is the only prison in California with a program through which inmates can receive an associate's degree by attending classes taught inside the facility by volunteer professors and teachers' assistants. Despite overwhelming evidence of the benefits of postsecondary correctional education, the Crime Control and Law Enforcement Act signed in 1994 by President Clinton prohibits all prisoners from receiving Pell Grants, the major source of funding for such programs (see Page 2004; and more generally Mele and Miller 2005).

cisco's *South of Market area (a neighborhood famously gentrified during the early years of the dot-com takeoff) that she realized she wanted to reorient her life:* "I would drive in to work every day listening to KPFA [a local progressive radio station], hearing about how horrible and screwed up our country is and then I would see it! I felt that going in to work and sort of living in this kind of sheltered world that was all about me and selling design was not fulfilling. So I decided *forget it, I'm gonna forget all this stuff, I'm gonna go back to school, I'm gonna study public interest law, and focus on prisoners' rights as an issue.*"

The subject of imprisonment already had hit close to home for Sarah since her brother had been incarcerated in the mid-'90s and was serving his time in "administrative segregation" (or solitary confinement) at California's notorious—and notoriously violent—Pelican Bay Prison.[5] *Although Sarah did not contest her brother's guilt, she objected to the harsh and degrading conditions of his confinement and of visiting, and she therefore arrived as a volunteer tutor at San Quentin in October 1999 with considerable empathy for her students in general. After a month and a half of biweekly forays behind bars, she found herself strongly drawn to one man in particular, Ben:* "I didn't really know what to do, and I wouldn't have pushed anything, but it was, I mean, I just really liked him. I respected him, he was fun, he was funny, he was intelligent, he was none of the things *that are the stereotypes of people in prison!* He's beautiful, he's kind and considerate and motivated and, ah, [we] love to talk about politics! That's where we really bonded, because, I would say after we had been working together for about three weeks, I started to share with him what I knew about political issues and social issues, and I started to recommend certain books for him to read."

From intense discussions of Howard Zinn's The People's History of the United States *the couple gradually moved to writing lengthy and impassioned love letters. After an absence while traveling abroad, Sarah resigned from the volunteer program and returned to San Quentin as Ben's personal visitor. By the spring of 2000 they were engaged.*

Compared to the relative "freedom" the couple enjoyed during their courtship evenings in the educational program (staff and students could bring books, paper, and writing utensils to class, talk in groups or one-on-one, and pass the time without constant surveillance by correctional officers), the

---

5. Pelican Bay State Prison, which opened in 1989 in northwest California near the Oregon border, is one of the state's most brutal correctional facilities. Riots, killings of inmates by correctional officers, and the "hiring" by correctional officers of inmate enforcers to inflict punishment on targeted prisoners have resulted in numerous investigations, including one by the U.S. Department of Justice into civil rights violations (Sward and Wallace 1998; Associated Press 2000).

constraints of being a prison visitor weigh heavily on Sarah, who remembers a precious moment unlikely to be repeated while Ben remains behind bars: "The last night that I saw him [as a volunteer], I went to the class and I was the first one to get there and I was waiting in the classroom and he showed up and nobody else was around. So we've spent, we had four minutes alone together, that's the only time we've ever been alone, was in that classroom that night, and that's bizarre to think that we've never been alone. You know, it's very sad too." The "constant struggle to maintain what little you have" that now characterizes her romantic life is a far cry from what Sarah had envisioned for herself: "I never would have dreamed in a million years that I was going to marry someone in prison, in San Quentin, who had an indeterminate sentence. It just was not on my strategic plan when I graduated from high school and tried to figure out what my life was going to be like!" Yet, since adolescence finding her soul mate has been a top priority and she is overjoyed at having finally met the man of her dreams: "I think about my life, and I easily have spent the past seventeen years looking and yearning and waiting and wanting the love of my life . . . seventeen years really looking for the person that I was going to fall in love with, and always wishing and wanting and hoping and wondering who was that person, where is he now, what is he doing, what does he look like, where is he from, what's he about, that constant searching, at the same time going through the continual disappointments of meeting men who were not Ben, and not fulfilling, and abusive, or just unhealthy for me."

For Sarah, the comparison between her past boyfriends and her fiancé is stark, and not incidentally linked to the hardship the latter has endured: "I look around me at what's out there in the world—I dated a lot before I met Ben—worthless! Worthless! Totally worthless! I'd love to shout this to the world: Men out there are worthless! And it's just amazing how it takes something, a significant, dramatic change in one's life to make them a decent, good human being. That's sort of a sad commentary on our society quite honestly." Indeed, "one of the main reasons that I got involved with Ben, why I stay involved with him, and why many other women stay involved with their [incarcerated] significant others, is because the men that they're involved with treat them beautifully. . . . The way that Ben treats me, I would never have gotten that from any guy running around out here in the free world." When describing what she was seeking in a spouse, she returns to the theme of experiencing adversity: "I wanted to meet a man who had a deep appreciation for life. And not only a deep appreciation for life, but a clear understanding of what was really important. Not all the money, and high-paying job, and the big house, and the fancy Porsche, the hair plugs, and the personal trainer— you know what I'm saying? Not all of that. But somebody who really knew *what was important in life and had really suffered and out of that suffering, and out of that pain, had grown as a human being and as a spirit."*

"At times I can't even believe that I'm doing this, I really can't, it just amazes me that it's me," Sarah confesses. "Sometimes I feel like I'm talking about somebody else. Sometimes I feel like I'm watching someone else's life! . . . It's almost like I'm not even in control, I'm not even the one making the decisions. It feels so much like the decisions have been made for me, it's fate! And, I'm just, I've just made the decision to go along with what I believe is my fate and my destiny."

Although her immediate family has warmed to her relationship (to varying degrees: her mother attended the couple's wedding and her father maintains a strong bond with Sarah but has yet to venture to see his son-in-law), Sarah can imagine the reaction of skeptics: *"I mean most people look at this, and anybody who's practical and anybody who's realistic will look at this and go, 'You are totally out of your mind!' . . . And no, it doesn't make* practical, scientific, mathematical *sense, but a lot of things in the universe don't make sense or can't be explained, and this is one of them. . . . I am not a religious person and I don't ascribe to* any *religion. Even though I'm Jewish I don't even believe that, but I see myself as spiritual and I have to look at this and go, okay, you know what? This is,* this is fate, *this is destiny, this is what was meant to happen. That's just how it's been mapped out."*

Implicit in this conviction is the assuredness that her present situation is temporary, a mind-set she shares with other lifers' wives: *"I mean really, these women would not be married and involved with these men for the period of time that they have if they did not believe and have hope that somehow, some way these guys were going to get out. So there is a strong faith."* Above all, though, her reasoning is simple: with *"all of the unknowns, and all the unpleasantries, and all the pain, and all the frustration, why do I do it? One simple reason:* I love him. I absolutely love him."

Although unique in its details, Sarah's profile shares underlying commonalities with the histories of thirteen other participants: Aisha, Basalisa, Bernice, Blessing, Darla, Laura, Lynn, Mai, Laila, Queenie, Sophia, Stephanie, and Tee. Each of these women is financially self-supporting, working primarily in white-collar or pink-collar fields such as computer networking, communications, administrative clerking, fund-raising, child care, and nursing. Basalisa, Blessing, Darla, and Tee received some undergraduate education; Queenie and Stephanie were months away from finishing bachelor's degrees at the time of their interviews, and Queenie had been accepted to a master's program; Sophia had a bachelor's degree; and Lynn had a master's in rehabilitation counseling. The majority have either no children or adult children, although Sophia and Stephanie are hoping to conceive with their spouses after the men are released. Most significantly, all of these women met their beloved after the men had been sentenced to prison, and all but Basalisa and Mai married or have plans to marry behind bars. Basalisa, Bernice, Blessing, and Laura are partners of Death Row inmates, while the husbands of Darla, Lynn, Laila, Queenie, Sophia, and Tee are serving life sentences. Aisha's spouse is sentenced to twenty-four years, and only Mai and Stephanie could expect that their loves would be paroled by 2005.

Women with these demographic profiles raise questions about why someone with a wealth of options available to her would choose to bind herself to a partner with essentially no options at all.[6] But as Sarah's narrative indicates, when accounting for their relationships women follow myriad lines of focused reasoning, drawing on previous life experiences and desires to participate in specific social and emotional trajectories.

"To Be Involved with Somebody in Prison Is an Act of Courage":
Political and Spiritual Conviction

According to Sykes and Matza (1957, 669) people invoke an "appeal to higher loyalties" to justify the claim that "deviation from certain norms may occur not because the norms are rejected, but because other norms, held to be more pressing or involving a higher loyalty, are accorded precedence." In their framework this entails "sacrificing the demands of the larger society for the demands of the smaller social groups to which the delinquent belongs such as the sibling pair, the gang, or the friendship clique." Women who form romantic attachments to men they meet behind bars offer a contrasting case, appeal-

---

6. The general public is often baffled and titillated by such stories: "No Shortage of Women Who Dream of Snaring a Husband on Death Row" proclaimed a *San Francisco Chronicle* headline (Fimrite and Taylor 2005) in the wake the arrival of Scott Peterson, who was convicted of killing his pregnant wife and unborn child, at San Quentin. In the article, criminologist Jack Levin attributes women's pursuit of men on Death Row to "love [of] celebrity status. . . . These are the same women who might correspond with a rock star or a rap artist." In a *Guardian* article "Why Are Women Drawn to Men Like This?" (Mina 2003), American and European women's active pursuit of relationships with Death Row prisoners are attributed to desire for feelings of "vicarious murder" and "hybristophilia," the condition of becoming "sexually excited by violent outrages performed on others."

ing to the priority of the larger societal norms of justice or religious devotion over the smaller-scale norms of marital privacy and physical intimacy, thereby valorizing daily self-sacrifice in the pursuit of wider social rectitude.

Marvin Scott and Stanford Lyman (1968, 52) note that "[o]ne variable governing the honoring of an account is the character of the social circle in which it is introduced"; or, in Ken Plummer's (1995, 87) words, "for narratives to flourish there must be a community to hear." The invocations of social justice or piety indeed are most accepted in the arenas of the "higher loyalties" to which they appeal: prison-related activist circles and religious or spiritual networks. Eleven of the women in this category (all except Lynn, Mai, and Tee) participate regularly in some form of activism, whether attending anti–death-penalty rallies and conferences, speaking at public hearings in the state's capital on prison issues, or writing letters of protest to wardens about the unfair or ill treatment of their spouses, and all fourteen are at least intermittently conscientious about voting, volunteering, or working professionally for social change. Ten repeatedly refer to religion or spirituality as important forces in their lives, whether as a bedrock (Basalisa, Blessing, and Lynn are born-again Christians; Aisha and Laila are practicing Muslims; Tee is a Jehovah's Witness) or a more diffuse philosophical guide (Darla, Mai, Sarah, and Sophia periodically attend church or spiritual retreats, consult spiritual leaders, or study spiritual texts).

For some women preexisting civic or religious engagement plus a particular interest in prison matters prompted them to first enter the correctional institution and facilitated their meeting of otherwise socially isolated men: Aisha met her husband while lecturing on nutrition at a county jail, Sophia encountered her spouse during her years volunteering for a carceral Alcoholics Anonymous program, and Lynn was introduced to her fiancé through a prison ministry program. For others, more general feelings of compassion or charity led them to reach out to prisoners, and in time they became romantically attached, politically energized, and/or religiously grounded. Basalisa, who was recently "born again" and who now criticizes the injustices of the correctional system in great detail, told how she met her "best friend" of ten years:

I met him through an ad in the newspaper. And at the time I wrote to him I always wanted to do something for people, you know, I like to help people and I thought it would be nice to write to somebody in prison. I picked his ad because specifically he wasn't looking for a woman. He was looking for a male or a female, somebody to, you know, just exchange ideas with. And so I wrote to him. And after about a year, I visited him. And from his letters I found out he was *very* different than what I had in my mind, my impression of what prisoners were, you know, they were like most people's, just some horrible monster in there.

Similarly Darla, who had been married for fifteen years to a police officer before meeting her current husband while working an administrative job in a prison, gradually became politically aware through personal experiences and conversations with her incarcerated spouse:

When I first went to work there [at the prison], we were programmed by the staff to not trust and to hate all inmates. And I found that the ones you couldn't trust were the guards! They were the ones that were stealing money out of your desk, or food out of your desk, or beating up inmates that were handcuffed. You see a complete different side of it than you would, you know, than people think! . . . I was married to a policeman, not saying he was corrupt but they're just like anybody else, and the same with the inmates, they break laws, they do things wrong, and now, where I work now [in a state government office], I see it firsthand all the time. . . . I wouldn't have probably noticed it if I hadn't met [my current husband], but, you know, sometimes he'd point out stuff and I'd think, "Well, of course you feel that way, you're in prison!" But that's not the case. It's really true!

The remainder of the women in this category were introduced to their partners through family or friends (themselves either prisoners or relatives of prisoners), sometimes as an explicit romantic arrangement but more often with an intent to provide the inmate with a pen pal or visitor to mitigate his loneliness. In these cases backgrounds of political activism or religious ministry and histories of having incarcerated family members or friends destigmatized women's choice of partner among some or all of their social network, as illustrated by Queenie's account of how she reconnected her daughter's fiancé to his incarcerated father—a man she subsequently met and then married a year later:

I kept saying [to my daughter's fiancé], you know, "Where your dad?" And he wouldn't like say anything. So finally one day [my daughter] said, "Mom, his dad's in prison." So I called him back out here, and I said [*sternly*], "Come here." I said, "Let me understand this. Straight face-to-face with me, *where is your dad?*" [slurring the words "Well, he's in San Quentin" together] "Wehe'sinmhm." I said, [*sharply*] "What?" "Wehe'sinmhm." [*chuckles*] You know, he was kind of mumbling the words, and I said, [*firmly*] "No, *where is he?*" He said, "He's at San Quentin." I said, "Well, why are you walking with your shoulders down?" I said, "Don't you know her dad [Queenie's late husband] did twelve years [in prison]?" And all of a sudden his shoulders went back and he was like, [*brightly*] "No!" And I said, "Well, he did." I said, "So don't *ever* walk with your shoulders down. *Don't ever.*" I said, "Why aren't you communicating with him?" I said, "No, *now.* Set down right now this minute and write him a letter."

Studies consistently document the lack of shame or stigma among family members of people incarcerated in connection with political conflicts (Rolston and Tomlinson 1986; Coulter 1991; McEvoy et al. 1999) and note that detention often provokes "women's own entering into the political arena in solidarity with their imprisoned kin" (White and Reynolds 1994, 42). Such a stance takes on peculiar form in the United States, a country that minimizes its internal conflicts and has not had a recognizable large-scale domestic battle since the civil rights movement—and even during the 1960s and early 1970s U.S. correctional institutions contained far fewer political prisoners than they did *politicized* prisoners who had been convicted of "ordinary" crimes and then constructed their radical identities once behind bars (Cummins 1994; see also Jackson 1970; Cleaver 1978). For many, then, the "appeal to higher loyalties" of political dissent involves "an idealist inversion of positivist imagery" through which "crime [becomes] either the expression, symbol or equivalent of political resistance or the product of the political order of capitalism" (Cohen 1997, 228); similarly, the serving of a sentence perceived to be overly punitive (such as condemnations to life or death in prison) may be considered to grant de facto political status to the inmate.

A parallel suppression of shame and stigma occurs when prisoners enter the embrace of religious institutions, particularly the Christian church. Religious ministry guiding "fallen sinners" to see the errors of their ways is at the very root of the penitentiary system (Rothman 1971; Ignatieff 1978), and prison chaplains, Sunday services, and Bible-study meetings are as integral to the correctional facility as locks and bars. The bulk of worship services are provided by volunteers from organizations such as the Rock of Ages Prison Ministry, a Baptist Mission Board that "labors to preach and witness of Jesus Christ within the state and federal prisons of America" in thirty-six states (Rock of Ages Prison Ministry 2003). Support for the incarcerated and their loved ones exists on the other side of the walls as well, in the form of church-based programs for prisoners' families offering transportation to remote institutions, counseling sessions, crisis intervention, prayer groups, and other services (Families and Corrections Network 2001). Indeed, even in a climate of massive social spending cutbacks and political conservatism, George W. Bush exhorted his "armies of compassion" (that is, faith-based organizations) to remember the incarcerated and minister diligently to their children (Bush 2001a, 2001b).

The psychological importance of being able to valorize one's decision to partner with a prisoner in political and/or spiritual terms is underscored by Tee: of the fourteen women in this category she was the only one who did not connect her relationship to a political or religious stance (although she and her husband are Jehovah's Witnesses) and the only one who endured chronic debilitating depression. In 1996 Tee suffered the double murder of a young woman who was "like a daughter" to her and the woman's three-year-old child, a tragedy that irrevocably altered Tee's perception of the "shared background expectations" (Scott and Lyman 1968, 53) against which she and other prisoners' wives situate their accounts of their relationships. This cognitive shift left Tee feeling unjustified in the campaign for the rights of prisoners and adrift among her peers:

One time I went to Sacramento [the state capital] just to go hear some stuff that was goin' on, you know, like a protest or whatever, and *I just totally felt* for those victims' rights people! And I was like, I don't belong here! Because I don't, I'm in the middle, you know? I understand how they feel, and I understand how we feel, but [*pause, then plaintively*] we really don't deserve anything! [*gravely*] [My husband] took life. That person can never be with their child, that person can never be with their family, they can never have intimacy. They're gone. . . . And actually most people, most wives of inmates, they don't agree with me at all, my stand on the whole thing. Cuz they're like totally for their, you know, for their side. [*forlornly*] I'm kinda different cuz I'm in the middle.

Victimization need not fracture the rationalization for involvement with a prisoner. Blessing, whose brother was killed in an unsolved homicide several years before she met her Death Row husband, appealed to Christian forgiveness for her sibling's murderer—and by implication for her spouse: "Someone killed my brother, and I never felt that they should be killed, because that's not going to *do* anything for me. . . . I think that the person should be punished, but not for the rest of their lives. People make mistakes—and yes that's a *serious* mistake, for sure! I mean, I don't justify anybody killing for *anybody*. But people do change."[7] Blessing's articulated empathy for her brother's unknown killer, interwoven with her active involvement in the anti–death-penalty movement and her nurturance of her husband, evoke Plummer's (1995, 33) contention that, in the telling of a personal story, "[t]here is a self-consciousness at work. . . . There is a sense of an identity . . . hidden from the surface awaiting clearer recognition, labeling, categorizing. . . . And there is a solitude, a secrecy and a silence, alongside a longing to shout." At home alone on the eve before her marriage, Sarah soaked in a bathtub and pondered her upcoming act: "And I'm sitting there thinking, 'I can't believe how *brave* I am to be doing this!' You know? And so at that moment it just sort of struck me what a leap of faith this was that I was taking. And it didn't scare me. It was a nice realization, cuz it was sort of the first time that I acknowledged what a courageous thing this is for me to be doing. I mean, just to be involved with somebody in prison is an act of courage."

Sarah's thoughts reflect what is described by Stanley Cohen and Laurie Taylor (1992, 56) as "self-conscious reinvestment," a tactic used in the "mental management of routine" that involves acknowledging the peculiarities of one's situation and committing oneself to enduring within those conditions:

Within the maximum-security wing, the prisoners' ability to relativize their experience reduced anxiety and tension. Their recognition that their environment with its phenomenal qualities was one amongst many such environments and their further realization that this recognition guaranteed them a higher degree of self-consciousness than that which had been enjoyed by men in those other environments, proved comforting. Self-consciousness of their predicament provided the opportunity to establish themselves against it, it protected them from the fear that their behaviour was determined by the structure and culture of the setting. It did not mean however that they now acted against the institution, it more usually meant that they went along with its edicts with an easier heart, reassured by the distance which they could mentally maintain from its social arrangements.

The "self-conscious politicization" or "self-conscious religiosity" exercised by women in this category provide similar means of distancing—

7. Interestingly, neither Tee nor Blessing claims the status of "other victims of crime" appropriated by some families of prisoners (see Howarth and Rock 2000) in their positions as wives of inmates, indicating that those who are both victims and family members of serious offenders perceive important distinctions between the two roles.

from denunciations of their loved ones as "bad men," from accusations that they are "wasting" their prime years on highly limited relationships, from the hardships and humiliations of visiting—by framing their partnerships in the contexts of the fight against social injustice, the contribution to a larger good, and the enactment of loving kindness or godliness. They also furnish a justification for lack of interest in "free" men. Stephanie, a criminal justice student who portrays herself as upwardly mobile and deliberately avoiding the domestic abuse and early pregnancy patterns that burden other members of her family, simultaneously dissociates herself from her university peers and resists her friends' attempts to introduce her to collegiate men ("Just because I'm college educated, I don't feel that I have to stick with those kind!"). Instead, she chose to marry a recidivist prisoner whom she met through her sister's incarcerated boyfriend, a decision grounded in her politics of race and class:

My husband, he's been in and out of jail since he was like a juvenile, since fourteen! That's basically all he knows. . . . I know how hard it is for black people, you know, minorities, and I know that the reason why a lot of people might commit crimes is because of, like I said, for survival, what might have happened to them that messed up their mind emotionally when they were younger. I don't like the criminal justice system, I feel that it's racist, it's another form of slavery. You know, you have slaves, which are the incarcerated people, and you have the overseers, and the masters who are the correctional officers and the warden! That's how I look at it. And that's how it's run, it's just a high-tech form of slavery.

In addition to appealing to a higher loyalty of social justice, Stephanie's account invokes two other techniques of neutralization: the denial of responsibility (minorities commit crimes for survival; people's minds might have been "messed up" when they were younger) and the condemnation of the condemners (the criminal justice system is racist; incarceration is slavery). Likewise, Laura's exoneration of her fiancé and her justification of her dedication to him uses the denials of injury and victim, as well as the condemnation of the condemners to situate her love on a higher moral plane:

I mean, yeah, I may be in love with a man who was convicted of murder, but [hesitates slightly] he hasn't done anything to me and nothing that I've seen! And as far as I'm concerned, I believe he is innocent. But even if he weren't, I'd still love him! He'd still be wonderful! He wouldn't have changed who he is! Right? You know, and I figure, there's been some people in the world that have done some awful things to me, I *forgive* them! I don't wish them anything bad! In fact, I actually feel sorry for them! You know? I feel sorry for them because they'll never have, ever have, what we have!

Laura's rejection of the idea that her fiancé is a "bad" or immoral person not only declares him as worthy of love, it also juxtaposes him against the other men to whom she could be married, those wed to other women who will "never have what we have." More than any other category, these fourteen women consciously and repeatedly compare their partners to "men on the outside"—an assessment that leaves them feeling quite content with their lot.

"So Much Drama and Bullshit": Disillusionment with "Free" Men

For the majority of women in this category, falling in love with a prisoner marked a notable transition from a more mainstream way of life, often one that had included a conventional domestic marriage: Blessing and Sophia had lived with previous partners; Aisha, Bernice, Darla, Laura, Lynn, Mai, and Tee had been divorced; and Basalisa and Queenie were widowed. There was overwhelming agreement among these participants (with the exception of Basalisa and Queenie, who had loving memories of their late spouses) that the tribulations and humiliations intrinsic to communicating with and visiting prisoners were preferable to the troubles wrought upon them by the previous men in their lives. Mai, the veteran of an eight-year marriage to a man she described as "abusive emotionally," maintained that her romance with an inmate in an out-of-state federal facility is the "most intimate relationship I've ever had":

[My partner] had asked me on the phone, he goes, "What do I contribute to your life, and what do I *bring* to you?" And I said, "What you bring to me is the qualities that I have not known in men in the free world." Quote-unquote the free world. And I said, "You bring to me honesty, communication, respect, and understanding." . . . I'm the kind of person that, I really don't get involved in relationships per se. Because, honesty and communication are just traits and qualities that I very seldom find. I can only speak from experience, and I haven't had a lot of involvement with men outside of my race, so I can only speak from a black woman's perspective in dealing with black men. And when you talk about trust, honesty, and communication, *you can forget it.* . . . I'm forty years of age, I would like to be in a relationship, but it's just, brothers come with so much drama and bullshit.

According to Orlando Patterson (1998, 3), "Afro-American gender relations, and consequently their marital and familial relations, have always been in crisis." In dissecting the causes of this predicament, Patterson examines the existing or projected lead of African American women in education, economic earnings, and life expectancy, arguing that "the very success of Afro-American women in the wider world exacerbates what is their greater gender problem—that between them and Afro-American males in all their sex roles and at all periods of the lifespan" (1998, 24). Searching for the root of such troubled relations "inevitably [leads] back to the centuries-long holocaust of slavery and what was its most devastating impact: the ethnocidal assault on gender roles, especially those of father and husband, leaving deep scars in the relations between Afro-American men and women" (Patterson 1998, 25). Yet Patterson has little to say about the influence of imprisonment—particularly the skyrocketing levels of mass incarceration—on African American gender divisions, a curious omission in light of Loïc Wacquant's positioning of "the prison in the full lineage of institutions which, at each epoch, have carried out the work of race making by drawing and enforcing the peculiar 'color line' that cleaves American society asunder . . . [namely] slavery, the Jim Crow system, the urban ghetto, and the novel organizational compound formed by the vestiges of the ghetto and the expanding carceral system" (Wacquant 2000a, 98–99). In their rejection of "free" men and their valorization of prisoners, participants indicate that this fourth "peculiar institution" (Wacquant 2000b) paradoxically works to facilitate male-female interactions by regulating men's behavior.

The median age at first marriage has been steadily increasing in the United States, rising from 24 years for women and 26 for men in 1990 to 25.1 years for women and 26.8 years for men ten years later (Fields and Casper 2001). Marriage rates among African Americans have been consistently lower than among their white or Hispanic counterparts since the 1940s, and their "marital disruption rates have always been unusually high" (Patterson 1998, 56). Literature examining the diminishing rates of matrimony among poor women and African American women tends to focus on "a shortage of marriageable men" (Lichter et al. 1992), conceived in terms of educational or economic status (Wilson 1987; Bulcroft and Bulcroft 1993) or the sheer number of available mates (McLaughlin and Lichter 1997). However, among those partnered with long-sentence prisoners the decision to rupture or to not form marital ties with free men stems less from perceptions of practical shortcomings than from dissatisfaction with the dearth of emotional rewards. In Laura's words: "I've been married twice. And in plenty of relationships it was always you gave a lot and he gave nothing in return, pretty much. And these were all men on the outside! They used you, lied to you, cheated on you. . . . I've been used by every single man I've ever known on the outside." Basalisa too declared: "I used to date a lot. *A lot*. And most of the guys I met were just like really jerks. They were either trying to impress you so they could have sex with you or just impress you because they didn't really have any kind of life of their own and they wanted you to think they did." Such condemnations of free men are juxtaposed with praise of the emotional availability and communicativeness of prisoners. Bernice proclaimed: "It takes most people a lifetime to get what we've got. That's how I feel. . . . In the twenty-two years I was married, I'm not saying it was bad to be married the whole time, but I've gathered so much [more] in this two-and-a-half [years] than I have in the twenty-two years. *Communication!* . . . This is the *best* relationship I've had with a man. We know each other completely. I can come to him with anything. I mean he's my strength."

Much of the criticism of African American men by their partners centers on their "absenteeism": "Far too many black men who praise their own mothers feel less accounted to the mothers of their own children," observes Patricia Hill Collins (1991, 116). Indeed, one study (Turner and Turner 1983) found that the majority of black female respondents categorized "most men" as irresponsible, unreliable, and untrustworthy. However, these complaints seem to cross ethnic boundaries: Laura is white, Basalisa is Hispanic, and Bernice is black (all three are involved with black men). Edin (2000, 124–25) describes similar negativity in the characterizations of men by low-income black, white, and Hispanic women, one of whom offers this bleak summation: "Either they leave or they die. The first thing is, don't get close to them, 'cause they ain't no good from the beginning." In contrast with men who continually let women down by physically disappearing or emotionally withdrawing in times of need, a man guaranteed to be in a specific place and likely to be eager to engage in lengthy conversation becomes precious. Laura elaborated:

I know I've never, *never* been with another man that has ever been so giving and loving. Like when things are going hard on me and life's really tough and everything's breaking down around the house and I'm gettin' a lot of BS [bullshit] at work and everything, he doesn't just say [*patronizingly*], "Oh, that's too bad," or [*weakly*], "Gee I'm sorry," or something like that, he *stops* and he *thinks,* he thinks about it, he analyzes the situation, and then he gives me advice! I mean good, sound advice. . . . He's there for me in a way that no man has ever been there for me. And isn't *that* odd, because he's never been "there!"

As discussed in chapter 3, although contained in a hypermacho environment, inmates are largely restricted in their expression of conventional masculinity toward their partners. Unable to woo her through sexual prowess, financial support, or even displays of physical force (visiting rooms are notoriously considered "off limits" for fighting since brawls would jeopardize highly prized visiting privileges) and emasculated by forced obedience and humility in the face of correctional officers, a man soon learns to exercise his own quasi-feminine charms in pursuing and sustaining the interest of his intended. The theme of prisoners being "unlike other men" in their command of interpersonal skills, decorous behavior, and "womanly" pastimes appeared repeatedly in participants' accounts of their partners. Darla enthused: "My husband crochets, believe it or not! . . . He's very soft-spoken and very gentle. You think of somebody in prison as being real mean, rough, and, and, you know, [*laughing*] tattoos all over their bodies! Whatever, I mean, you can imagine the image of people in prison, but he was very the opposite, he was very gentleman[ly] and very soft-spoken, and he always was helping everybody else."

Likewise, Basalisa explained how she gradually fell in love with her pen pal as she discovered his feminine side:

When you spend a lot of time with someone and the time is mostly spent in conversation, you learn a lot about what's inside a person. When the sex thing isn't there to get in the way. He wrote a lot of poetry. And I thought, oh, that's pretty cool, you know, it's not really a *guy* thing, you know, not [like] any of the men that I've met. And I liked what he said, I liked what he thought, I liked the things that he was able to express about himself and his feelings about what he cared about. They were things I cared about too.

The ongoing exchange of communication and caring coupled with the interdiction of sexual contact lead to a phenomenon of *the prisoner as girlfriend* in which women portray incarcerated men in feminized terms and speak of their relationships as they would a close friendship that is assumed not to include the sexual, emotional, or practical complexities of cohabitation. Many women openly acknowledge the role played by the enforced chastity of a prison relationship, and while they are ambivalent over such prohibitions and often articulate strong desires to be intimate with their partners, they also hail the virtues of nonbodily expression in developing solid, long-lasting relationships. In speaking positively of extended courtships, voluminous exchanges of letters, and the postponement of sexual congress, women echo the tenets of Victorian romance that "[t]rue love is permanent, constant, and elementary, an affair of the heart and soul, not of the body and desire," and that intercourse—although special and even sacred—is "not, however, a way to demonstrate and sustain love" (Seidman 1993, 42). In Sarah's words:

And you know it's funny because if we were living like say a hundred years ago or two hundred years ago, *waiting,* you know, the courtship period and waiting for the person that you love was really sort of the status quo of the times. I mean, to have delayed gratification now is unheard of, especially in our culture. And that's really what this is . . . [two hundred years ago] a couple might have experienced unrequited love for their entire lives and *never* ended up together because of class differences, race differences, who knows, you know, family feuds, whatever. So that's why I have to kind of try to step out of this absurd world that we live in and say okay, what is this really? Well, it's definitely delaying the gratification, delaying the payoff, you know, *not* taking the easy road out because I believe that the benefits that I can reap by waiting are going to be so much greater than just settling for something that is immediate and I can have now, but isn't going to be *anywhere* as fulfilling as a relationship and a life with Ben.

In her study of clients of sex workers, Monica Prasad (1999, 200, 206) documents the valorization of commercial sex exchanges for their "lack of romance"—which "is read as a lack of hypocrisy"—and suggests that in contemporary free-market society "romantic love might sometimes be subordinated to, and judged unfavorably with, the more neutral, more cleanly exchangeable pleasures of eroticism." Interestingly, partners of convicts often employ a parallel argument for the separation of physical entanglement from romance (while championing the latter), finding the "sexless marriage" imposed by imprisonment to be appreciably straightforward and authentic:

And so, what I get out of this [relationship] is a man that I love like I've never loved anybody, who loves me the same way, who has for me all the elements of romance that could possibly exist, without sexual sin, without all the stuff that muddies the water in relationships, you know? Cuz you know, you start injecting that stuff and it's hard to separate what's real and solid, and really a foundation versus what's just, you know, goo-goo ga-ga feelings, what's lust, what's this, what's that. So I get that, and plus I have a man who can actually sit down and teach me something from the Word of God. (Lynn)

This is the way a relationship really *should* progress. We got to know each other. It wasn't like, as [my fiancé] put it, "Oh, he's good in bed, she gives good head— let's get married!" You know? [*laughs*] Which is unfortunately, a lot of people, they *think* they're in love, but they never bothered to get to know someone before they're having sex and getting transmitted diseases and everything else! I mean, I'm not saying I've never done stuff, you know, jumped the gun either, but, I now *choose* to be celibate. (Laura) [8]

Among women in this category, suspicion concerning the negative ways sex altered relations with men ran deep. Past experiences with male infidelity and "being used" for sex soured participants' attitudes in similar ways to those documented by Edin (2000, 125), some of whose interviewees "instrumentalized their relationships with men to the point that they didn't 'give it away anymore,' meaning they no longer had sex without expecting something, generally something material, in return." The women in Edin's study identified the avoidance of marriage or serious relationships as their primary way of protecting themselves from the hazards of sexually unfaithful men. However, for women in relationships with prisoners, the struggle to hold men to conditions of love and monogamy with respect to sex becomes a nonissue since the majority of couples are ineligible for family visits and men who can participate are only allowed to do so with a legal spouse. [9] The result, according to Aisha, can be transformative:

This was the first time I had ever had a relationship with a man where the physical wasn't like right up there in my face. I mean it wasn't, because it wasn't possible. So, what that does is it forces you to build on something deeper and more meaningful than the physical, than sex. . . . There's a certain beauty to that. I wish every

8. In the admittedly staged circumstances of a *Larry King Live* program filmed inside of San Quentin, prisoners serving life sentences themselves put forward similar arguments. Responding to Larry King's assertion that incarceration prohibits wedded couples from enjoying "the bliss that marriage can bring," one prisoner asserted, "No, but you would be amazed at how close two people can become when sex isn't part of the picture, and when you can communicate honestly and openly and *intimately* through letters and conversations in the visiting room." Later in the program, another man echoes this opinion: "[In the general society] you don't really get to talk to each other, converse, spend time with each other—and in here relationships *are built* like that. Yeah, I would like to have family visits, but I've also learned that there's so much more to life, Larry, than just sexual intercourse" (transcribed from *Larry King Live*, aired June 7, 2006).

9. This discussion only concerns men's sexual involvement with women. Obviously men may engage in sexual activity with other men with fair impunity (although homosexual acts in California prisons are illegal), a fact that most women recognize in the abstract but deny as likely for their own partners (Comfort et al. 2000).

woman could experience that, because it makes you feel different, as a woman, when you're respected and loved without that, you know? So, all in all, I feel like I have a really beautiful marriage, a wonderful husband, and I'm happy.

Mai, who spoke with bitter disappointment about her history with various Lotharios, views her use of the correctional apparatus to "manage" men's sexual behavior more pragmatically: "Once you give yourself to a man intimately, they cut out. That's how I feel. So [*firmly*] *that's* another reason why I deal with [my partner]. Because the time, the years that we've been dealing with one another? We can't have physical intimacy cuz we're not married. *So it's safe for me.*"

Women's reliance on the prison to create conditions of "safety" extends to another area Edin (2000, 125–27; 2005, 94–97) identifies as a disincentive for marriage: domestic violence. Tee became pregnant at age fourteen and quickly married her nineteen-year-old boyfriend; after seven years she escaped this "terribly abusive" relationship and spent the next thirteen years raising her daughter on her own and avoiding any involvement with men. In 1991 she felt ready to venture into matrimony once more and allowed herself to be set up with a close friend's brother who had been sentenced to life in prison in 1981 (her current mother-in-law orchestrated the introductions). The couple first met in March and married three months later. Tee spoke passionately about "love at first sight" and repeatedly claimed her husband is her "soul mate," but at the same time she acknowledged that his circumstances played a part in her willingness to commit: "I really think that part of the reason why I married [my husband] too is because, when you get deep into your psyche, is because I felt *safe*. [*pauses, reflecting*] That he couldn't abuse me like my ex-husband did. . . . I think that that safety, I think it was kind of a security blanket for him to be in here [in prison] and not to be able to abuse me like my ex."

Overall, the women in this category uniformly expressed high levels of satisfaction with their partners and demonstrated strong romantic commitment to their beloveds. Although all stated that they desired their partners' release from prison and complained about various institutional constraints, they also acknowledged that the penitentiary was the mitigating factor that permitted their relationships to blossom through its shaping of men's behavior. In Laila's summation:

I think both of us [she and her husband] had holes in our hearts, and holes in our lives at that point, and I think that sometimes you can give it whatever name you want to give it, but when the chemistry is right between two people, for whatever reason, it's right. And it doesn't always have to be what people think it has to be. And we understood what it was, we realized that on the streets we might never even talk to each other. But we fit right now. And our situations fit, and we liked each other as people, and then we realized we were falling in love with each other.

"Taking All Our Black Men Away"

Twenty-four-year-old LaShawn and her twenty-six-year-old husband Darrell have known each other for "six years and change": the couple met in a barber shop when LaShawn took her baby for his first haircut, and they married just over a year before I encountered the bride in the Tube. If not for her husband's whereabouts, LaShawn would seem a model of upward mobility: coming from a stable working-class background (her mother is a secretary at a university and her father, now retired, worked at a major chain supermarket for twenty-six years), the teen mother returned to high school a week after giving birth in order to graduate on time, then went to college for two years, and now works long hours as a unionized public-transit bus driver, bringing home $35–$40,000 a year. Darrell shares her trajectory of solid education and hard work: his father was in the military, and after attending Catholic schools as a child Darrell graduated from a predominantly black university in the Midwest, after which he worked as an accountant for a janitorial service and later as the manager of an IKEA warehouse. Owning two cars and having purchased a small apartment together in Oakland, the young African American couple enjoyed moderate financial stability and looked forward to increasing their investments while providing a good quality of life for themselves and their only son.

The first setback came in 1996, when Darrell was accused of plotting a crime committed by a group of his friends. According to LaShawn the convicted offenders testified that her husband was not involved but the police insisted this was a cover-up, a conflict that dragged the trial proceedings out over a period of eighteen months—during which Darrell remained in the county jail and only saw his family for thirty minutes at a time during bi-weekly noncontact visits. This was the young man's first arrest and he had hired his own lawyer rather than rely on a public defender, but after a year and a half the combination of depleted finances, a desire to return home, and the realization that one way or another he was serving time led him to accept a plea bargain for a four-year sentence. With credit for time already spent in custody and for good behavior, he was released nine months later with two years of parole. There were no further problems for a year: the young couple settled back into the routines of work and family time, with Darrell assuming primary responsibility for child care since his hours were flexible and LaShawn was driving her bus from noon to 9 p.m. five days a week.

Steady employment and a quiet lifestyle minimized the rigors of parole supervision: "He had been doin' so good, you know how they supposed to go check in with the parole officer every month? His parole officer tol' him he didn't have to, he could just fill out paper[work] every month." But exactly three hundred and sixty-six days after Darrell's release, the parole officer phoned to say that the young man needed to stop by the office for his annual review. Upon arrival, he was handcuffed and arrested for violation of parole. The issue in question was a trip to Disneyland the week before for his son's birthday: Darrell and LaShawn claimed that he had been given verbal authorization to leave town when he wanted as long as he continued "to program" (stay out of trouble and hold a job), but the parole officer—who had discovered Darrell's absence when he phoned IKEA looking for him—argued that no such permission had been granted. "I guess the parole officer was tryin' to clear his butt," LaShawn speculates, referring to the laxity of her husband's supervision. "Because he hadn't did the review and my husband was outta town, he wouldn't be able to do the review till after his [first] year [of parole] was up. It's lookin' bad on the parole officer, it's lookin' like he hasn't been doin' his job, hasn't been checkin' up." Despite testimonies at a Morrissey hearing [10] from his wife, child, and employer arguing that his absence had been family and not crime related, Darrell was returned to custody in September 2000 for his remaining year of parole.

LaShawn sees the role played by ethnicity as highly consequential in Darrell's initial conviction and his parole violation. Speaking of the Morrissey hearing, she notes: "His parole officer is white. . . . The only white people that were there that were on his side was the people from his job. Everyone else who came in, it was me, his mother, my son, you know, we're all black. So it was just, it was a very *uncomfortable* situation. I was *really* nervous. I didn't want to be there." Her husband's court and prison experiences have left her furious with the criminal justice system, which she bitterly condemns as racist and illogical: "Here you have a man. All he did was go outta town. He was workin', he has a family. . . . Instead of tellin' this man, you know, 'Okay, you did something wrong, don't do it again, but you need to be there to take care of your family' . . . Here you would take this man, the breadwinner of this family, from that family! Okay, you did cause a triple effect: you got another man in jail. You got a single parent now. You got a child without a father. And if I was on welfare, you know, here I am back on the system. To me, they're not*

---

10. The case *Morrissey v. Brewer* (1972) established minimal due process requirements in parole violations proceedings. Morrissey hearings are informational hearings designed to establish that violations are based on verified facts.

tryin' to help the problem takin' all our black men away an' lockin' 'em up! [heatedly] You know, when they should be there with their families! The society say, you know, that they're not there providin' for their family, but when they are there tryin' to be there to provide for their family, look! You take 'em to jail for some, [stammering with anger] some, some bullcrap!"

LaShawn anticipates that with credit for good behavior her husband will serve just six months, but nonetheless his reincarceration has served a hard blow. On a practical level the industrious mother once again has had to assume sole financial responsibility for the household, selling her own car and working overtime in order to be able to make payments on her husband's truck, his credit cards, and their mortgage; she also changed her work schedule to the 5 a.m. to 3 p.m. shift and dropped out of a stenography program at a local community college in order to care for their son after school. Emotionally, entanglement with the criminal justice system makes her feel that her hard work is for naught: "This is not somethin' I want to go through, I'm tryin' to move forward in life, this made me feel like I was moving backwards. And it was just very disappointing, very, very disappointing." Her past efforts to avoid this predicament make her current frustration especially keen: "Before I got married I'd have boyfriends who would go to jail. And I would leave 'em alone, cuz I kept sayin', 'I don't want to mess with a man in jail! I don't wanna mess with a man that goes back and forth to jail!' So I'd be like, 'I'm not getting into this pattern!' . . . You know, all the men in my family work, all the men in my family, they take care of they kids, and they weren't back and forth to jail, so I always said I wanted to marry the man like my daddy, like my grandfather. I wanted to associate myself with men like that."

LaShawn's criteria for a mate ultimately distanced her from her childhood sweetheart and the biological father of her son—a "party-party, kick-it-with-his-friends" character eight years her senior—and drew her to her "family-oriented," "homebody" husband. She still believes she made a good choice. Trouble with the law, she explains with a mix of resignation and outrage, is not limited to hoodlums and gangsters: "Black men have trouble with the law, everywhere, all the time. I mean, you could be a businessman. Went to college, graduated! You know, and they could be drivin' their BMW, Mercedes, or not even driving! They could just be walkin' down the street, dressed nice, you know, fitted down! And they automatically gotta be sellin' drugs, automatically gotta be doin' somethin' that they're not supposed to be doin'. Here you are, po-lice officer hasn't even spoke not one word to this man, has never seen this man before, will automatically assume the worst."

Although disapproving of Darrell's friends, whom she holds responsible for his first arrest ("I think it's time for them to just go they separate ways"), she repeatedly defends her husband and pledges him her full support: "I couldn't *blame* him, *because I know he hadn't been doin' anything wrong, cuz it was my idea to take my son outta town. . . . If he would have came back to jail for something he* did, *you know, actually committin' a crime? I don't think I would have been as understanding. . . . [But] since this is somethin' he didn't, it's, you know, not his fault, this is some chumped-up charges! You know, I'm gonna be* more *than supportive. . . . So since it's not somethin' that he did, he didn't do anything he shouldn't'a been doin' in my eyes, you know, I'm gonna be behind him a hundred percent, you know, do whatever I have to do to make this time as easy as possible for him."*

Describing Darrell's many good qualities—his intelligence, his commitment to fatherhood, his marital fidelity—LaShawn's voice waxes tender, then somber: *"If he hadn't'a been to jail he'd be the perfect man!"* she sighs. *"That's the only damn fault he has."*

———

Like LaShawn, half of the research participants made a decision to "stand by their man" during his periodic bouts of incarceration: Alice, Beth, Cindy, Crystal, Fern, Gina, Jamie, Jasmine, Jeanette, Jenna, Josephine, Karen, Linda, Mimi, Natasha, Nicole, Pat, Samantha, Sandra, Vanessa, Veronica, Vicki, and Yaz. All of the partners of these twenty-four women except for Alice's husband had been held behind bars at least once before their present stints; ten women were unable to remember exactly how many times their partners had gone to jail or prison during their relationships; and thirteen portrayed their mates as having spent their adolescent and adult lives circling "in and out" of correctional facilities. Eighteen of the men were presently in prison for violating the conditions of their parole, with seventeen of the twenty-four serving sentences of between three and twelve months and another six with penalties between one and three years. Veronica's husband, who had been sentenced under the "three strikes" law, was the notable exception to these relatively brief stays: after going to jail and prison approximately seven times during their seventeen-year marriage for offenses related to his drug addiction, his third felony conviction (this time for burglary and receiving stolen property) landed him thirty-six years to life.

In contrast to Sarah and her peers, the women in this category span the socioeconomic spectrum: Jenna, a thirty-five-year-old woman of mixed parentage, owns a construction company and three shopping centers and estimates her own worth at five million dollars; Crystal, a twenty-one-year-old bank teller also of mixed parentage, aspires to complete her college degree and become a child psychologist; Linda, who is white and in her mid-fifties, has had a twenty-five-year career as a truck driver; Josephine, an assembly-line worker, tells a story of returning a pair of underwear she purchased for herself for fifty-one cents to the store because she needed the money to buy her son a birthday present; while Veronica, a forty-seven-year-old Hispanic woman, became homeless due to incapacitating depression after her husband's trial and at the time of her interview had been living for nearly three months in a tent in a public campground with her children and grandchildren. Women in this category also vary widely in their reactions to their partners' return to custody, with some suffering extreme physical and mental health complications or disruptive financial problems after the men's arrests and others claiming that prison-related absences had little practical impact on their own daily lives. However, all agree that they look forward to a time when the cycle of imprisonment ends and the men "settle down" and assume roles as involved husbands and fathers. All also framed their explanations of their partners' predicaments in the context of "mass incarceration," referring repeatedly to their fatalism about men's likelihood of avoiding imprisonment and their perceptions of the U.S. criminal justice system as a corrupt instrument of oppression.

"They'll Lock People Up for the Littlest Reasons"

There are a thousand women here [at New York City's Rikers Island jail] today, half of whom have children—kids visiting fathers who once visited *their* fathers here. . . . There is no sense of regret in the women, no hint that they feel they have selected the wrong man to father their children. This experience, this day, is just a fact of life.

GREG DONALDSON, *THE VILLE: COPS AND KIDS IN URBAN AMERICA*

As stated in chapter 1, 12 percent of African American men ages twenty-five to twenty-nine were behind bars in 2005 (Harrison and Beck 2006), while 20 percent of black men and nearly 60 percent of black male high-school dropouts born between 1965 and 1969 had been to prison at least once by 1999 (Western, Pettit, and Guetzkow 2002). The implications these figures have for the likelihood of *knowing* a black man who has gone to prison or jail are obvious, with the chances being that anyone acquainted with more than a few African American males who did not complete high school will have a personal connection to the carceral world. Among the twenty-four women in this category, seventeen identified their partners as African American, four as white (those in relationships with Fern, Linda, Veronica, and Yaz), two as white Hispanic (Sandra's boyfriend and Vanessa's husband), and Crystal identified her husband as African American and Hispanic. Only Jasmine had no other family members or friends who had ever been incarcerated, and seventeen participants had at least one (and often multiple) other close relative or previous romantic partner who had been behind bars at some point. Beth, a thirty-seven-year-old African American receiving under $5,000 a year in government aid who characterized her fiancé's history of imprisonment as "just a constant thing" (at the time of her interview he was serving three months for a parole violation), also had an ex-husband, eldest son, brother-in-law, stepfather, and uncle (the latter two having committed a crime together) who had all served hard prison time. Natasha, a twenty-six-year-old black woman barely subsisting on seasonal work at the post office during her boyfriend's ten-month sentence, was overwhelmed by a question about other incarcerated relatives and listed the people whom she knew at San Quentin alone: "I asked my cousin how to get here, cuz she come here all the time cuz *her* husband is here. . . . I know my brother-in-law is here. And my godson's father is here. My uncle just left here! So, a few people. I *might* know some more people here [*giggles*], I just don't know! . . . I think I might have some cousins up here, cuz I haven't seen 'em in awhile!" When she visited her boyfriend in the Santa Rita county jail Natasha found a similar familial and social network:

My sister, she was visitin' her boyfriend, so I was visitin' my boyfriend . . . and then I have a friend, her boyfriend was in there, and we'd go up there together, you know. I see people there that I know, I see a whole ton! When I was goin' to Santa Rita, I seen all these people that I know! I was like, "*God!*" I was like, "What you doin' up here?" They was like, "What *you* doin' up here?" It was a whole buncha people. I seen my cousin up there: "I didn't know that he was up here!" "Girl, yeah, he been up here for *a while!*" [11]

11. Natasha's earnest description of her unexpected encounters with friends and family at correctional facilities corresponds almost exactly to aspects of a long, mocking narrative Mai provided about her observations of other visitors on her first trip to San Quentin. On this occasion Mai, who had not yet met her incarcerated partner, was accompanying a friend visiting her husband:

I went inside, and I had never been in a prison before in my life. So we're walking down this long corridor, and I see all these hoochie mamas, and when I say hoochie mamas, you know the sisters with the big butt, with the *tight stuff* and *cleavage!* All this hair and these nails, and you know [*very animated and raucous, switching voices to indicate dialogue among several people*], 'Girl, honey!' 'Ooh, girl! I saw you up at San Quentin!' 'Girl, I saw—' 'Didn't I see you at Santa Rita?' 'Girl, yeah.' 'But your man over here now?' 'Girl, yeah.' 'Child, can I ride down with you next time?' You know, it was that kind of thing. . . . And I'm goin', oh, okay, where the camera? Okay, we're on *Candid Camera*, where's the camera? And I'm goin', I can't believe this! I cannot believe this shit! This is like something out of a bad blaxploitation movie!

Carter Hay (1998, 426) notes that "[a]ccording to the normative validation thesis, perhaps the most deleterious reaction to deviance is *not reacting to deviance*. When violations of moral norms evoke no corrective reaction, those norms are no longer meaningful." The casualness with which Natasha speaks of the imprisonment of her relatives and her expressed attitude toward her own boyfriend's incarceration (when asked if she knew why he had first gone to prison, she replied "I didn't even ask, I just let it go") give evidence of such a nonreaction and validate Alfred Blumstein's (1998, 132) conjecture that "it is possible that the great expansion of imprisonment has diminished its deterrent effect by eroding its stigma component." Tellingly, only Alice shared LaShawn's principled avoidance of lawbreaking men; the remainder of the women in this category entered their relationships knowing that their partners had histories of incarceration (many of the men had been recently released from custody and were on probation or parole from the start), and none of them identified the male's criminal record as a disincentive. These reactions challenge the null hypothesis assuming that all ex-convicts are inherently undesirable as mates and recall Walter Miller's (1958, 5) caution that deviance is "approached most productively by attempting to understand the nature of cultural forces impinging on the acting individual as they are perceived *by the actor himself* . . . rather than as they are perceived and evaluated from the reference position of another cultural system."

Goffman (1963, 4) asserts that stigma is a "special kind of relationship between attribute and stereotype." A crucial step in destigmatizing an attribute therefore is to distance it from negative stereotypes and resituate it in a neutral or positive context. Personal familiarity with prisoners can counteract their societal stigma to some degree as their dishonored identity is understood not to override or preclude more positive traits. But cultural perspectives about why or how someone becomes incarcerated may play an even more determinant role, influencing people who previously have not had direct contact with the criminal justice system. Like LaShawn, Alice was a member of the upwardly mobile "new black middle class" (Landry 1988; see also Pattillo 1999) before her husband arrived at San Quentin; prior to this, his first arrest, the young man had been a construction worker while Alice stayed home minding their two-year-old son. In Alice's family only one uncle had been imprisoned, and she took pride in her upstanding husband's ability to stay out of trouble and provide for his wife and child. In her view, his three-year sentence (imposed for a variety of charges incurred "a long time ago") is unwarranted, but also unavoidable, in a society intent on the incarceration of minority men:

They was like, "He got a lot of cases, and never been in jail before," so I guess they just wanted him. . . . It's mostly blacks and Mexicans in jail. And they're just, basically, they're just *locking people up*. Instead of building schools, they're building more prisons. They'll lock people up for the littlest reasons . . . you can do any little thing and get three strikes. You know? And you'll be locked up forever. And I don't think that's right at all. But I don't understand why they're locking everybody up. I really don't know. It's sad though, it's really sad. Cuz *a lotta people* are in jail. . . . But you know how they be. When they want you locked up, *they will lock you up*.

Feelings of helplessness or predetermination with respect to criminal justice involvement are not unique to the U.S. phenomenon of mass incarceration. Janet Foster (1990, 152–53) observes a similar pattern among two generations of inner-city dwellers in England: "Delinquency was often regarded by both generations as simply a product or hazard of living in the area which parents could do little about. Fathers in particular adopted a seemingly abstract concern for their children, where they theoretically wished to see them legitimately employed and law-abiding, but accepted their delinquency with an almost fatalistic inevitability if it occurred."

However, the current penal incarnation of "American exceptionalism" is distinctive from its European counterparts in the length of its punishments and the sheer numbers of people it involves (Tonry 1999, 3–47; see also Lipset 1996, 46–47). As a result, women like Alice and LaShawn simultaneously commit themselves to middle-class lifestyles and values and resign themselves to the inexorableness of their husbands' imprisonment. What Jerome Miller (1996, 5) describes as "the social disaster . . . overtaking black males in the United States," that is, their disproportionate rates of incarceration, underpins the most prevalent account among women for their partners' temporary absences: according to Vicki, a thirty-nine-year-old African American sporadically employed in cafés and bookstores whose boyfriend is serving one year, "If you black you goin' down. *You goin' down*. Don't matter." During her interview, Pat complained about the police not bothering certain people while persecuting others. When asked what she thought explained this discrepancy she replied bluntly: "Blackness." Later, she rejoiced that her husband would soon finish serving his full sentence, meaning that he would not be on parole following his release:

Yes, he's *maxing* out. [*slowly, with emphasis*] *He will not be on parole anymore.* So it's nothin' they can do to him! They can't just pull him over for walkin' down the street bein' a black man. They can't stop him just for ridin' a bike or just for drivin' a car, I mean, you know, they can stop him but they can't send him to jail because he *won't* be on parole! They can't say it's a violation. You know, ridin' a bike without a helmet, or throwin' a cigarette butt on the ground, you're *violated*! . . . A black man walkin' down the street, if he just happen to leave his wallet and don't have his ID, they can violate his parole for *that*!

Regardless of their own ethnicity, participants partnered with black men consistently castigated the police and criminal justice system as racist, indicating that it was nearly impossible for an African American male to evade harassment and arrest. Jasmine, who is Palestinian American, was incensed by the treatment of her boyfriend:

JASMINE: When he's out he doesn't do anything wrong! He's not doing anything, you know, illegal, he's not doing anything he's not supposed to be doing. It's just places at the wrong time that he's at. . . . Wherever he goes it's hard, and his appearance I guess doesn't look too nice for cops to just pass by him and, "Oh, okay, he's fine!"
MC: What does he look like?
JASMINE: He's just a big black guy. That's all. He's African American, real big. So they look at him like, "Oh, okay!" You know? "Let's mess with him! Let's get our commission off him!" So, it's hard for him. And he can't help it. . . . Just stupid stuff cuz he has tattoos an' he's a big guy. An' he's black, basically. An' I'm not gonna say all cops are prejudiced, but the ones *I* came across were.

Jasmine's and Pat's declarations make clear that they do not believe their partners' arrests result from criminal activity but rather from being in the wrong place at the wrong time in the wrong skin, namely being a black man in today's America. Women involved with white or Hispanic men also offered accounts of an illegitimate criminal justice system, but identified aggressive policing and corruption, rather than racism, as the source of their partners' troubles:

And then to be watched through the next three years [while my husband is on parole] and harassed. You know? It's like God forbid we go out to dinner, have a few cocktails, and stumble out the door, and *boom!* [*snaps fingers*] Forget it! He's goin' back in, and he's lookin' at another five years! I mean, and that's *seriously* how strong it gets. I know most people'd be like, "Oh, well, then you must've had somethin' in your pocket or you're doin' somethin'!" *No,* it's that simple! 'Kay? You wanna have one of these fuckin' asshole cops have a bad day? That's how simple it's gonna get. (Yaz, twenty-nine-year-old Hispanic personal trainer, husband awaiting sentencing)

I'm so horrified by the *injustices* of the system that the anger takes over. I'm just so upset with people that they're letting this state turn into a *socialist* state. [*shouting*] A police-run state! That's what they want, that's what they're trying to do! . . . There's no-good sheriffs all over, I mean dirty sheriffs, the *whole* system needs to be investigated! (Linda)

The vast majority of participants who claimed that their men had been imprisoned for "nothing" had partners who were serving time for parole violations, or PVRC: Parole Violators Returned to Custody. As Joan Petersilia (1999, 503; see also Petersilia 2003, 77–91) explains, in addition to the standard requirements of parole,[12] authorities can demand "gainful employment," "no association with persons of criminal records," "pay all fines and restitution," and "support family and dependents" of their supervisees, conditions with which virtually all ex-convicts would have serious trouble complying. Indeed, in the year 2000, 89,346 out of 117,227 parolees, or 76 percent, were returned to custody in California, 73,330 of them (82%) for reasons other than a new crime (Camp, Camp, and May 2002, 190, 198). Being returned to custody without a new case does not automatically absolve someone of illegal activity—in some situations, the district attorney may opt to revoke parole in lieu of prosecuting the latest offense (Petersilia 1999, 483)—but for many women the absence of a criminal charge stands as evidence that their partners are placed under overly strict and wholly unfeasible conditions. Nicole, a twenty-year-old African American nurse's assistant, explains how her boyfriend received an eighteen-month sentence for violating his parole:

And I was kinda mad because he was like, *it wasn't his fault,* it was just, he was there and then this other guy was doin' some stuff [had drugs on him] and the po-lice,

---

12. "Common standard parole conditions include that one should report to the parole agent within twenty-four hours of release, not carry weapons, report changes of address and employment, not travel more than fifty miles from home or leave the county for more than forty-eight hours without prior approval from the parole agent, obey all parole agent instructions, seek and maintain employment or participate in education/work training, not commit crimes, and submit to search by police and parole officers." (Petersilia 1999, 503)

you know, drove up on him. And whatever the other guy had, he dropped it on the ground. And then when the po-lice came up, [my boyfriend] was there and the guy was there, so, instead of just takin' one guy, they took *both of 'em*. You know, he was just like trapped up in that, you know, so I was like, "Oh my God, so you're in there for *nothing!*" He was like, "Pretty much, yeah! I shouldn't've been there, you know." So next time he know not to go there no more!

Although at times these protestations seem disingenuous (Yaz, for example, had been arrested alongside her husband when the police caught the pair with stolen property, drugs, and a gun), the distinction between whether or not a man bears responsibility for his arrest is paramount in women's minds and may determine the degree of support they provide during his incarceration. Gina, a twenty-two-year-old African American receptionist whose husband is serving an eighteen-month parole violation for driving a stolen vehicle with a suspended license in the company of a friend possessing a gun, refused to participate in family visits because she faulted her spouse for their predicament: "I didn't want to do any conjugals. I didn't do any conjugals because I feel that if I give you a conjugal then that's like you're being rewarded for something that you shouldn't be rewarded for. For me I believe what he did was wrong and he's on punishment for it. It's just like a child, you know, if you were going to punish a child and then give them candy, they would never know they did anything wrong. You know? So, he's on punishment!"

Similarly, Crystal had visited her husband only three times during his previous three-year sentence because she held him accountable for his arrest. However, now that he is serving five months for a parole violation she views as a dishonest maneuver on the part of his negligent parole officer, she spends the entire day with him every Saturday and Sunday: "He didn't come here because of him doin' somethin' wrong. You know, just a *stupid little violation*. So I didn't feel like it was his fault this time. And before it was his first time bein' in prison and it *was* his fault! . . . The majority of people that are in prison, let me see, the majority population is black and Hispanic. You know, that's mainly it. You don't really see too many whites. . . . *I* don't even feel like we have a *justice* system anymore."

The vocabulary used to discuss motivational accounts ("justifications," "rationalizations," "denials") places those doing the accounting on the defensive, implying that they are obscuring facts or exaggerating their own victimhood. Without extensive background information it is impossible to determine who is entirely blameless, but high-profile cases such as the shooting of unarmed West African immigrant Amadou Diallo (Sachs 2001), the Los Angeles Police Department corruption imbroglio (Purdum 1999), or the beating by police of a sixty-four-year-old man in the streets of post-Hurricane Katrina New Orleans (Hauser and Drew 2005)—not to mention studies of vast ethnic- and class-based inequity in the criminal justice system (Miller 1996; Cole 1999)—lend credence to women's assertions of the authorities' wrongdoing or malfeasance. In one case I unexpectedly confirmed a participant's protestation of innocence: during her interview Karen, a twenty-two-year-old African American, explained that she and her husband had been arrested together, but she professed their complete innocence and claimed that the police officer had framed them: "The guy [the police officer], he lied in my report, saying that he found some stuff [stolen credit cards] in my purse. And I'm like, that *cannot* be true because all I had in my purse was my wallet and some check stubs, you know, my little lipstick and stuff like that! I'm like, how could he, I mean, that's just, *how could he do that?*" As a result of the arrest Karen spent one month in jail and was sentenced to three years of felony probation; on her release she learned that even though her employer of eighteen months had held her job for her, she could not resume work because as a security guard she was not allowed to be on probation. When asked how long her husband would be in San Quentin she replied that he had not been sentenced yet "because the guy who arrested us, he's on the run. . . . He's in Mexico or something." When I excitedly pressed her for details, Karen bemusedly gave a physical description of the arresting officer that exactly matched that of Francisco "Frank" Vazquez, an Oakland policeman who had recently fled south of the border after he and three colleagues were indicted on over sixty charges of misconduct including "conspiracy to obstruct justice, kidnapping, assault, filing false police reports, filing false documents and making false arrests" (Nieves 2000).[13]

"I Knew What I Was Saying 'I Do' To"

The condemnation of the criminal justice system as racist and unjust is by far the most common account used by the participants in this category to frame men's roles in the events that led to their incarceration.

13. Although I gave Karen the phone number of a legal advocacy group that was filing a class-action suit against the officers and encouraged her to contact them so that she could clear her record, she gave little indication that she would do so and expressed her fatalism that her circumstances could not be changed.

However, participants also neutralize their partners' lawbreaking in ways that resonate with the feminine attributes of compassion, self-sacrifice, and the prioritization of others. Both of Samantha's parents have been repeatedly incarcerated since her birth twenty years ago: her father nearly lost his life when his throat was cut in San Quentin in the 1980s, and her mother's drug addiction had landed her back in jail three weeks before Samantha's interview. Samantha, who is white and works as a housecleaner, became engaged to the twenty-three-year-old black father of her nineteen-month-old son against her parents' wishes: "My dad *number one* doesn't like the fact that I'm with him because he's an African. He has a *real* problem with the race issue. And then number two he doesn't like it because he's in jail and he thinks that I'm wasting my time." Samantha fervently explained why her fiancé cannot be held liable for his four incarcerations during their two-and-a-half year relationship (she estimates he has been free for eight or nine months since they started dating) and why she will continue to stand by him if he returns to prison:

I'd say he started [going to correctional facilities] like around, like [when he was] eight years old. I don't blame *any of it* on him though. [*sympathetically*] He was brought up in a group home! If you've known institutions all your life and you've been *institutionalized*, you know what I mean? It's like, it's all you *know*! He doesn't know what it's like to be out on the streets and have a family! He knows what it's like to deal with stuff in there [San Quentin]! [*pause*] It's *hard* for him. It's easier for him, I think, to be in jail, than it is for him to be home.

Women's explanations of why they plan to continue their relationships often refer to popular culture enjoinments to follow the gender role of loving and devoted female. Jeanette, who characterized her marital fidelity as "doin' your wife job," feels depleted by her husband's frequent incarcerations and suspected sexual dalliances. Yet she insistently converted the denial of her spouse's responsibility for their connubial woes into a *claiming* of her responsibility to make the relationship work:

JEANETTE: [W]e can't change the one we with, either we have to deal wit' it and work on it together, with him *or* her—it's either *stick in or get lost*! So I don't know, I don't think I'm gonna waste five years and just give up and walk away and give somebody else my husband. . . . Stay behind your husband and do what you gotta do. We can't change men. *We cannot.* So, like Jerry Springer say [*spiritedly*], "Either deal wit'it, or *step on*!" [*both of us start laughing*]

MC: Is that what he says?

JEANETTE: Yeah! Those were his journalist words. His thought of the day. Jerry Springer, at the end of his show, he breaks it down, tell you how it should be and what to say—I love it! At the end of it, yes, it's words of encouragement: "A woman allows herself to go through exactly what she lets herself." . . . So [*with steely determination*] I'm gonna get a marriage outta this.

Despite Gina's displeasure at her husband's imprisonment—and her efforts, described above, to further punish him by refusing to participate in overnight visits—she too assumed responsibility for her relationship, claiming that she immediately knew that the handsome man who had caught her eye two years earlier was an ex-convict: "When we met it was like the way he *walked,* I was like, 'Ooh, he just got out of jail!' . . . I really can't be mad because it's not like it's the first time [he has been incarcerated]. And you know, when I said 'I do,' I knew what I was saying 'I do' to *before,* you know? Before I even said 'I do.'" The couple wed in January 2000 at San Quentin, and Gina spoke unenthusiastically about married life:

It's kind of like now, it's like before I met him [when] I was on my own. . . . So I'm used to being basically by myself. And then it's like, by him being in jail, it really doesn't faze me either way, cuz it's still like, you know, I'm by myself! Yeah, I say, "That's my husband," but it doesn't feel like a marriage! Or, then maybe I don't know what a marriage is supposed to feel *like,* you know? . . . It still feels like we're dating! [*laughs*] At the end of the day, he goes his way and I go mine.

Gina's assertion that her husband's absence "doesn't faze" her calls to mind the "denial of injury" and "denial of victim," techniques used to neutralize forced separation by mitigating the impact it has on women: "It doesn't bother me," "I'm used to it," "I've learned to handle it," "It doesn't make any difference." These justifications fall under Cohen's (2001, 7) category of "interpretive denial" wherein "the raw facts (something happened) are not being denied. Rather, they are given a different meaning from what seems apparent to others." These responses usually arise in tandem with fatalism about the inescapability of men's incarceration, revealing ambivalence as women at once claim that "there's nothing to be done about it, but it doesn't bother me anyway." Sandra, a twenty-one-year-old Hispanic woman who works for "*way* under ten thousand" dollars a year as a cashier supporting a four-year-old son and a fourteen-month-old daughter, cannot remember how many times her boyfriend (currently serving six months at

San Quentin) has been incarcerated during the last four years of their relationship:

Yeah, getting into trouble, and it seems like during a certain time like everybody's in jail and then everybody gets out and then everybody goes *back* to jail. . . . It's kinda stressful, but, I don't know, there's just nothing you can do anymore, you're so used to it. . . . Cuz he just keeps coming in and he just keeps coming in and out. I can't get used to him [at home] because once I start getting used to him, it's like he's gone again for another five months, another six months, two months, then he gets out, and then he'll be out for who knows how long.

Although the twenty-four women in this category looked forward to their partners' releases and stoically hoped for an eventual period of settling down (if not always believing that it would occur in the near future), many acknowledged some benefits to their current situations, primarily the control it gave them over their households. Edin (2000, 121, 123) notes: "When we asked single mothers what they liked best about being a single parent, their most frequent answer was, 'I am in charge,' or 'I am in control.'" Furthermore, the "often difficult life experiences of these mothers had convinced them of competencies they might not have known they had before single motherhood. Because of these experiences, their roles expanded to encompass more traditionally male responsibilities than before." Jeanette, while conventional in her desire to be a "beautiful, nice wife" and sorely lonesome for her spouse, chafed at her husband's reassertion of dominance over household matters on each return from prison: "When they leave and they're gone for a long period of time an' you're used to handling your own, a woman is used to handlin' they own, the bills, *everything*. That's somethin' else hard, for someone to come back in, and try to *run it*? You let 'im, since I guess he's my husband now, but that's kinda hard too to switch. Okay, it's been like this for hecka months. Now you wanna come in and *switch*?"

Vanessa, a twenty-four-year-old Hispanic dental assistant who married her high school sweetheart (now serving six months for a parole violation), discovered untapped inner resources when her husband went to prison and she found it particularly difficult to relinquish control of their daughter's upbringing the first time he returned home:

VANESSA: Disciplining our daughter—I had been the only one, you know? When he came out he had a totally different idea on how to do things, and I was like "Whoa! Whoa, wait a minute!" And then that was hard for me to kinda step back and let him handle it also. You know what I mean? Him have his own issues with her. It was me and her, you know? I didn't want anybody else yelling at her! [*laughs*] Even though, you know, *that's* her *dad,* but I just, I just felt like, *no, that's my* baby! And so that was really hard.

[. . .]

MC: Do you think that your husband's incarceration has changed you?

VANESSA: Yeah. Yeah. I'm more independent I think than other, like, girlfriends my age and stuff. I can do it! You know? I don't have to worry about anybody taking care of me, I know that I can pretty much, I mean I've done it before and I can take care of myself. I think it's also made me—when I was younger I used to feel like I always needed somebody, like a partner, with me. And him being away, I think that, you know, it made me feel like it's not really necessary to see him every day or talk to him every day. And I don't know if that was just the way my personality was gonna be, you know, or if this situation, you know, has helped that.

Finally, hints of domestic violence appeared in multiple interviews, suggesting that in this category too women may view the prison as a device for managing abusive men. None of the twenty-four women said that her current partner was abusive to her, although several had left previous relationships due to violence: when Fern met her current fiancé she fled an abusive man whom she had wed twenty-six years before at age sixteen (and who threatened to kill her when she separated from him); Beth was severely beaten by her second husband and had to leave the state to escape him; Mimi found herself married to a batterer at age sixteen; and Jenna (whose lover is serving nine months for a domestic violence incident involving another girlfriend) and Pat offhandedly mentioned abuse at the hands of previous spouses. In addition, three women made comments indicating the possibility of violence or sexual exploitation in their present relationships: Jasmine became involved with her boyfriend when she was fifteen and he was twenty-seven; during his stays at San Quentin he exercises significant control over her, wanting to know where she is at all times and using his phone calls to verify that she is at home whenever she is not visiting him or working. Crystal told several stories of her husband's vicious fights with other men, cautioning, "And, it's terrible, because he's *crazy!* You know, he has a *very bad temper.* And I mean it's like, don't do somethin' wrong to him cuz he *gonna* go off on you!" Likewise, Karen warned that her husband "is very hard to control. *Very* hard to control. Once he's, once he's just mad or somethin' happen, he's basically the type to like to have his way all the time." Although Karen only described verbal arguments with her spouse, she acknowledged that he was placed on psychiatric medication following a suicide attempt during a previous incarceration and said that she wished he would have continued this treatment after his release. Such histories and indicators of violence suggest that numerous women in this category may in fact rely on periods of incarceration to interrupt untenable situations when their partners are at home—a strategy characteristic of the women described in the following section.

"You Just Can't Throw It Away"

In the five years I have known Erica she always and adamantly has been "between thirty and forty—I haven't reached forty yet!" and "a member of the human race—although according to society I'm an African American woman." She and her husband Leon have been together since 1983 and married in the early 1990s; although she has never told me the story of how they met, she once showed me a photo of a handsome young couple posing in front of a prison gate and commented, "This is how it started: me and him in jail." Efforts to tabulate how often during their relationship Leon has been thrown behind bars yield similarly vague and inconclusive responses, with the likely answer being more times than Erica can—or cares to—remember. A rail-thin woman given to manic spurts of energy, Erica spends many of our conversations delivering lengthy and impassioned diatribes against her errant husband and the dysfunctions of the criminal justice system, complete with expansive gesticulations, theatrical pratfalls, and dramatic stomping or leaving the room for emphasis. Over time I realize that she usually phones me when she needs to blow off steam, and when transcribing our interviews I note that her preferred form of interaction is to lecture me at the top of her lungs with a "you" referring to Leon, thus creating a submissive and attentive conjugal stand-in who not only soaks up but actually tape-records her every word.

Erica's speech is peppered with self-help sound bites drawn from pop-psychology books, a wealth of Oprah-esque television shows, her preacher's Sunday sermons, and the various drug- or alcohol-recovery groups she periodically attends (once after vigorously informing me that a "real man" should avoid repeating his mistakes and "not go back and do the same thing over and over and over again, expecting different results," she winked at me slyly: "Got that from AA [Alcoholics Anonymous], by the way!"). When Leon is incarcerated, these support systems and vocabularies of self-actualization have a strong effect on Erica, who is remarkably successful at obtaining above-minimum-wage jobs in telecommunications, often as a phone operator or

163

call-center manager for wireless companies. Employment is central to Erica's ethos and her self-validation of being a worthy person—"Because see, companies hire you today based upon your integrity. Not just your skills! Your morals, your principles. That's how I get all of my jobs"—not to mention crucial for keeping her housed and fed as she lives paycheck to paycheck. In addition to steadily holding down jobs throughout the three-to-nine month periods when her spouse is away, Erica usually attends church and her twelve-step program meetings, socializes with friends, and spends time with her and Leon's seven-year-old daughter, of whom Erica's mother has legal custody.

The story dramatically changes when Leon comes home. Erica typically uses her extensive employment connections to line up work for her husband upon his release, and Leon typically loses this job a few weeks later because of insubordination or failure to adhere to a regular schedule. Home alone all day with nothing to do and feeling depressed, he returns to using drugs, paying for them by hocking possessions: "He went and sold his jacket, he started sellin' his watch, my watch that he bought me. Everything. All of a sudden I come home, everything had disappeared. So I knew that he had went back on the crack." Often Leon's next step is to steal his wife's car and disappear for days or weeks at a time, at which point Erica loses her job due to lack of transportation and stress-related maladies. Once things escalate to this level Erica usually appeals to the police for help, but she is realistic about why her case is not their top priority: "[Leon] disappeared for two months. Okay? No word, nothing. We put out a missing person's report after the first thirty days. Because that was his MO [modus operandi], to disappear for thirty days. . . . I wasn't about to go, you know, lookin' for a drug addict in alleys in the city [of San Francisco]. Which I've done before. And I'm sure I'm not the only one. But it had got to the point where, hell no, I'm not gonna put my life in danger looking for this man. The police were supposed to do that. But who's gonna look for a convict on drugs? Please! There are children that are disappearing, okay?"

Out of work, stranded without a car or other possessions that Leon sold (like her cell phone and pager), and preoccupied with finding her husband, Erica's life starts to unravel. She falls into debt, loses touch with her daughter, her friends, and her church, and sometimes relapses into alcohol and drug abuse, especially if she already had started using with Leon when he was home. Eventually, her spouse winds up on her doorstep, phones her from the county jail, or gets word to her of his whereabouts. In one episode, Erica received a tip from an acquaintance that Leon was living in a homeless encampment around Folsom Street in San Francisco and in the early morning hours of January 1, 2000, after a night of celebration, she decided to track him down: "He looked like a mixture between James Brown and Oscar the

Grouch on Sesame Street! He had lost all *of his weight. He could wear my pants, and I weigh a hundred and fifteen pounds. . . . He was funky, he was smelly, he had a very strong odor, probably like the Unabomber did!* [cracking herself up, clapping her hands and laughing] *In fact he looked like he could'a been related to the Unabomber! I mean he was* [strong emphasis] *ugly, okay? Just flat-out ugly.* [laughing] *Here I am all dressed up all pretty, coming from this classy club where it cost fifteen dollars to get in, you know,* [with broadcaster hype] *it's the year two thousand, a new millennium and thangs an' I'm havin' a ball! Okay? An' you out here in crack alley. Somethin' is wrong with this picture. Houston, we got a problem. . . . I said, 'Where the hell have you been living?' Excuse my French, but I went fifty-one fifty [referring to the San Francisco police radio code 5150 designating a mental health detention, used in slang to mean "crazy"]! And he said, 'I wanna come home.' I go, 'Home? What's that? This is your home!' He had some crack change in his pocket, like about five bucks, that he let me see. And I didn't want his money, I looked at him, and I* pitied *him. I, I could not believe that was the man I had married. I* couldn't *believe it! And then I felt* sorrow *in my heart for him, because of the Christ that lives in me—even though yes I cuss, I ask God to forgive me for that—but still, I have God in me. Cuz God is in your heart. But the fact of the matter is that, you know, I, I looked at him, Megan, and I was just* so *devastated."*

After these disappearances, Leon returns to an unstable domestic situation: Erica is unemployed and in financial trouble, she does not have job prospects for him, and now one or both of them are in the full swing of abusing drugs. Tempers soon flare, and violence follows. Erica, who freely admits to serving time in jail for assaulting Leon, offers tutelage on how she fends off her husband's attacks: "I go put on [the singer] Mary J. Blige [singing raucously] 'I should'a left your ass a thousand times before! Oh, I ain't gonna cry, ain't cryin', I ain't gonna cry no mo'!' And I blast it to the top! Of the roof! Okay? And I have hardwood floors! Okay? It's echoin'! [standing up and stomping around laughing] I jeopardized my apartment! For my life. Cuz see, we ain't supposed to have all that drama. You can get kicked out for that kinda mess [meaning she could get evicted from her apartment building for disturbing the peace]. But see, that's how I turn a bad situation to a good sit-, [fiercely] I'm gonna survive! I will survive! See? This is what women don't know how to do, you gotta draw attention to yourself, get some police there before somebody kill your ass. This guy is under the influence of crack and Lord knows what else. I don't know what he's gonna do to me! This is not my husband, this is not the man I married! I'm not even gonna try to talk to him like that! But I knew, [matter-of-factly] I got a knife, and I didn't have my Mace, but I got a knife, I picked up a knife, and I started boiling some water.

And I put some syrup in it, cuz my mom told me, 'If you don't have grits, just scald him with some syrup an' that'll stick to him and he'll wake the hell up and leave you the hell alone!' So if an intruder is in your house, always cut the hot water on an' put some syrup in there and just scald his, you know, set up little traps in the house for the scenario to go down."

Creating enough of a disturbance to provoke her neighbors into phoning for help is important for Erica, who says that she only dials 911 as a last resort: "If I was to call the police myself, and let him see me? That is saying I've gotta come and see you, I've gotta come and visit you [visit Leon while he is incarcerated]. I am responsible for sending you to jail. That is just a no-no. You don't do that. . . . Cuz it's like, that's what they want you to do. So you can feel obligated to go visit them. Yeah, yeah! So they'll create a scenario, making you call the police cuz they know they got to go back to jail anyway, cuz they done violated their parole, right? So they try to set you up. So I'm hip to that game!"

One way or another, law enforcement eventually does arrive and Leon is carted off to the county jail, charged with violating parole, and then sent to the penitentiary to serve another three-to-nine months during which he settles down, detoxes, and apologizes to Erica, begging her for another chance. Erica—who repeatedly manages to reestablish herself with a car (possibly by earning money in the underground economy—she acknowledges exchanging sex for money during certain periods) and later gainful employment—atones too, blaming herself for not being more accepting and supportive of her spouse ("I was pretty much just being selfish, thinking about myself and what he had did to me. And actually, spiritually, I should have been praying for him, praying for him to be free from whatever he was going through"). Prohibited from harming each other physically by the guards and bars, and with time apart to reflect on their mistakes and pine for each other's company, by the time of Leon's release date both parties have reconciled their differences and are eager for reunification.

Depending on where she is in this cycle, Erica offers different answers to a fundamental question: Why does she continue to actively pursue this relationship, especially when she often has other suitors competing for her affections? Despite her bravado when describing domestic altercations, Leon's tendency to violence and his history of jealousy-provoked rage are significant factors—as became evident during a conversation in which Erica berated herself for repeatedly allowing her husband back into her life while insinuating that she feared Leon might kill her if she rejected him: "I am very upset with myself! I'm uncomfortable with, with the fact that I keep [long pause], it's like, how much is it gonna take? . . . What I'm waiting on now is for him, I'm givin' him enough rope to hang hisself and I'm also surviving. There are *people now that are* dead [pause, measuring her words carefully], *behind leaving relationships* [ominously] *inappropriately." Yet Erica also recognizes that she further jeopardizes herself by maintaining contact with Leon when he is in prison, seeking him out when he has disappeared, giving him keys to her apartment, and otherwise trying to share her life with him. In one moment of self-analysis she proffered this insight, gleaned from her favorite book,* Women Who Love Too Much,[14] *to explain: "We [women] are focusing more on what we want to happen in the relationship, as opposed to what is* in actuality *happening. So in other words we're like blind, okay? And that's why we have family members that are not in love with these men that are tellin' us, 'You can do better.'" This coincides exactly with a scene Erica's lifelong friend Mai describes:*

I've been knowing Erica since before Erica was in love with Leon. And I think that that's a relationship from hell, because it causes her nothing but grief and turmoil and drama. So what kind of enjoyment can you *possibly* be deriving from that? You know? And I've asked her before, but, I remember her saying to me, she had a little figurine, and the figurine was a man sitting—an African American family—a man sitting in an easy chair, the wife with her arm around him, and the little girl on the floor. And she picked it up, and she started crying, and she started screaming at the top of her lungs, "This is *all* I wanted! This is *all I wanted!*" And I looked at her and I said [*with a hushed voice*], "But that's not what you have. That's *not* what you have. You've been in this relationship for thirteen years, your child is three years old, it's not what you have, so let it go."

Instead of "letting go" of her vision, Erica sticks to her belief that with dedication to Christian ideals and a firm will she can be the mistress of her destiny: "I take charge *of my life today! And that's what I'm tryin' to tell him* [clapping her hands together for emphasis], you gotta take charge! *You gotta be a* man! *I am a woman; I take charge of my life! I do not let people run it for me! I do not let people make decisions for me today!" Hence her conviction that Leon can reform his ways if only he will really try, her periodic self-recriminations for not having been the "good woman" to help him do it during his previous releases, and her recommitment during each incarceration to their life together: "I want to be with my husband. I want to be with the man that I had his baby with. I want to give this man an opportunity to be a productive member*

14. *Women Who Love Too Much: When You Keep Wishing and Hoping He'll Change* (Pocket Books, 1991), a "stunning bestseller classic" (according to its back-cover text) by Robin Norwood, addresses those for whom "being in love means being in pain" and promises that "women who love too much can recover—when they find the power to love themselves."

*of society and take care of his child. If I leave him now, he's just going to re-
gress, he's going to get worse. And so am I." And so, come Leon's next parole
date Erica's heart will have softened, her hope will be renewed, and her door
will be open: "All of the time and the effort, and the money, and the love,
that we have invested—that's worth more than gold. Because people don't
just be together for that long amount of time, and you just can't throw it
away. It's just something, it's just,* [with deep feeling] you just can't throw
it away."

———

In a society simultaneously engaged in widespread policies of mass
incarceration and welfare retrenchment (Piven and Cloward 1993; Katz
1996; Sidel 1998), the prison stands out as the most prominent, powerful, and "reliable" state institution in the lives of many low-income people (see Miller 1996, 132–36, 177, 241). As Elliott Currie (1998, 32–34)
observes:

The prisons became, in a very real sense, a substitute for the more constructive social policies we were avoiding. A growing prison system was what we had *instead* of
an antipoverty policy, instead of an employment policy, instead of a comprehensive
drug-treatment or mental health policy. Or, to put it even more starkly, the prison
became our employment policy, our drug policy, our mental health policy, in the
vacuum left by the absence of more constructive efforts. . . . *Prison, then, has increasingly become America's social agency of first resort.* (emphasis added in last sentence)

Eleven women—Ann, Brandi, Butta, Celina, Dawn, Jessica, Joy, Keisha, Kim, Millie, and Paige—share Erica's reliance on the correctional
facility as a "social agency of first resort" to help them manage the drug-
addicted, criminally involved, philandering, and oftentimes violent
men in their lives. Few were as candid as Erica in their interviews about
according this role to the penal institution—and most likely few are as
painfully aware as she is about their dependence on carceral control—
instead articulating similar justifications for their partners' imprisonment as the women in the previous category, principally castigating
the criminal justice system for its racist and unfair application of the
law. Indeed, passages from the majority of these interviews in which
the women defend their mates as principled men victimized by "the
system" are indistinguishable from those offered by LaShawn and her
peers. What differentiates this category are the internal contradictions
in their accounts: expressions of mournfulness at the loss of a partner

alongside memories of satisfaction or even happiness at news of his arrest; rifts in the relationships that are healed rather than exacerbated during his absence; condemnations of a "no-good" and "hard-headed" man followed by impassioned speeches of how he has been framed or why he deserves help; great optimism about future domestic harmony coupled with histories of life being calmer and both partners being more stable when the male is behind bars. Of all the participants' narratives, these twelve women's stories were the most paradoxical—but as Ann Swidler (2001, 24–40) observes, all "talk of love" to some degree draws on contrasting vocabularies and a patchwork of justifications to explain attraction and commitment. The question is thus not whether these women are confused or unreliable but rather what "incompatible normative expectations of attitudes, beliefs, and behavior" (Merton 1976, 6) drive them to offer certain accounts at certain moments.

The majority of the men in this category regularly went to prison for violating parole: at the time of the interviews, all were serving between four and twenty-four months for parole violations with the exceptions of Millie's husband (sentenced to six years) and Jessica's boyfriend (sentenced to one year) for intent to manufacture drugs, Kim's fiancé (serving six months on an unspecified new charge), and Butta's husband (who had accepted a plea bargain for twenty years for charges related to selling drugs and fleeing the police). Seven of the women (Ann, Butta, Erica, Jessica, Keisha, Millie, and Paige) directly linked their partners' repeat offending and violation of parole to untreated alcoholism or drug addiction. It is important to note that I had ongoing contact with several participants in this category after their partners were released from prison, which enabled me to record views that contrasted greatly with the rosy outlook they described during the incarceration period. As noted, the categories deployed in this chapter are loosely bound and it is quite possible that women in the previous category had similar experiences of disenchantment and recourse to the criminal justice authorities as the dozen women discussed here that did not arise in the single interview I conducted with them, and thus the following arguments could apply to a larger proportion of the overall sample of participants.

In laying bare their difficult navigations between expectation and disappointment, the twelve women fluctuate repeatedly between belief that a man's incarceration will somehow address his unemployment, substance use, or violence problems and despair when these troubles persist following his release. Such cycles call to mind Beth Richie's (1996, 4) study of battered women detained in New York City's Rikers Island and her concept of "gender entrapment," which she uses to

169

analyze how the limited life opportunities available to abused African American women cause them to resort to criminal activity. Although not all are African American and not all are partnered with abusive men, the women in this category show signs of being "entrapped" in their relationships by weak or nonexistent social services and a powerful penal system, the combination of which at once binds them to their mates and ensures that the men's mental health, substance use, unemployment, and other socioeconomic needs go unaddressed. The fact that these women and those in Kathryn Edin's (2000) study contend with similar issues in their dealings with the opposite sex (Edin's domains of affordability, respectability, trust, control, and domestic violence) but that the latter choose *not* to commit to the men in their lives underscores the significance of the intermediary role played by the penitentiary in encouraging and sustaining carceral dyads.[15]

Affordability and Respectability

The participants in this category are primarily poor, with Keisha, who makes $35,000 annually by working two service-industry jobs, netting an income nearly double that of the top salary of any of the others. Celina, Dawn, and Paige are unemployed and receive under $5,000 a year in government assistance; Ann, Kim, and Millie work full-time for annual salaries under $10,000; while Brandi, Butta, Erica, Jessica, and Joy have yearly incomes fluctuating between $10,000 and $20,000 depending on their employment status. Like the women in Edin's work who found men to be more fiscal hindrance than help, the majority of these participants gained no economic advantage through their partnerships. Only Celina's, Dawn's, and Millie's spouses were contributing financially to the household before the time of their arrests (the men worked, respectively, at Home Depot, at a gym as a fitness trainer, and on his parents' cattle ranch); Ann's unemployed husband provided essential care for their five children, which enabled Ann to work the day shift as

15. While Edin specifically addresses women's choices not to marry, her analysis can be generalized to the desire to "commit to" a partner with the hope of marrying since those in Edin's sample actively expressed skepticism about whether their relationships would endure and spoke freely about desires to remain single. This differs greatly from the women in this category, who largely were already married or intended to wed their partners: Ann, Butta, Dawn, Erica, and Millie were legally married to their spouses; Celina and Paige referred to their partners as "my husband" although they were not officially conjoined; Keisha was engaged and Brandi anticipated marriage; Joy desired more commitment than her lover was willing to undertake; and only Jessica and Kim were dubious about their continued involvement, saying it largely depended on their boyfriends' behavior after release.

a cashier at a grocery store (when her spouse is incarcerated she switches to the 6 p.m.–midnight shift); while Keisha's fiancé took over the duties of a traditional housewife: "[My fiancé would] watch my kids while I go to work, and clean the house and cook and massage me when I come [home]." The remaining seven men provided neither financial nor practical support on a regular basis, and indeed four of them were sources of considerable financial loss when they periodically stole money, belongings, or vehicles from their partners, usually in connection with their drug addictions. Given these circumstances, the economic ramifications of a man's incarceration on most of these women did not entail the proverbial "loss of the breadwinner." Indeed, since Millie's husband had been spending a considerable portion of his income on drugs, only Celina and Dawn felt overwhelmed by financial hardship as a direct result of their spouses being sent behind bars—and both of these women already had been living in poverty before their husbands' departures.

However, despite the lack of monetary contribution from the men prior to their incarceration and the expenses women faced feeding and housing them, the economic drain of maintaining contact with a prisoner detailed in chapters 3 and 4 (the high costs of collect calls, the pressures to send packages and to deposit money in inmates' accounts, plus the significant expenses of visiting) usually meant that the imprisonment period was *not* easier financially for women and thus did not alter the "affordability" of their boyfriends, fiancés, or husbands in a practical sense. Instead, the relational dynamics around economic issues changed in ways that gave a context of "respectability" to the partnership and valorized the women's support of their men. Edin (2000, 120) documents the linkage of a man's economic viability and his ability to confer "respectability" on his wife: "[Single] mothers said that they could not achieve respectability by marrying someone who was frequently out of work, otherwise unemployed, supplemented his income through criminal activity, and had little chance of improving his situation over time." Faced with high rates of male unemployment and criminality, therefore, "[m]ost mothers weren't willing to sign an apartment lease with the man they were with, much less a marriage license." On the whole, women with incarcerated partners shared the desire of Edin's interviewees for their mates to participate in the wider societal labor force, yet when the men went to prison the women's expectations diminished noticeably: out of all fifty participants only Darla argued that her husband should work and cover his own expenses, with the rest of the women not caring about or not counting on their partners' ability to hold a job while behind bars (although ironically for a handful of men their stints in prison were the *only* times that they held jobs). For many this lack of expectation stemmed from the practical constraints governing prison labor, namely the relative scarcity of jobs, the prohibition of prisoners under certain security classifications from working, and the extremely low wages paid for most institutional duties (thirty-five cents an hour at San Quentin). Others actively opposed their partners' penal employment, viewing prison work as collusion with the enemy and participation in a form of labor exploitation reminiscent of slavery. In either case, participants did not stigmatize unemployed prisoners as being lazy, noncommittal, or "hard-headed" about working—characterizations they did apply to jobless men in the outside world.

The radical shift in women's expectations for men's labor-force participation when their partners go to prison signals the role of the penitentiary in changing the meaning attributed to men's "acts of omission" (Brooks and Silverstein 1995, 281) such as unemployment, lack of fathering, and relationship inadequacies. Speaking in retrospect about when the men were last released or in anticipation of their homecomings, women in this category share the attitudes of Edin's interviewees and communicate strong yearnings for their partners to settle down, find work, and attend to their families—and they express scarce sympathy for the parolees' shortcomings if they are unable to do so. Yet during the men's sojourns behind bars the women temporarily absolve them of many such responsibilities, acquiescing that it is no longer the heavily constrained prisoner's fault that he is "omitting" these roles from his life, for, indeed, how could he enact them under his present circumstances? Such pardons are facilitated both by the stories of redemption told by prisoners (as discussed in chapter 3), who express newfound devotion to the partnership and avow that they truly wish and intend to mend their ways if only their dedicated mates will help them do so, and by the cultural scripts described in the previous two sections asserting that prisoners are honorable men who ran afoul of a racist or unjust system.

Hence the twofold way in which incarceration confers "respectability" on troubled relationships: first, by furnishing a culturally acceptable and "manly" excuse for a partner's joblessness, his lack of interaction with his children, and his financial drain on the household (attributes that were disparaged as "not being a man" when he lived in the outside world), and, second, by positioning the inmate as a "reformed soul" who is now committed to the values of marriage, family, work, and sober living, as so eloquently expressed in his letters and phone calls.[16] In this context, the beleaguered woman who labors to put food on the table is no longer a dupe supplying drug money and free shelter to a disrespectful and disreputable man, but rather a "good woman" working hard for the benefit of her family, including her attentive and appreciative (although temporarily distant) partner. In addition, rather than having her money ignominiously stolen and wasted on street drugs or sex workers, the woman has control of her expenditures and can direct her finances toward the emotionally gratifying purchase of communication, food, and nurturance through phone calls, packages, and visits. As discussed in previous chapters, these displays of "standing by your man" confer moral righteousness on the woman and bolster her self-image as a loving and loyal mate—a characterization that can help sustain her through a subsequent round of rejection and disappointment. Paige, whose fiancé disappeared within days of his release from San Quentin, taking with him a car Paige had borrowed from a friend, consoled herself by emphasizing her selfless devotion:

It's like, [sarcastically] hello? I waited seven months for this? [philosophically] I waited, and I wouldn't take that back because you know what? That's the woman I am. I waited cuz I wanted to wait. Okay? So there's nothing that I would do differently about that, at all. Cuz I know I'm good. I know that I fucking did what I said. I was faithful, I've still been faithful! To this fucking very moment! You know? And I still will be because I'm fucking stuck on him.

Paige's experience with the release of her partner illuminates the conundrum that a man's affordability and his respectability (and thus the respectability of the relationship) are contingent on his carceral status, and are sure to be lost when he is sent home with no drug treatment, job prospects, or other rehabilitative services.

Trust and Control

We have a lot of men that's very immature that don't know how to treat a woman, you know. For mine's, I know that his head was hard! An' he didn't listen. So, this is his punishment. . . .

16. In cases when men are drug addicted, imprisonment also can impute a more respectable physical appearance (one remembers Erica's colorful description of Leon's "funkiness" when she found him in the homeless encampment). As Philippe Bourgois (1995, 109) documents, addicts returning to the streets from prison are noticeably more robust than their "free" counterparts—much to the befuddlement of crack dealers attempting to screen out undercover officers: "The most frequent confusion [over who was an authentic customer] arose over men who had just been released from prison and had not yet destroyed their bodies on crack. . . . [A crack dealer assessing a prospective customer commented] 'He musta just came outta jail because that nigga' looked fresh union. That nigga' was healthy.' "

It's a lot of good men behind walls! You know, it's just that it took them *to be* behind the walls to wan' to get theirself in order. An' that's sad.
BUTTA

As in the first category of participants, women in this category express notable disillusionment with "free" men and compare them unfavorably with prisoners. However, unlike Sarah and her peers, these women generally are speaking about the *same* men, whom they feel change significantly—and for the better—during their periods of incarceration. When Brandi first met her current boyfriend while hanging out in her neighborhood she did not like his personality and did not pursue his affections; years after their initial meeting he contacted her while locked in a correctional facility, and it was only then that their romance blossomed. Brandi calculates that the young man has been in prison for all but four months of their two-year relationship, and she spoke dispiritedly of his shift in demeanor when he last came home from a Southern California penitentiary: "It was just a difference, the way he would act. He wouldn't be, it's like, he was gettin' *harder,* back to the way he *used to be* I guess. Cuz he was real nice and stuff when he *first* got out. Then he started to change." Similarly, Celina, whose partner stayed out of prison for almost twelve consecutive months during the first three years of their relationship, described the time of their cohabitation as being full of "yelling and screaming and fighting and arguing and stuff like that." Even so, home alone with two sons under the age of three and deeply moved by her lover's "melodious" and repentant letters from San Quentin, Celina optimistically awaited his return: "I feel like I'm just passing time until he comes home. . . . I can't wait till he gets home so we can just have fun again and just be a family again, and be productive and all that." A month after her partner's release, the young mother sounded exasperated and depressed:

[*listlessly*] He like, *took over.* . . . I mean, he's takin' care of business an' stuff, but I feel like I'm like *takin' second wheel,* like he took over everything and I'm just like on for the ride. [*pause, growls in frustration*] . . . It's not a fairy tale like I thought it was gonna be. But, it's cool though. We're just tryin' to make it. Once you put all the elements of tryin' to *survive* and *make it* it's like totally different, it's not like the same thing as when they're in jail and stuff. So, [*dully*] I don't know. It's okay, but, *I don't know,* somehow I think I was disappointed, but then, I just hold on and just don't even trip off of it no more.

Celina's comments echo those of Jeanette and Vanessa from the previous category in her longing to continue to exercise control over finances, child rearing, and other household decisions once the man returns to the home. As Martin Moerings (1992, 256; see also Bourgois 1995, 229) records, women's "role transitions" when their partners are incarcerated often elicit untapped capabilities:

Not all women [whose partners are imprisoned] have negative stories: Some women successfully tackled their problems and became more independent. They were forced to make decisions on matters that used to be their husbands' responsibility. The situation is different where women feel relieved at their husbands' absence from home: The detention offers them the opportunity to lead a life with more freedom, without the frequent strain of the relationship.

Like the women in Ann Davis's (1992, 83) investigation of the financial impact of men's imprisonment on their mates, none of whom "reported a feeling of increased personal financial security following their partners' release," Keisha was initially disturbed by the arrest of her fiancé but soon learned to relish her self-sufficiency: "I mean when he first came in [to prison], I'm like, he was payin' the bills and he was doin' this and he was doin' that and now he gone, who gonna do it? Then I just have to realize, I don't supposed to never look up to no man to do anything for me, and that's one thing my mama *always* told me, 'Don't look for a man to do anything for you, you do it for yourself.' So, now I'm doin' it for myself!"

On their release from prison, men's disruption of women's autonomy and household control—often at the cost of the women's economic stability and quality of life—engenders feelings of resentment and powerlessness in their partners, especially if the men anchored them in the relationship during the incarceration period with assurances that their circumstances would improve. As Celina aptly pointed out in her above comments, contending with an ex-felon who is struggling to find work, control a drug habit, avoid the temptations of the street, and subdue his violent temper is "totally different" from interacting with this man when he is housed, fed, and restrained by the penitentiary. When men fail in their efforts at self-rehabilitation, or when they show no motivation to make such efforts in the first place, the women who believed their promises and staked their future happiness on their guarantees angrily turn on their partners, often looking to the criminal justice system to validate their sense of betrayal by punishing the man who has done them wrong. After yet another demoralizing failure to settle in to domesticity with Leon, Erica reveled in his shipment by the Department of Corrections to a facility in Southern

California instead of placing him in his customary environment of San Quentin:[17]

ERICA: They shipped him all the way to the *far depths of hell* this time, which [*gleefully*] I'm *so happy* about!

MC: Why?

ERICA: Because! [*laughing heartily*] He's up there by like, San Diego, like Mexico, an' he's up there with all these ah, you know, Hispanic Mexican people, gangs, and he's, he's *scared shitless! Okay?* Because he's, he's not of that culture. And that's uncomfortable [for him]. And they're crazy.

MC: And why are you happy about that?

ERICA: Because, it takes something like that maybe to [make him] *wake the hell up!* Maybe, maybe, you know, he, he brought this on hisself! And it's like, I'm, I'm really kind of *satisfied* with the situation because, I don't know *who* decided to ship him to the far depths of hell, but I wanna really personally *thank him.* [*more subdued*] However, I do not want anything to happen to my husband, I don't want him to get killed up in there, it's not that serious. Okay? But, nevertheless, he was taking for granted that they were always gonna send him to San Quentin.

In contrast to the women in the previous category, Erica and her peers generally supported the arrest and incarceration of their partners, agreeing with the law-enforcement authorities that the men were guilty of wrongdoing and deserved punishment. Yet the nature of the men's offending in the women's eyes was often manifestly personal and not the legal reason for their detention, a distinction that permitted the coexistence of rationalizations claiming men's innocence and victimization by the system. Kim, a twenty-one-year-old African American, worked four nights a week from 9:30 p.m. until 8 a.m. packaging groceries for an Internet-based food delivery service and repeatedly seemed to be on the verge of dozing off during our interview; her brief and lethargic responses nonetheless clearly communicated her pleasure that her fiancé now had the opportunity to contemplate his infidelity from behind bars:

KIM: It [his incarceration] brought us closer together, so if it hadn't been for him comin' here we probably wouldn't even be together right now.

MC: Why do you say that?

17. Leon's placement in a distant facility almost certainly occurred out of administrative necessity (overcrowding at Bay Area prisons and space available elsewhere) rather than for punitive reasons. Prisoners are not sent to specific correctional facilities as punishment per se, although people with high security classifications may land in notoriously fearsome prisons and those suspected of gang membership or who are alleged to be threats to other inmates and correctional officers may be placed in the Security Housing Unit (SHU) at the remote and brutal Pelican Bay facility.

KIM: He needs to sit here and *think*. This is his first time just ever sittin' down. When he's out he's been workin' or whatever, but he still hasn't sat down and *think*.[18] That's what he's doin' now. Nothin' but time to think!

[. . .]

MC: How did your life change when he came here?

KIM: A lot of stress went away. *For me!* [*we both laugh*] For me!

MC: What kind of stress?

KIM: Just emotional problems. Problems, period. A lot of problems. And when he came here, it was just cool. [*chuckles, pause*] Cool for me.

MC: So what's your life like now?

KIM: It's the same, just without him. [*chuckles*]

[. . .]

MC: Do you feel like you've changed at all since your fiancé's been in prison?

KIM: Um, no. [*pause*]

MC: Did it change any of your attitudes about things?

KIM: No, I just started eating more and I started gaining more weight!

MC: Why?

KIM: [*chuckles*] Cuz I was less stressed!

MC: And what kind of things were stressful before?

KIM: [*bluntly*] Cheating.

MC: So when you first heard he was arrested, how did you feel?

KIM. *Happy.* [*giggles*]

[. . .]

MC: Are you lookin' forward to him comin' out?

KIM: Yeah.

MC: What's the main reason?

KIM: Cuz I wanna see how much he changed. That's the only reason. [*chuckles*]

MC: And what are you gonna look for?

KIM: *A better man.*

MC: What do you mean by a better man? What makes a man better?

KIM: I just wanna see if he's gonna *just* be with me, that's all. That's all I worry about.

Although hopeful immediately before a man's release from prison, the women in this category express disappointment about the lack of leverage they have in controlling their partners' sexual, drug-related, and violent behaviors and frequently resign themselves to ceding authority over their men to the penitentiary. This resignation typically stems

18. Later in the interview Kim says that her fiancé has not held a job during their two-and-a-half-year relationship except when he has been incarcerated, implying that the work she refers to here is in the illegal economy.

from long histories of being failed by inadequate or nonexistent support services that inculcate a fatalistic realism about the (un)likelihood of receiving help from social institutions other than the penal system. Ann is a thirty-year-old Hispanic mother of five children ages four to thirteen. She single-handedly supports her offspring by working as a grocery-store cashier for under $10,000 a year following the termination of her state assistance under the Welfare-to-Workfare program. She has an eighth-grade education and has been living away from her parental home since age sixteen due to her mother's schizophrenia, which rendered the mentally ill woman unable to care for her family. Ann's first husband was ferociously abusive and her current husband, with whom she has had a twelve-year relationship, has struck her hard enough to cause bruising on multiple occasions; after the first time he hit her Ann tried to leave the relationship by obtaining a restraining order, but she wound up reconciling with him because she could not find legal help to assist her in recovering her daughter, whom the husband was keeping away from Ann as a means of enticing his wife to return to him. This man first went to prison in 1996 when he was sentenced to eighteen months for selling amphetamines to support his own drug habit. In the next four years he served four more sentences for parole violations, usually for dirty drug tests, and in one instance Ann's mother tipped off the parole officer that her son-in-law had been getting high because she wanted him to go to prison to detox. Ann, who has struggled with her own drug addiction, described the pattern that occurs each time her husband returns home from prison and the psychological pain he inflicts on their children:

[*weary, flat tone*] I was like, "I'm gonna tell you what's gonna happen. You're gonna get high. You're gonna start selling. And once you start selling, we're gonna start arguing, you're gonna start going out and not coming home. You're gonna meet somebody else who's gettin' high with you, cheat on me, and go to jail." And that's, and it happened just that way. [*pause*] Just that way. And, now he's back [in San Quentin] and [*pause, sadly*], my kids go through it when he's high. Because they know when he's high, my older ones, cuz they could tell, you just, you could tell when someone's on drugs. And they're like, [*said slowly, exaggerating, like a tedious list*] they don't like *all* the people coming in and out of our house, once he starts *selling,* people start *knocking* on our door all the time, asking if he's home, coming by *late at night.*

Judith Clark (December 1995–January 1996, 35), who is serving a seventy-five-years-to-life sentence in New York State's Bedford Hills

Correctional Facility, lucidly documents "the tragic paradox of imprisonment" for incarcerated mothers who were too consumed by drug
addiction, criminality, and sheer survival before their arrests to tend
to their children. The penitentiary, "which tears women from their
children and their mothering roles, [brings] some sense of relief in its
terrible wake. Deprived of their children's daily presence, but also free
of much of what distracted them, the mothers can finally think first
about their children." Clark describes the prison as a "punitive parent"
(1995, 310) that imposes welcomed restraints on chaotic lifestyles, a
characterization echoed in John Sloop's (1996, 2) account of a Texas
woman who tearfully praised her strict home-surveillance and drug-
testing program: "This program has been like a parent to me, the parent I never had" (see also Duncan 1996, 24–31). For the women in this
category the criminal justice apparatus intervenes in situations that
have failed to attract other institutional responses, enabling women to
regain control of their households and reestablish trust in their relationships—in highly relative terms.

Domestic Violence

Ann, Dawn, Erica, Jessica, and Keisha discussed violent incidences with
their partners, while Brandi, Celina, and Joy hinted at, but did not acknowledge outright, emotional or physical abuse. In a particularly awkward but revealing conversation, Linda, who had introduced me to Jessica, a twenty-five-year-old unemployed white woman whose boyfriend
was sentenced to one year after burning down his family's house while
manufacturing drugs, interrupted her friend's romantic reverie with a
reminder of Jessica's boyfriend's past behavior:

JESSICA: [I miss my boyfriend] especially when I'm going through my hard times,
   cuz like, he was always the one that would always, be my savior, you know, no
   matter—
LINDA: [sarcastically] He was always the one to tell you how *dumb* you were!
JESSICA: [ignoring Linda] And you know, regardless of whatever, he always was there
   for me, and I don't have anybody now.
LINDA: Yeah, nobody to beat up on you!
JESSICA: [laughing nervously] Shut up, Linda! [addressing MC] We got into a fight
   once, okay? And he, and he—
LINDA: He beat the *shit* out of you!
JESSICA: [laughing] He didn't beat the shit out of me!
LINDA: He did!

JESSICA: We got into a really big argument, he took my shoes, I remember that.

LINDA: *I* remember what he did, he *beat* the hell out of you!

JESSICA: And um—

LINDA: You called me up cryin'! "Waa-waa-waa! Come get me!"

Other women were forthright about violence in their relationships. Keisha, for example, spoke openly about how her fiancé came to be behind bars for assaulting her: the couple had been arguing over Keisha's suspicion that her fiancé, with whom she had recently had a baby, was cheating on her after he returned to the house late one night drunk and smelling of perfume. When her fiancé grabbed her and yanked her backward by her hair, Keisha "cracked him upside his head with a VCR . . . I *knocked him out*" and then picked up the phone, warning him, "I know what I'm gonna do! I'm gonna call the po-lice on you! You gonna get outta my house *tonight*!" By the time the police arrived both parties had calmed down; the officers decided not to arrest Keisha for her fiancé's injury, but since the young man was on parole they booked him on a violation. The episode left Keisha conflicted, believing on the one hand that she was wise to defend herself (as a child she bore witness to her father's battering of her mother, a trauma she refers to often) and on the other feeling responsible for her fiancé's incarceration, acknowledging her unpunished violence toward him:

[My fiancé] always told me, as long as we been together he always told me, "If I gotta get to the point where I gotta hit you, I'm gonna leave you alone. And I promise that." And I mean, I been goin' by that! So, that's why when he did it [grabbed her hair] I was just like, "*What*? You pullin' my hair, you fixin' to get to the point!" Cuz it start from your hair an' then it gets to a swat, an' then it get to a sock! I know about that [from seeing my mother abused]. [*pause*] But his, his mom tol' me, she ain't never seen him beat up his wife, or, you know, his friends, or his other girlfriends. You know, this is the first time, on his *whole record* this is the first time he ever been in jail for domestic violence. So it was like a shock to me! . . . I don' feel guilty, because I feel that he shouldn't'a pulled my *hair,* but I feel wrong because, if I wouldn't'a kept goin' on, I probably could'a just tol' 'im to leave and then we'd probably be still together. Because I done put, threw his clothes, I done that before, I done set [his] clothes on fire, I mean, *everything*! Me and him done been through *a lot,* and this is the first time he ever went to jail for anything we did.

Despite the spiraling levels of aggression in her relationship and her strong desire not to repeat her mother's experiences, Keisha says that she has never contacted any domestic violence prevention services (she does not know of any available to her) and that when she or her friends require help they telephone the police as a first recourse: "Sometimes I think the po-lice can be a real asshole, but then, when you need 'em, they do be there." Richie (1996, 130) finds a similar primacy of the criminal justice system in women's management of violence, but with a crucial distinction: some members of her sample of women relied on their *own* incarceration for respite when going to "jail became one of the few sources of safety from abusive male partners that they could envision." The discrepancy between the ways these two groups of women use penal control for personal protection (the former as a means of removing men, the latter as a means of finding refuge from them) is intriguing, especially given their commonalities in defending their partners. Both Richie's (1996, 70–80) and my participants balked at directly phoning the police to arrest a man, particularly an African American man, due to their strong feelings about institutional racism, injustice, and the socioeconomic disadvantage burdening black males. Those who had called the police felt ambivalent or remorseful, usually vowing that they would not do so again and trying to compensate for their actions by providing abundant financial and emotional support to their partners throughout the men's imprisonment. Dawn, a fifty-five-year-old white woman involved for ten years with an abusive African American man, explained why she only once had made a criminal statement against him (when she was "out of it" from taking medication): "[I] believe that [my husband] really needs a good break in life, you know? It's *very* hard being a black man in this country. *I* wouldn't want to be a black man in this country for anything! . . . I don't trust them [the police], frankly! And, in this situation—I might have trusted them in other circumstances, but not when there's an interracial thing."

"Preoccupied with the negative social circumstances, and deeply loyal to the African-American men" (Richie 1996, 71), women's tales of men's difficult life histories and limited life chances resonate with a pattern Goetting (1999, 7) identifies:

For many women a twist of pity enters the battering equation early on. This man may present himself as sad and wounded by mistreatment: perhaps he was abused as a child or by another woman or at work. Whatever his source of pain and injury, it is the love of this woman alone, he says, that can deliver him from his tortured existence. He convinces her that he needs her unconditional love for his very survival. . . . When pity becomes a factor in the battering, guilt emerges as a powerful retention force: How could she be so heartless as to compound his misfortune and pain with her abandonment, especially if there are children involved?

Sandwiched between conflicting desires not to abandon or betray their partners but also to defend themselves against physical harm, the women in this category have discovered a criminal justice "escape hatch" that permits them to temporarily rid their households of violent men while maintaining their mates' honor: the oft-maligned parole violation. Under the conditions of parole, having "police contact"—that is, drawing the attention of law-enforcement authorities for any reason—can be grounds for a violation and return to prison. Thus, if a battered woman can either wait out her partner's roundup in a police sweep (a near inevitability in low-income neighborhoods) or plot to attract police attention (using strategies such as those described by Erica), she can be practically guaranteed a period of relief while the man cycles through the correctional system. Meanwhile, the fact that he technically is guilty only of violating parole and has *not* been incarcerated for abusing her facilitates the woman's defense of him as a man wronged by a hyperpunitive system and preserves harmony between them because she did not bring charges or testify against him. Paradoxically then, the parole system functions as both a safety net in the absence of other social services for women involved with abusive men *and* as a mechanism that perpetuates the relationship by virtually assuring periods of respite during which "loving contrition" (Goetting 1999, 11) can occur.

———

In chapter 1, I noted that the disintegrative repercussions of incarceration and the integrative functions of the prison-as-peculiar-social-service coexist, and as many of the case histories, field observations, and interview quotations presented in this chapter show, women at once condemn and extol the criminal justice system for its intervention in their personal lives, and both resist and assist the correctional authorities charged with supervising, restraining, and punishing their partners. Returning to the concept of "sociological ambivalence" elaborated by Merton and Barber (1976), it is clear when one considers the processes in the social structure that underlie most women's ambivalence toward the prison that the oddly beneficial functions of the penitentiary arise predominantly in the absence of social-welfare institutions traditionally charged with such roles: job-placement and drug-treatment programs, mental-health services, domestic violence shelters, and individual and family counseling. The interconnected cutback of the social-welfare state and expansion of the penal state that has been occurring in the United States since the 1980s has virtually erased these services from the public sector, diverting those who can afford to pay for therapy and treatment to private clinics and leaving the rest to turn to the one government-funded resource that is still robustly in operation: the correctional facility.

Furthermore, when reflecting on this chapter's three categories of orientation one realizes that they correspond to a trio of family types delineated by Thompson and Morris in the little-known *Report on the Work of the Prisoners' Wives Service* (Thompson and Morris 1972). These types, which consolidate Morris's eight more intricate types detailed in her earlier work (1965), can be understood as clusters of protective factors, predictors, and indicators of degrees of secondary prisonization. First, these researchers identify "families with a problem" (Thompson and Morris 1972, 3), and indeed, for the women in the initial category—financially secure, predominantly well educated, with few or no dependent children—the incarceration of a beloved is the central "problem," or issue, around which they organize their lives. Returning to Clemmer's (1958, 301–2) schema of factors affecting the degree of prisonization among inmates (summarized in table 1, chapter 1), one sees that these women correspond to the profile of someone less likely to become severely institutionalized since their white-collar work situations, political activism, religious involvement, and preexisting social networks protect them from total integration into the prison culture or acceptance of its dogma and keep them connected to primary or semiprimary groups away from the penitentiary. For them, having an imprisoned partner usually remains an exceptional and unforeseen, rather than ordinary, life circumstance, and although they "wise up" (Clemmer 1958, 300) to the dictates of the prison regime through their frequent and prolonged contact with it when visiting and communicating with their loved ones, they are self-reflexive in their critiques of the politics and impacts of carceral control. However, although Sarah and her peers are not secondarily prisonized to a strong degree in their nonconjugal social relations, their self-concepts, or their life expectations, their vociferous denunciations of men "on the outside" as compared to men behind bars signals the near-total prisonization of their romantic existence.

The second category of women roughly corresponds to the type of those for whom incarceration is one part of a complex web of difficulties (labeled "problem families" by Thompson and Morris). Virtually all of these women contend with racism, intergenerational criminality, and their partners' recidivism; for many these hardships are compounded by poverty, inadequate family and social services, harassment at the hands of criminal justice authorities, and controlling or abusive mates. In contrast to the wives of lifers and Death Row convicts, the women in this category lack the social and economic capital to shield themselves from secondary prisonization, and indeed are often "groomed" from early ages for this process through their contact with imprisoned kin and associates. For most, the scarce opportunity to form relationships with people outside of a "carceral community" of probationers, parolees, inmates, and their visitors brings the effects of secondary prisonization to bear on daily interactions and activities. Although those like LaShawn and Alice with more advantageous socioeconomic circumstances are less vulnerable to secondary prisonization and may attempt to disassociate themselves from a prison primary group, the pervasive fatalism in this cohort about the inevitability of a partner's arrest and confinement demonstrates their "acceptance of," or resignation to, what remains "an inferior rôle" (Clemmer 1958, 300) in spite of their efforts to recast it as heroic or inconsequential.

The final category recalls the third type, that of families "showing such symptoms of instability and disorganisation before imprisonment that the departure of the husband may alleviate the problem, at least temporarily, and the wife may be in a better position to manage than previously" (Thompson and Morris 1972, 3). Contending with poverty, domestic violence, their own or their partners' mental-health and substance-use issues, and other ills in the absence of state social assistance, Erica and her peers depend on—and indeed reach out for—penal intervention as a primary resource for imposing a semblance of order on tumultuous and troubled existences. Here one finds the highest levels of secondary prisonization, as women commit to institutionalized men, become unable to sustain a life apart from the penitentiary, and engage the criminal justice system as a protective intervention in their relationships, finding a semblance of stability, control, and safety in its long shadow.

SIX

The Long Way Home

In chapter 1, I proposed to examine the relationships of women with incarcerated partners with the social institution of the prison using the concepts of sociological ambivalence and secondary prisonization. The chapters that followed revealed that such an analysis yields powerful examples of the convoluted and counterintuitive roles the penitentiary plays in women's lives, as it at once subjects them to punitive management, penetrates their domestic spheres, "feminizes" their partners, drains their economic resources, facilitates the enactment of idealized romantic scripts, and, in some cases, protects them from conjugal abuse. The fifty women interviewed for this research varied in their tolerance of and dependency on the correctional facility's intercession in their lives, with some viewing the prison's primary "good" as being its transformative effects on men's communication and emotional responsiveness, and others embracing its attributes more fully, finding the time they spent behind the walls a welcome alternative to the punishing conditions of their devastated home neighborhoods. Importantly, none of these women were *wholly positive* or *wholly negative* about their experiences with the prison, and by extension with incarcerated men, underscoring my original assertion that profound ambivalence characterizes secondary prisonization as it is a status of "being both ways" (Clemmer 1958, 109–10).

A central conclusion of this study is that *women partners of prisoners are themselves changed* by their interactions with the correctional facility. In *The Prison Community*, Clemmer (1958, 87) describes "a slow, gradual, more or less unconscious process during which a person learns enough of the culture of a social unit into which he is placed to make him characteristic of it. . . . We may use the term *prisonization* to indicate the taking on in greater or lesser degree of the folkways, mores, customs, and general culture of the penitentiary." From altering their style of dress, the food they eat, and the hours they keep, to valorizing the benefits of enforced celibacy and the correctional chastising of men, women who maintain contact with incarcerated partners become "characteristic of the penal community" (Clemmer 1958, 84) in ways that over time connect them ever more deeply to the carceral apparatus.

My analysis has a variety of implications for contemporary debates and future investigations. Applying the concept of secondary prisonization to the experiences of women with incarcerated partners elucidates that, rather than being a remote and self-contained microcosm, the correctional facility exerts a persistent influence over the lives of those who sustain relationships with inmates. This realization therefore expands and complicates the reentry discourse by underscoring that, when a felon is released, both his family and his residential neighborhood typically have been prisonized to a degree that the dividing line between "inside" and "out" is significantly blurred. The dominant model therefore should not be one of people being taken from "the community" to be incarcerated out of sight and out of mind until they are released and reintegrated back into society. Instead, as this study has shown, one sees a continual flow of people moving in and out of correctional facilities, some for short stays and others for long ones, forming various networks that traverse carceral borders and that are subjected to punitive measures in the domestic and communal spheres. Additional research in a number of areas—the scope of women's roles as the partners of prisoners, the depoliticization and disenchantment of populations heavily affected by incarceration, and the international context of secondary prisonization—would further highlight the broad impact of mass incarceration and provide indicators for changes in public policy.

The Scope of Women's Roles as the Partners of Prisoners

As discussed in chapter 3, a woman may attempt to use packages and personal contact to coax her partner into being a "docile body" (Foucault 1977, 135–69) who will "do his time" calmly and without incident and thereby minimize his risk of falling victim to violence or incurring disciplinary penalties that extend his time behind bars. In doing so, the woman works in concert with prison administrators, who may even "up the ante" by instituting conjugal visitation (Goetting 1982, 63) or improved visiting facilities (Rideau and Wikberg 1992, 197–98) in the stated belief that special privileges give well-tended-to men further incentive to avoid trouble in order to preserve their rights to interact in some intimate manner with outsiders. During the incarceration period women therefore serve in the curious role of external "prison mate," a hybrid status of devoted loved one and rule enforcer that benefits the inmates *and* the penal institution as wives, fiancées, and girlfriends supply the labor and funding for the influx of rewards that keep prisoners on their best—or at least, better—behavior. Hence, women are not prisonized solely in the roles of secondary *inmates*, but simultaneously in the roles of secondary, or surrogate, *correctional officers*.

Women's practical participation in the institutional management of prisoners begets the questioning of their roles in other dimensions of the criminal justice process: their influence over the outcomes of their partners' trials and sentencing, and their simultaneous positions as auxiliary parole officers and de facto parolees. In the first instance, limitations on inmates' telephone privileges and the volume of calls typically required to make headway in legal matters result in many women shouldering primary responsibility for contacting and liaising with attorneys when jailed or imprisoned men are contesting new charges, preparing for Morrissey hearings, or filing appeals.[1] This situation usually prompts—or forces—women to become the organizational center of their partners' legal efforts, and in interviews numerous women spoke of compiling extensive files of key telephone numbers, records of case-related conversations, witness statements, and other documents assembled on behalf of the defendant. Many also said they kept track of court dates, relayed messages among the involved parties, and arranged for family, friends, co-workers, and employers to attend hearings as demonstrations of support. Further study is necessary to map out how common these forms of assistance are, how they vary across economic and ethnic groups, and what role they play both in the delivery of legal services and in sentencing outcomes. Because the vast majority of offenders are too poor to retain private lawyers and therefore are represented by harried, overworked, and notoriously incompetent public defenders (Cole 1999, 76–95), the supplementary legal work pro-

---

1. As described in chapter 5, Morrissey hearings are informational hearings designed to establish that parole violations are based on verified facts.

vided by partners is likely to fulfill a similar purpose as their contributions to prison discipline through delivering goods and services, that is, it functions as a stopgap measure in an underfunded and overburdened justice system.

Also of importance in legal matters is women's influence on men's decisions to accept plea bargains. Franklin Zimring, Gordon Hawkins, and Sam Kamin (2001, 67–68; see also Feeley 1992, 185–94) point out that harsh sentencing laws such as California's "three strikes" provoke increased levels of plea bargaining among defendants eager to avoid conviction for specific crimes that incur steep penalties. This is corroborated by several of my interview participants, who report that the threat of long mandatory sentences inflames a generalized fear that causes them to strike their own bargains with their mates so that the men will swiftly "settle" their criminal affairs rather than risk the dire consequences of a trial verdict. When she learned that her partner was facing a sentence of forty-to-eighty years if he took his case to court, Butta advised him to avoid disappearing into the bowels of the correctional system by accepting a plea bargain of twenty years, telling him, "You need to just go ahead and take this deal. Because if you don't take this deal, they gonna forget about you." According to Butta, "After we talked about it, he turned around and said, 'Well, will you marry me?'" and she promptly agreed: "I didn't waste no time. And we got married the day he got sentenced." In a similar (although less dramatic) arrangement, Alice convinced her recalcitrant husband to consent to a three-year sentence:

[My husband] kept fightin' [his case]. . . . He kept pursuing it, and one day they was like, "We're going to take everything to trial." And I was like, "*Please* don't take it to trial." . . . [The plea bargain] wasn't sounding good to my husband, he was like, "Why should I take three years, and I didn't do anything?" But I was really sad, [and] the *real* reason why he took it [the plea bargain] is because I was really sad, and I was like, "Well, if you take it to trial, *I* know what you didn't do and *I* know what you did do, but just since they're so screwed up, what if you take it to trial and get *a long time*?"

Alice felt strongly that because her husband had accepted the plea bargain primarily to pacify her fears, her part of the "deal" was to visit him regularly and keep him well supplied with packages and mail. Thus the circumstances of his sentencing strengthened her emotional and practical commitment to him and served to draw her more deeply into the clutches of the penitentiary. Stories like Butta's and Alice's highlight a pressing need for research into the impact of women's counsel in men's decisions not to take their cases to trial and the repercussions of these agreements on legal trends, romantic partnerships, and the absorption of women into the penal sphere.

A second set of roles that requires examination is that of women as auxiliary parole officers and secondary parolees. My research indicates that women approach the rigors of the postrelease period with a mind-set similar to that which guides them during their partners' incarcerations: as Josephine announced, "We just gonna do it one day at a time to get through this, you know. Just like we did this prison time, we'll do this parole time too!" Numerous participants explained that they typically contacted their partners' parole officers prior to the release date in order to establish their domiciles as the men's legal residences, verify contact information, and discuss possible work opportunities. Some women went further and spoke on behalf of their partners to past or potential employers, attempting to secure the parolees' hiring—or at least a placement interview—in advance. In addition, many participants said they assumed responsibility for keeping track of the dates and times of supervision meetings, made sure the ex-convict attended these sessions (often by accompanying him to them), and tried to enforce the conditions of parole by urging men to find and hold down jobs, stay away from drugs, alcohol, wayward friends, and ex-felons, and to stick close to home. Karen, who was inspired by her younger brother's successful quest for work at Wal-Mart following his release from jail, described the pep talk she planned for her husband once he was discharged from San Quentin:

I'm gonna kick him to a job! . . . [I'll tell him] "Hurry up and get a job! No kissing-lovey-dovey nothing, *no*! Just go find a job, then when you find a job you can relax a little bit." . . . I'm like, "You *will* get hired. You just have to have faith," you know? I mean, maybe sometime you probably have to stop wearing your little afro that looks all thuggish and comb it out or something, you know? Or get it braided. . . . As long as you look decent enough to work there, that's all that matters.

Future studies of women's involvement in the parole process need to cover three key areas. The first is to assess how genuine these claims of assistance and encouragement are, since separation during imprisonment and hope for the future may lead women to aggrandize the degree of their retrospective or prospective support or to minimize their contributions to episodes of criminal behavior. (Here one remembers Celina's dejection over not having more say over her partner's behavior after his release, or Erica's periodic joining of Leon in violent or drug-related activities.) In addition, it is important to map out the specific types of help wives, fiancées, and girlfriends provide for their partners. If women are assuming responsibility for men's legal paperwork, job and housing placements, sobriety, health and mental-health care referrals, enrollment in educational programs, and the like, then they have in effect shouldered the social-work functions discarded by parole officers when the latter's profession was reconstituted in the early 1980s as a managerial and law-enforcement position primarily concerned with drug testing and rearrest (Simon 1993, 169–201). In such cases, women once again would be supplying the resources and labor for the meagerly funded "rehabilitation" the criminal justice system rhetorically claims to offer to their men but fails to provide (Lynch 2001; Petersilia 2003, 88–90).

Whether or not women actively attempt to boost compliance with parole conditions, spending time with a parolee effectively subjects someone to that person's terms of supervision. This situation raises a second issue calling for further study: women's roles as secondary parolees. Police and parole officers are permitted to search the cars, residences, and belongings to which ex-offenders have access, and forbidden items (such as weapons, including kitchen knives over certain lengths and various other household utensils or tools) and forbidden people (under California law, parolees are not allowed to fraternize with one another) can result in an automatic violation and a return to custody for the supervisee (Petersilia 1999, 503–4). Celina's complaints about the infringements on her privacy illustrate the sacrifices exacted from someone living with a newly released prisoner:

We could be just getting done doing things [*intonation suggests she is referring to having sex*] or you know, having our little intimate time, and here comes somebody knocking at the door at seven o'clock in the morning and whatnot. . . . They have a key to our gate at the bottom of the door, cuz it's like there's a gate and then there's the upstairs where you can come in, so he [the parole officer] has the key, so he comes and he knocks on our door [*she knocks loudly on the table to demonstrate*], and so by then I'm like, man! I feel so, you feel so violated, you just feel like, God, I can't even have no privacy!

The third aspect of parole that merits further attention is women's reliance on the ever-looming possibility of a return to custody as an "escape hatch" to remove violent or disruptive men from the home. As discussed in chapter 5, although women typically try not to telephone the police directly for help with an abusive mate, they may scheme to bring him into contact with the authorities in order to have his liberty revoked. In pilot interviews that I conducted, one parole officer working in northern California revealed that her parolees' partners sometimes would phone her to report the men's illegal behavior and then would react with false surprise and conspicuous indignation when she arrived at the residence to investigate the claim. Thus wives, fiancées, and girlfriends of released prisoners may at once collude with and be scrutinized by their partners' parole officers, a conglomeration of relations that—like their prisonization as secondary inmates and adjunct guards—they adopt through their proximity to and participation in the support, supervision, and sanctioning of previously incarcerated men.

"I Just Watch Her Dumb Ass Do It!"
Depoliticization and Disenchantment

In chapter 5 I documented how the wives of men who are serving life sentences or who are on Death Row tend to see their partners' predicaments as part of a larger political battle and thus participate in various forms of activism. However, although women in relationships with lower-level offenders or parole violators frequently denounce the criminal justice system as racist and unfair, their sentiments do not translate into concrete political engagement. Historians have pointed out the key role played by activist friends and relatives outside of the penitentiary walls in generating media exposure about prisoners' grievances, spurring administrative responsiveness to inmate demands, and raising general public concern for the plight of the incarcerated.[2] Given the extreme rates of incarceration in the United States and the ever-escalating severity of sentencing legislation, one might expect that those whose lives are touched—let alone besieged by—the country's "justice juggernaut" (Gordon 1990) would be on the front lines of any "critical resistance" (to borrow the name of a national anti-incarceration group) against the state. Instead, the women partnered with routine parole violators or recidivist prisoners met my questions about political activities with blank stares, halfhearted shrugs, or mild irritation.

---

2. For an analysis of Californians' support of prisoners during the 1960s and 1970s, see Cummins (1994); for a discussion of Vietnamese Communist agitation over prison issues during French colonial rule, see Zinoman (2001).

Two building blocks for an investigation into the low rates of political engagement reported by the majority of prisoners' partners emerged in my research. The first was many women's characterization of political petitions, protests, and demonstrations as futile. Vicki gave a lengthy and telling account of her disdain for such activities:

MC: Have you ever participated in any demonstrations or protests about prisons?

VICKI: Nuh-huh.

MC: Why not?

VICKI: Cuz, have you ever had a outcome that came out good when somebody was doing that shit? I'm not goin' ta stand around in the hot sun if that shit ain't gonna do no good! [*pause, scoffs*] Nuh-huh!

MC: So it's not worth it?

VICKI: [*scornfully*] No! No. Cuz I haven't seen nothin' bein' done by that. They stand outside, people gettin' executed and they [*full of wrath*] *still* gonna get executed, so, [*sarcastically*] "Come with the *posters!*" [*we both chuckle*] I mean cuz people, their mind is already made up, so they basically making you look like an ass. Cuz they know what they want to do! They let you stand outside, they let you do all that shit, but they know the bottom line [is that] what they *wanna* do they *gonna* do in the end. So, that shit is extra, I ain't fixin' to giv'em no laughs off me! Cuz that's all it be. My friend [*laughs*] participate. She's white, and she's hella cool, she's gay or whatever but she's like my best friend, and we was working in Jack London Square [a shopping area in Oakland where Vicki worked in a bookstore] and I look out the window, and she comes [*mocking voice, husky with laughter*] with a *big sign*, I was like [*firm voice, slow and stern, separating the words*], "If you don't put that *sign down!*" I banged the window!

MC: What was it a sign for?

VICKI: I can't, oh, it might'a been affirmative action. . . . So when she came with the sign she just looked at me like, [*perkily*] "Here I go!" Cuz she protests *everything! Everything!*

MC: And you don't—

VICKI: *No!* Look, *she protests, and there ain't no change!* I just watch her dumb ass do it!

Mobilizing populations who are most in need of changes in social policy but have the least time for or faith in political action has been a classic problem for grassroots organizers (Fuchs, Shapiro, and Minnite 2001), and the case of prisoners' partners and families presents a difficult task. On the one hand, sentiments of alienation from and scorn for activist action are not surprising among low-income and marginalized people whose lives are already packed full of pressing concerns about housing, food, child care, and employment. On the other hand, many women do indicate strong political awareness and perspicacity when they talk about criminal justice issues such as policing strategies, sentencing policies, mass incarceration, and the death penalty as being driven by efforts to contain and control African Americans, to amass political power, or to avoid treating people's mental-health or substance-abuse needs. Judging by my interviews, living in the long shadow of the penitentiary has put incarceration on women's political radar but has left them unconvinced of the promise of collective resistance. Further research into prison activism or the lack thereof among inmates' partners may reveal not so much depoliticization as disenchantment sown by fatalism, exhaustion, or fear of criminal justice retaliation.

The second building block for this investigation is more counterintuitive. For the past decade, the primary grassroots opposition to corrections in the United States has clustered around the notion of the rise of a "prison-industrial complex." Purported to be the post–cold war era substitute for the "military-industrial complex," the prison-industrial complex allegedly propels the mushrooming of the carceral population through an unholy alliance among prison-industry profiteers, custodial bureaucrats, and politicians who reinforce one another's interests by fueling public fear of offenders, advocating tough-on-crime policies, and constructing and filling penal facilities at heretofore unknown rates (Davis 1998; Goldberg and Evans 1998; Schlosser 1998). The prison-industrial complex relies on the prosecutorial approach described in chapter 1 that denounces all things correctional as malevolent and assigns all prisoners (and by extension, their families) a status as "victims of the system." Such proclamations disregard the possible advantages of incarceration in the forms of sanctuary from deadly inner-city violence, forced reduction of substance abuse, or the provision (even if substandard) of clothing, shelter, meals, and health care.[3]

My analysis of women's participation in penal management and the prisonization of their intimate ties places partners of prisoners at loggerheads with the prison-industrial complex ideology, demonstrat-

3. Charles Faupel (1991) argues that incarceration can offer a positive interruption in criminal activity; for autobiographical accounts of prison-as-salvation following years of trauma and bloodshed, see the memoirs of Nathan McCall (1994) and Sanyika Shakur (1998); for discussions of prisoners as the sole group of people in the United States constitutionally entitled to state-sponsored medical treatment, see Hammett (2000).

ing that carceral and family life are not two separate entities pitched against each other but rather symbiotic institutions at the bottom of the class and caste structures (see Wacquant 2000a). If women rely on the correctional system for help with emotionally difficult, financially draining, or physically abusive men, then it may be that they do not want to "tear down the walls" alongside prison abolitionists, knowing that to do so would remove a serviceable instrument in the organization of their personal lives and leave them more vulnerable to harm than they already are. To not acknowledge this need indicates a truncated comprehension of the multifaceted and contradictory social roles of the penitentiary and significantly mutes the potential for effective penological and societal change. To avoid repeating the mistakes of their predecessors, who greatly reduced the populations of mental hospitals only to find large numbers of former patients wandering homeless in the streets (Scull 1977), prison abolitionists and activists must take into account the full scope of meanings and functions the correctional system assumes in poor people's lives, and work to create strong alternative channels for handling the surfeit of problems currently contained by the penal Pandora's box.

Secondary Prisonization and Mass Incarceration: Looking beyond the United States

The United States began establishing itself as a penal outlier years before hitting the benchmark of two million bodies behind bars. From the late 1970s, just when Alfred Blumstein and his colleagues (1977) were theorizing the long-term stability of incarceration rates, changes in U.S. sentencing policies propelled the skyrocketing of those rates to levels five-to-twelve times higher than other Western countries (Tonry 1995, 81–124; Baum 1996; Mauer 1999, 142–61). But the peculiarities of U.S. "penal exceptionalism" are not contained solely in the criminal justice system: "The United States spends less on social welfare programs than most other industrial democracies. . . . The social safety net for the poor is weaker in the United States, and poor Americans are poorer than the poor in these other countries" (Mayer 1995, 137–38). In contrast to "European countries [where] social assistance is viewed as a right, irrespective of the causes of poverty" (Duncan et al. 1995, 90), Americans hold dear the creed of "individualism" that admonishes people to "pick themselves up by their bootstraps" and fend for their own (Cullen 2003).[4] Indeed, the tellingly named Personal Responsibility and Work Opportunity Reconciliation Act signed into law in 1996 by President Clinton, a Democrat, moved to end "welfare dependence" by dismantling the federal administration of state assistance, establishing a five-year lifetime limit on benefits, and eliminating guarantees of help to even the poorest of families (Sidel 1998, 201–27; DeParle 2004). Meanwhile, Americans from all income groups live without the free access to medical care and higher education available to many of their European counterparts, and "family policy" in the form of child allowances, subsidized child care, or systematic after-school programs effectively does not exist.

Given the triple distinctiveness of the United States with regard to its penal, welfare, and family policies, the need for comparative research on partners of prisoners across countries is obvious. The full impact of mass incarceration can only be assessed by controlling for the phenomenon itself, and studies conducted in nations with lower imprisonment rates, less onerous sentencing regimes, and more generous social welfare provisions are bound to illuminate the particularities of Americans' responses to the sweeping confinement of their brethren. One paramount difference is the *scope* of the issue: the sheer size of the U.S. carceral population results in significantly higher numbers of women being drawn into contact with the criminal justice system, a fact that has repercussions on the organization of family and social networks around shared experiences of secondary prisonization and thus on the (de)stigmatization and normalization of imprisonment.

Another discrepancy is the dire straits of the American poor, who live under such miserable conditions that spending the night in a prison trailer seems pleasant and having a partner incarcerated for six months can ease financial strain. Although this may be the case for small groups of their foreign counterparts, welfare and family policy in other Western countries protects the majority of those in the lower reaches of the social structure from such penury and provides for the

4. In David Downes's (2000, 63–64) assessment, this makes the United States a "macho" society:

When economic strength and cut-throat profitability are the drivers of conduct; when job stability and decent wages are a folk memory; when skilled professionals can be told to clear their desks within the hour; when you are only as good as your last deal; and when secrecy in takeovers, asset stripping and head-hunting are conducted with the sublime disregard for ethics, then the basis for some sort of Kantian respect for persons in social relationships can hardly be said to exist.

alternative handling of social problems through drug treatment, job training, mental-health counseling, and domestic-violence services. Thus one can hypothesize that even if the incarceration rates in Europe or Canada suddenly ballooned to match those of the United States, the national contrasts would remain because the people affected would be unlikely to perceive the correctional facility as a primary site for social assistance. Meanwhile, those who do have imprisoned loved ones in countries committed to welfare and family support draw on greater resources than their U.S. peers, enabling them to better insulate themselves from the economic impacts of incarceration and the emotional absorption of the carceral "home."

Considering the U.S. phenomenon of mass incarceration from an international perspective exposes the flawed logic of those who would posit that if low-income women are finding assistance through the incarceration of disruptive or hazardous men, why not advocate for wider-sweeping arrest and detention policies, longer sentences, and more prisons as a means of providing "protection" for the poor? The fact that a close investigation finds counterintuitive "benefits" to incarceration does not override the much more obvious and amply documented destructive effects of forced separation and confinement on family ties (Braman 2004; Western, Lopoo, and McLanahan 2004), children's welfare (Eddy and Reid 2003; Parke and Clarke-Stewart 2003; Johnson and Waldfogel 2004), and community life (Clear 2002; Lynch and Sabol 2004). As is evident throughout the data presented in this book, women's expressions of relief at or acceptance of their partners' imprisonment are consistently interwoven with statements of remorse, longing, fearfulness, and depression, in clear recognition of these negative effects. Indeed, as stated at the beginning of this book, women are not choosing incarceration *over* therapeutic or social-welfare services, nor do they tout it as a desirable or effective means of controlling their men, protecting themselves, or improving their lives in the long term. On the contrary, women turn to what would otherwise be their option of last resort because criminal-justice intervention has become the only reliable method of obtaining help (as succinctly expressed in Keisha's blunt statement: "The po-lice can be a real asshole, but then, when you need 'em, they do be there"), and although their hopes for the future rise while their partners are serving time, women describe the periods of reunification after the men are released as disappointing and frustrating repetitions of the behaviors that landed the men behind bars in the first place.

In the words of Pat Carlen (2005, 6), the prison is an institution "whose primary function, to keep people confined against their will, necessarily (*not* contingently) perverts any of the other, more therapeutic functions claimed for it." Decreases in social funding and increases in penal funding might result in correctional facilities being incidentally charged to do the work of schools (Gerber and Fritsch 1995), of health clinics (Glaser and Greifinger 1993; Hammett 2001), or of detoxification centers (Butzin, Martin, and Inciardi 2002; Goodrum et al. 2003), but the official purpose of a prison system is to punish the guilty and all other tasks will forever be compromised by that driving mission. By extension, therefore, secondarily prisonizing women by keeping them enmeshed in and dependent on the criminal justice system as they attempt to create a safe, healthy, and sustainable existence for themselves and their families condemns these women to degraded proxies of the services they need and thereby ensures their stagnation in a "carceral community" even as they dream of a life beyond bars.

Appendix 1:
Setting and Methods

Description of the Study Site

San Quentin is the oldest prison in California and was built using convict labor between 1852 and 1856. The prison originally operated under a private leasing system but came under state control in 1860; since 1927 it has held only male prisoners. There are three distinct housing areas within the institution. The oldest buildings of the prison are multitiered cell blocks arranged in a rectangle around an open central space. Men who have been sentenced to death, officially referred to as "condemned" prisoners, live in East Block, the eastern wing of this rectangle. Medium-security convicts, including men serving life sentences who have been classified as being at low risk for escapes or violent incidents, live in North Block. The remainder of the cell-block units constitute San Quentin's Reception Center. Because convicts in the Reception Center are awaiting the classification of their security levels, the entire unit operates under high-security standards: prisoners wear bright orange jumpsuits for easy identification, are locked in their cells twenty-three hours a day, and have restricted access to phones and visitors. Prisoners generally spend from eight to sixteen weeks in the Reception Center, after which they are integrated into the general population (either at the Reception Center prison or another institution), placed in protective custody, or sent to a Security Housing Unit, depending on the outcome of their classification procedures. Approximately half of San Quentin's daily population consists of Reception Center inmates.

The East Block, North Block, Adjustment Center (solitary confinement), and Reception Center housing areas, along with the dining halls, church and other worship spaces, a hospital, several administrative buildings, the education buildings, and "the Yard" (a large exercise area with a running track and basketball courts), are bordered by a high wall patrolled by armed guards. Just beyond this wall lies H-Unit, a level II housing area constructed in the mid-1990s.[1] H-Unit residents sleep in bunk beds in open dormitories, eat in a dining hall located in the complex, exercise in their own yard, and are confined by razor-wire fences and correctional officers in gun towers. On the other side of the H-Unit perimeter, the low-security inhabitants of "the Ranch" dwell in barracks and do not need to traverse any wall or fence when leaving San Quentin to go to their off-site jobs for the California Department of Transportation. The back border of the Ranch nearly reaches a busy public boulevard that leads to several local shopping centers, two major highways, and a ferry terminal.

Description of the Fieldwork

In April 2000 I came to San Quentin to begin nine months of intensive fieldwork. I began by hanging out in the visiting center during the four visiting days each week (Thursday through Sunday), working to build rapport and trust with women coming to the prison. I often took public transportation to San Quentin and in doing so encountered visitors at the bus stop. On days when I drove to the prison I offered rides to visitors, which provided us with a reprieve from the correctional environment and also enabled me to see women's home neighborhoods.

After spending roughly a month at the visiting center, I began to accompany women into the Tube, the concrete corridor in which all

1. Security levels in California state prisons are calibrated on a scale of one (minimum) to four (high) plus special categories for Death Row and Security Housing Units (maximum-security solitary confinement), with most institutions housing two or three levels of security. Each level corresponds to the following housing requirements:

Level I—Open dormitories without a secure perimeter. Level II—Open dormitories with secure perimeter fences and armed coverage. Level III—Individual cells, fenced perimeters, and armed coverage. Level IV—Cells, fenced or walled perimeters, electronic security, more staff and armed officers both inside and outside the installation. SHU—Security Housing Unit. The most secure area within a Level IV prison designed to provide maximum coverage. (California Department of Corrections 2000) visitors must wait before they are permitted entry to the prison. There is no reason for anyone to be in the Tube other than to enter San Quentin, but sitting with women while they waited for their visits provided a means of casual inclusion for me, and after several weeks I had become a regular fixture in the corridor. I undertook a methodical observation of this area, arriving early in the morning and "camping out" for six- or seven-hour stretches to watch the dynamics among the visitors and correctional officers entering and exiting the hallway throughout the day. I often knew several women present, and I would sit or stand with them and participate in their discussions; when I did not know anyone, I would either strike up a conversation with someone or just sit quietly and observe, whichever felt most appropriate. I was forthright about my observations and interviews in conversations with people. I informed all of the regular visitors whom I knew that I was preparing a PhD dissertation and eventually a book, and they were generally appreciative of my efforts; several of them volunteered to be interviewed and were instrumental in recruiting other participants.

As described in chapter 2, the Tube is a zone of stress and confusion, particularly for newcomers who are not acquainted with many of the prison's rules and procedures. Although I knew much of the information visitors required, I did not want to disrupt the "natural" rhythm of the Tube during my observations. I therefore adopted a tactic of non-intervention when there were other people in the Tube whom I knew could assist new visitors, permitting me to watch their interactions. Whenever someone directly approached me for help or whenever no one else was available to intercede, I always aided visitors to the best of my ability. During moments when the Tube was empty, I would jot down notes, which I wrote up in full each evening. I continued my observations in the Tube and my field notes until the end of my fieldwork period (December 2000), spending between one and four days a week in the corridor for a total of 256 on-site hours. The number of days each week and the amount of time each day I devoted to observations varied according to my progress recruiting interview participants, my interview timetable, and my arrangements to spend time with visitors at venues other than the prison.

Three months after I concluded my primary fieldwork, I wrote a letter to the San Quentin administration requesting permission to interview members of the correctional visiting staff. I explained that I was a doctoral student completing a dissertation on women with incarcerated partners, and that many of the women I had interviewed for my research visited men at San Quentin. Somewhat to my surprise, I was granted an interview with a person who previously had worked for two years as the visiting lieutenant, the correctional official in charge of visitor processing and all visiting areas (in the interest of maintaining confidentiality, I will not specify during what period). I was not allowed to tape-record this interview, which occurred in an office inside of the prison, but I took extensive notes during and immediately following our conversation. The lieutenant answered my questions about visiting policies and procedures in detail, but was notably less talkative when I probed for opinions or observations. This interview therefore served primarily as a means of clarifying facts about visiting regulations.

Interviewee Recruitment

Alongside my ethnographic observations, I conducted in-depth, tape-recorded interviews with fifty women with incarcerated partners between May 5, 2000, and December 15, 2000. I initially encountered forty-three of these women in the Tube or at the visiting center, usually on days when they had come to San Quentin to visit their partners;[2] four were people I had known from my previous work, and the remainder were new contacts made during my observation period.[3] The only eligibility criterion I used was that the woman considered an incarcerated man to be her partner, whether that meant they were legally wed, in a committed relationship, or casually dating.[4]

From my prior contact with women with incarcerated partners, I knew that they typically feel suspicious or fearful of outsiders due to their acrimonious experiences with criminal justice authorities and other state agents. They perceive unknown interviewers as intrusive and threatening, and under these circumstances resist research participation or incline toward superficial "best-case scenario" portrayals of

2. One interviewee, Jenna, came to see the exterior of San Quentin when she learned her boyfriend would be transferred there several weeks later; another, Yaz, was performing community-service work at the visiting center and, when I told her about my research, she informed me that her boyfriend was incarcerated elsewhere.

3. Although they were aware of my research, I did not actively recruit women I had known from my previous work for interviews because I felt conflicted about shifting the nature of my relationship with them from one of service provider and client to one of researcher and interviewee. Also, since my earlier work had involved going into the prison visiting areas during visiting hours, I knew the husbands of many of these women and did not want to impose on their privacy. The four women whom I did interview volunteered to participate when I discussed my project in general terms with them.

4. I did not inquire whether the interview participants were biological or transgender women; none of the participants identified herself as being transgender.

their lives, resulting in the production of social artifacts. In addition, as Richard Sparks (2002, 578) notes, "[p]risons are even more apt than most other institutions to generate lines of conduct that from afar look bizarre, irrational, self-confounding. The rules of engagement that obtain within them are obdurately impenetrable other than by close and extended involvement at first hand." By being consistently present in the Tube, interacting publicly with regular visitors in ways that demonstrated their confidence in me, remaining up to date about visiting requirements and visitors' concerns, and offering assistance to people who needed help, I worked to convey my personal commitment to the families of prisoners, sympathy for their difficulties, and desire to better comprehend their situations. Over time, these efforts strengthened my relationships with visitors and resulted in a relaxed, friendly rapport with my interviewees, nearly all of whom had observed me in the Tube or talked with me on several occasions before our recorded conversation. Out of all fifty interview participants, I had repeated interactions (frequent conversations in the Tube, shared bus rides, phone calls, or social outings) with nineteen women.

I used a combination of convenience and snowball sampling methods to meet my research participants. One of my prime recruitment strategies was to intercept women who were temporarily turned away by the correctional officers and told that they had to wait for several hours before they could enter the prison. The situation occurred when visitors arrived during the 4 p.m. count described in chapter 2, when their partners were at work or school, or when the men's court or medical appointments interfered with visiting hours. Despite San Quentin's relative proximity to several major Bay Area cities, many women chose to stay near the prison rather than go home and come back when their visit was postponed. When I encountered women waiting to enter San Quentin I would describe my study, find out if they were visiting a romantic partner, and ask if they were interested in participating in an interview. The majority readily agreed, often saying they were glad to have an activity to occupy their time. Only three women declined to be interviewed, one because she wanted to distance herself from other visitors and two because they were not inclined to "talk about my business." Altogether, I recruited twenty women for interviews using this method (see table 2). I spoke with most of them in a quiet, private room at the visiting center, although a few participants preferred to speak with me on the porch of the visiting center, in their cars, or sitting at the edge of the visitor parking lot overlooking the bay.

Table 2. Recruitment of interview participants

Method of recruitment	Participants	N
Approach during delay of visit	Alice, Ann, Beth, Brandi, Cindy, Crystal, Gina, Jamie, Jasmine, Jeanette, Josephine, Karen, Keisha, Kim, Lynn, Natasha, Nicole, Sandra, Vanessa, Vicki	20
Miscellaneous outreach efforts	Basalisa, Blessing, Butta, Celina, Fern, Jenna, Joy, LaShawn, Linda, Millie, Mimi, Paige, Pat, Queenie, Samantha, Sarah, Yaz	17
Known from previous work	Dawn, Erica, Sophia, Tee	4
Snowball sampling	Aisha, Bernice, Darla, Jessica, Laila, Laura, Mai, Stephanie, Veronica	9

I drew an additional seventeen women into my study through various outreach techniques. Fourteen women responded favorably to my request for an interview after informally discussing my research with me in the Tube or at the visiting center. Four of these participants (Blessing, Basalisa, Joy, and Millie) made subsequent plans to come to the visiting center for an interview before or after visiting their partners. I interviewed three women (Butta, Celina, Mimi) at restaurants over meals before I drove them home from the prison. Yaz arranged for me to meet her at her workplace, and we held the interview at a nearby café, while Queenie—a regular visitor with whom I had a strong relationship—hosted our five-hour meeting in her home, after which we met her daughter for dinner at a local eatery. Five other interviewees (Fern, Jenna, Linda, Pat, and Samantha) decided that it was most convenient to talk with me over the phone and invited me to call them (with the permission of each woman, I tape-recorded all phone interviews).

Among the remaining three women recruited through outreach efforts, Sarah phoned me after seeing a note I had posted in the Tube (a technique I abandoned after a month, when Sarah was the only person who had responded). I initially interviewed her in her home, subsequently meeting with her socially multiple times and conducting a second recorded interview with her in May 2001 following her marriage. LaShawn, who had seen me repeatedly in the Tube, left her young son in my care one afternoon when she could not bring him into the prison because she had forgotten his birth certificate at home. When she rejoined us after her visit, she told me that both a correctional officer and another visitor (whom I had interviewed previously) had vouched for my reliability, but that her husband had scolded her: "You left my son with some woman and you don't even know her name?" LaShawn laughingly told me that she had tried vainly to explain the foundation of her trust in me to him: "But she's *always* there!" To thank me for babysitting, LaShawn drove me home and offered to participate in a phone interview, saying, "You helped me out and now I can help you out." The final participant in this group, Paige, and I rode the bus together numerous times and had many phone calls during her boyfriend's six-month sentence for a parole violation; we kept in touch after his release, and I interviewed her in early December 2000, two months after her boyfriend had been rearrested and returned to custody.

I knew four interviewees (Dawn, Erica, Sophia, and Tee) from my previous work at San Quentin. Dawn and Tee recognized me in the Tube and arranged to meet with me for interviews after I explained why I was there. Sophia and I spent many hours away from the prison together; at her initiative, I interviewed her at her house on the day of our first outing together. Erica and I had been keeping in touch with each other since 1995, and although her husband was not at San Quentin during the period of my fieldwork, he was imprisoned at and released from California's Centinela State Prison in 2000. Erica, an eager research participant, came to the visiting center for an initial interview and frequently prompted me to tape-record our conversations during the ensuing phone calls and meals we had together.

I recruited the final nine interviewees using methods of snowball sampling by requesting contacts from people who were already involved in or familiar with my research. These introductions ranged from the semiformal (an introduction through a colleague) to the casual (a visitor giving my phone number to a friend) to the impulsive (during a phone call with Linda, she abruptly passed the phone to her friend Jessica, telling me, "Here, this little girl's boyfriend is in jail! You can interview her right now!"). Through this method, I included seven women whose partner was incarcerated at an institution other than San Quentin: Correctional Training Facility, California Correctional Institution, Deuel Vocational Institute, Folsom State Prison (all California state prisons, in Soledad, Susanville, Tracy, and Represa, respectively), an out-of-state federal prison, and two county jails.

Interview Structure and Participant Demographics

The interviews ranged in length from forty-five minutes to three hours, with an average of ninety minutes. All interviews were conducted individually except for Bernice's and Laura's because the two friends carpooled to the prison regularly and requested that they be interviewed together to avoid making each other wait before the three-hour journey home. I conducted each interview and personally transcribed all of the recordings verbatim. Most interview participants chose their own pseudonym for the study; when someone did not specify a pseud-onym, I assigned one to her. During the interviews, I followed a semis-tructured format touching on five core themes, but encouraged women to digress and to talk about what they felt was important for me to know. The core themes for the interviews were:

1. *Relationship with the incarcerated partner*: history and status of the relationship, maintaining contact while partner is incarcerated, how current relationship compares with past relationships.
2. *Interaction with the prison authorities and state authorities*: experiences with prison officials, parole or probation officers, and police officers, perceived impact of in-carceration on home community, political outlook, and activism.
3. *Impact of incarceration on self and home*: changes in home life when partner is in prison, perceived impact of partner's incarceration on participant, participant's children, and other important people in participant's life.
4. *Social networks and resources*: participant's living situation, relationship with kin and friends, social activities, and support system.
5. *Demographic and social profile of participant and partner*: age, ethnicity, educa-tion, income, and work history of participant and her partner, number and ages of children, who else known to participant is or has been incarcerated.

From the collection of demographic and social information, I was able to compile a descriptive profile of the study sample, presented in tables 3 and 4.

San Quentin does not keep statistics on prison visitors. Therefore, it is impossible to compare the demographics of my interview partici-pants with those of the visiting population at large. However, a cross-sectional survey of female visitors at San Quentin conducted in 1998 by Olga Grinstead and colleagues (2001) provides a useful comparative demographic profile (see table 5). In Grinstead's study, a team of in-terviewers stationed themselves at the doors of the Tube and waited for women to leave the prison, at which point interviewers would ap-proach them and ask them to participate in the survey. Over the course of five days, 153 women agreed to do so. In addition, during this re-cruitment process one researcher counted all of the women leaving San Quentin (including those who refused to participate and those who left when an interviewer was not available) and categorized them by

Table 3. Select characteristics of participants and partners

Characteristic	Participants	Partners
Ethnicity (%)		
African American	50	70
White	30	16
Hispanic	12	8
"Other"	8	6
Age (%)		
19–25	36	22
26–35	22	42
36–45	26	22
46–55	14	10
60	2	—
not stated	—	4
Yearly income (%)		
<$5,000	12	
$5,000–$10,000	24	
$10,000–$15,000	10	
$15,000–$20,000	16	
$20,000–$25,000	4	
$25,000–$30,000	10	
$30,000–$45,000	6	
$50,000–$100,000+	6	
not stated	12	

apparent ethnicity. Based on this count, Grinstead and her colleagues estimate that of 981 women exiting the prison, 34 percent were African American, 39 percent were white, 20 percent were Hispanic, 4 percent were Asian, and 3 percent were "other" or mixed. Because the demographics of their survey participants were similar to those of the larger group, the researchers suggest that their sample is representative in terms of ethnicity (Grinstead et al. 2001, 60–63).

Curiously, although my ethnicity demographics vary slightly from those gathered in Grinstead's cross-sectional survey (with 13 percent more African Americans, 8 percent fewer whites, and 4 percent fewer Hispanics participating in my research), they correspond almost exactly to those Grinstead and I (Comfort et al. 2000, 68) previously documented in our 1996 study of eighty-six women with incarcerated partners, in which 54 percent of the sample was African American, 27 percent white, 13 percent Hispanic, and 6 percent "other" or mixed. Meanwhile, my interview participants tended to be younger (36% compared to 24% under the age of 25) and poorer (36% versus

Table 4. Social Characteristics of Participants and Partners

Name of participant	Age	Relationship to partner	Occupation	Annual income (in thousands)	Participant's ethnicity	Partner's ethnicity	Partner's sentence[a]
Alice	22	wife	unemployed	$15–$20	African American	African American	3 years
Aisha	46	wife	nutritionist	not stated	mixed parentage	African American	24 years
Ann	30	wife	grocery store cashier	$5–$10	Hispanic	Hispanic	2 years
Basalisa	55	"friend"	computer networker	$20–$25	Hispanic	African American	Death Row
Bernice	44	fiancée	nurse's assistant	$25–$30	African American	African American	Death Row
Beth	37	fiancée	unemployed	< $5	African American	African American	3 months (PV)
Blessing	38	wife	company representative	$40–$45	African American	African American	Death Row
Brandi	20	girlfriend	hairstylist	$10–$15	African American	African American	1 year
Butta	32	wife	administrative assistant	$15–$20	African American	African American	20 years
Celina	23	wife	unemployed	< $5	African American	African American	6 months (PV)
Cindy	46	girlfriend	chef	$5–$10	African American	African American	8 months (PV)
Crystal	21	wife	bank teller	$20–$25	Mixed parentage	African American and Hispanic	5 months (PV)
Darla	50	wife	government employee	not stated	white	white	25-to-life
Dawn	55	wife	unemployed	< $5	white	African American	4 months (PV)
Erica	late 30s	wife	various	$15–$20	African American	African American	multiple PV during fieldwork
Fern	43	fiancée	substance-abuse counselor	$25–$30	white	white	6 months (PV)
Gina	22	wife	receptionist	$25–$30	African American	African American	18 months (PV)

Name	Age	Relationship	Occupation	Amount			Sentence
Jamie	21	girlfriend	store manager	$40–$45	white	African American	1 year (PV)
Jasmine	19	girlfriend	unemployed	$5–$10	Palestinian American	African American	6 months (PV)
Jeanette	31	wife	home-healthcare worker	$15–$20	African American	African American	6 months (PV)
Jenna	35	lover	construction company owner	>$100	mixed parentage	African American	9 months (PV)
Jessica	25	girlfriend	unemployed	$10–$15	white	white	1 year
Josephine	35	wife	assembly-line worker	$15–$20	African American	African American	14 months
Joy	45	lover	security guard	$5–$10	white	Hispanic	9 months (PV)
Karen	22	wife	unemployed	< $5	African American	African American	awaiting sentencing (PV)
Keisha	20	fiancée	service-industry worker	$30–$35	African American	African American	1 year (PV)
Kim	21	fiancée	warehouse worker	$5–$10	African American	African American	6 months
Laila	early 40s	wife	account manager	not stated	African American	African American	life
LaShawn	24	wife	bus driver	$25–$30	African American	African American	6 months (PV)
Laura	38	fiancée	post office worker	$50–$55	white	African American and Hispanic	Death Row
Linda	mic-50s	girlfriend	truck driver	not stated	white	white	1 year
Lynn	38	fiancée	fund-raiser	not stated	white	African American	25-to-life
Mai	40	"love interest"	dance teacher	$10–$15	African American	African American	6–10 yrs.
Millie	34	wife	cashier	$5–$10	white	white	6 yrs.
Mimi	23	wife	unemployed	$5–$10	Native American	African American	6 months (?PV)
Natasha	26	girlfriend	seasonal worker	$5–$10	African American	African American	10 months (PV)
Nicole	20	girlfriend	nurse's assistant	$5–$10	African American	African American	18 months (PV)
Paige	29	fiancée	unemployed	<$5	white	African American	6 months (PV)

(continued)

Table 4. (*continued*)

Name of participant	Age	Relationship to partner	Occupation	Annual income (in thousands)	Participant's ethnicity	Partner's ethnicity	Partner's sentence[a]
Pat	34	wife	unemployed	$5–$10	African American	African American	9 months (PV)
Queenie	60	wife	retired	not stated	African American	African American	life
Samantha	20	fiancée	housecleaner	$5–$10	white	African American	8 months (PV)
Sandra	21	girlfriend	cashier	$5–$10	Hispanic	Hispanic	6 months (PV)
Sarah	31	wife	account manager	$100	white	white	15-to-life
Sophia	37	wife	nanny	$10–$15	white	Native American	life
Stephanie	25	wife	security guard	$15–$20	African American	African American	4 years
Tee	42	wife	nurse's assistant	$25–$30	white	African American	life
Vanessa	24	wife	dental assistant	$15–$20	Hispanic	Hispanic	6 months (PV)
Veronica	47	wife	unemployed	<$5	Hispanic	white	36-to-life
Vicki	39	girlfriend	seasonal worker	$10–$15	African American	African American	1 year
Yaz	29	wife	personal trainer	$15–$20	Hispanic	white	awaiting trial

[a] PV = parole violation

Table 5. Comparative characteristics of San Quentin visitors

Characteristic	Grinstead et al. (N=153)	Comfort (N=50)
Age (%)		
18–25	24	36
26–35	27	22
36–45	32	26
>46	16	16
Ethnicity (%)		
African American	37	50
White	38	30
Hispanic	16	12
Asian	1	0
"Other"	8	8
Annual income (%)		
<$10,000	18	36
$10,000–$19,999	26	26
$20,000–$29,999	20	14
$30,000–$40,000	14	2
>$40,000	16	10
Not stated	6	12
Have children (%)	83	80

Source: Grinstead et al. 2001.
Note: In their article, Grinstead et al. report the ethnicity characteristics from their entire sample (n=153) and the income, age, and child-rearing characteristics of a subsample of women visiting African American men (n=75). Through personal communication, I obtained all characteristics for their entire sample, which are presented in this table.

18% with incomes under $10,000 annually) than the women surveyed by Grinstead in 1998.[5]

Apart from these demographics, the fifty women I interviewed encompassed a range of diverse experiences. Among them were women who were long-time, frequent San Quentin visitors and who were new to prison visiting; who participated in noncontact, contact, and family visits with men from Death Row, the Reception Center, Mainline, H-Unit, and the Ranch; who owned vehicles and who were dependent on public transportation; who lived in houses, apartments, public-housing projects, and were homeless; and who were free to visit on

5. In our previous study, Grinstead and I did not gather information on participants' annual incomes. The mean age of participants in that research was thirty-three with a range from eighteen to sixty-three years (Comfort et al. 2000, 68), but no breakdown of those under twenty-five is available.

weekdays and who were only available on weekends. Their common intersection was that they all visited their husbands, fiancés, long- or short-term boyfriends, lovers, or "love interests" (as one participant identified her beau) behind bars, and thus had at least periodic, and for some, intensive, contact with the penal institution.

Institutional Policy Changes since 2000

Several notable policy modifications have been implemented at San Quentin since December 2000. Beginning in January 2004, the visiting days at most California state prisons were cut from three or four days a week to weekends only due to budget restrictions. The warden of San Quentin at the time, Jeannie Woodford, argued that having a mere two visiting days at San Quentin each week was untenable due to the relatively high volume of visitors. As a compromise, San Quentin was allowed to keep four days of visiting, but Thursdays became restricted to appointment visits only, and on Fridays the entry time was pushed to 1:30 for all Mainline visitors, with Ranch visiting being eliminated that day. This allowed San Quentin to reduce expenses by keeping the contact-visiting areas closed on Thursdays and holding all contact visits (North Block and H-Unit) in one room on Friday, cutting down on the number of correctional officers needed to supervise visiting. The Saturday and Sunday visiting hours remained the same as they had been in 2000 for all types of visits.

When Thursday contact visits were ended and the start of Friday visiting hours was moved to 1:30, the informal waiting line systems described in chapter 2 became more problematic due to the larger volume of people stacking up in the Tube: women who previously had visited on Thursdays and skipped Fridays flip-flopped their schedules, and those who used to time their arrivals to miss the 11:30 "rush hour" now found that they had to come earlier in the day in order to be processed into the prison before the 2:30 cutoff for the 4:00 count. The result was a Tube jam-packed with angry, frustrated visitors hours before visiting officially began. In response, the San Quentin authorities formalized the "numbers system" the women had previously operated by sticking their visiting passes under the pipe outside the processing-area door. At 11:30 a correctional officer begins handing out laminated cards with numbers on them to visitors who have already arrived; once they have received their cards, the women are free to leave the Tube and to return shortly before 1:30, when they will be called in order. Visitors who arrive after 11:30 can go directly into the processing area and request a card. This system has drastically cut down on the congestion in the Tube between 11 and 1 p.m., but by 1:30 the corridor is always teeming with women and children eager to enter for their visits.

Two final noteworthy changes concern packages and food for family visits. Women have lost the ability to customize these offerings for prisoners: first, packages must now be ordered through a designated company, which takes over the task of putting the items in the box and sending it to the inmate. These packages can no longer contain cigarettes, since smoking was banned in all California state prisons in July 2005. In addition, food for all family visits (including those on the Ranch) now must be ordered from the San Quentin cafeteria. As described in chapters 3 and 4, the preparation of packages and food assumed enormous meaning for women as ways of tending to their partners and expressing affection, and the depersonalization of these activities has been yet another source of disappointment for those attempting to maintain romantic connections across the bars.

Appendix 2: An Orientation to the Research Literature

This appendix provides more detail on the research literature on prisoners' families than could be given in the first chapter of this book. This is not a complete survey of the field, but rather a guide to the key works necessary to map out the analytical space in which this book is situated.

Pauline Morris's groundbreaking yet little-known study of 588 wives of male inmates in England and Wales, *Prisoners and Their Families,* was published in 1965. Remarkable in its scope and its methodological rigor, the book presents a nuanced analysis of "the economic, social and psychological problems and needs" of families of prisoners as well as an evaluation of "the social service arrangements currently available for dealing with such problems" (1965, 19). To conduct this research, Morris recruited a representative sample of 824 male convicts (including first-time, recidivist, and civil inmates) from seventeen prisons, then requested permission to speak with spouses who met the criterion that the couple had been living together for at least three months before the man's arrest. Having noted in her previous work with repeat offenders that "a high proportion of men appeared to have severe family problems," Morris (1965, 17, 9) embarked on her investigation with a strong claim for the need for a holistic approach to rehabilitation:

The experience of imprisonment does not occur in isolation for a man with a family, and the prison wall can never be a complete barrier to the emotional currents which flow between a man and his wife and children. Too often in prison work, the family is thought of as some external appendage, remote and irrelevant to the processes of treatment and training, rather than as a continuous influence upon the man in custody.

Through her extensive research, Morris (1965, 24-25) delineated a set of eight types of family situations into which she placed her participants:

1. "Families already separated before imprisonment";
2. Families with good relationships before imprisonment, but in which incarceration constituted a marriage-ending crisis;
3. Families with "severely strained" relationships before imprisonment, in which the incarceration added further strain, leading to marital breakup or to "psychological relief" and the "'opportunity' to break up";
4. Families with strained relationships before imprisonment, but which remain together "because there seems no alternative (such families may be tied by either financial or emotional dependency)";
5. Families with strained relationships before imprisonment, for which "prison brings additional material difficulties, but psychological relief. Contact between the parties is maintained during the separation and marriage is likely to be resumed as before";
6. Families with strained relationships before imprisonment, for which the acknowledgement of the offense "brings the partners together" so that "the marriage is strengthened";
7. Families with good relationships before imprisonment, "but [which] deteriorate as problems become intensified during the separation; nevertheless the marriage will be resumed";
8. Families with good relationships before imprisonment that "remain unimpaired, or where the relationship contains a certain amount of conflict which is tolerated before and during imprisonment, and where the marriage will be resumed with a similar degree of toleration."

Seven years after the publication of *Prisoners and Their Families* Morris directed the study that led to the *Report on the Work of the Prisoners' Wives Service* (Thompson and Morris 1972, 3), which consolidated the eight categories from her original typology into three specific groups: (1) "families with a problem," that is, families for whom incarceration is a distinct crisis; (2) "problem families" for whom criminality figures among a cluster of several serious difficulties (such as poverty, substance abuse, or domestic violence); and (3) families "showing such symptoms of instability and disorganization before imprisonment that the departure of the husband may alleviate the problem, at least temporarily, and the wife may be in a better position to manage than previously." In a similar genre, Morris also supervised Kate Vercoe's (1968, 38) National Association for the Care and Rehabilitation of Offenders (NACRO) report *Helping Prisoners' Families,* an examination of the available programs for offenders' kin that critiqued existing forms of assistance for being "supportive rather than manipulative, i.e., the emphasis is placed on material and personal help of an immediate practical kind rather than on attempts to make fundamental changes in the family functioning."

Publications on prisoners' families in the 1970s and 1980s were few and far between. Among the more analytical works were two studies of relatives of African-American prisoners that documented low levels of stigmatization or shame among their participants (Schneller 1978; Swan 1981) and Lennox Hinds's (1982, 9) critique of the "fragmented and uncoordinated" state of social services, which contributed to the distress of low-income and minority people with kin behind bars. Most other publications were largely descriptive, characterizing inmates' loved ones as "hidden victims of crime" (Bakker, Morris, and Janus 1978; see also Matthews 1983; Jorgensen, Hernandez, and Warren 1986, 52; Shaw 1987; Blake 1990; Light 1993; Carlson and Cervera 1991b). Stewart Gabel (1992, 307) correctly assessed this early literature as "heavily descriptive and anecdotal, with few empirical studies and significant methodological limitations," and critiqued in particular the small sample sizes, the lack of longitudinal studies or control groups, and the failure to account for variables such as prisoners' offenses, sentences, or preexisting relationships with their families.

The slow tempo of research continued into the early 1990s, quickening toward the middle of the decade as the numbers of, and hence the interest in, prisoners' children mounted. Although children had been a subject of attention since the 1970s (e.g., Sack, Seidler, and Thomas 1976; Fritsch and Burkhead 1981; Hughes 1983), this earlier work had focused narrowly on behavioral reactions to parental absence, while later book-length studies (Shaw 1992; Gabel and Johnston 1995) oriented their investigations around legal and policy issues, particularly those of care, guardianship, and visitation rights. This shift reflects the influence of research conducted by scholars of social service administration, especially Creasie Finney Hairston, dean of the Jane Addams College of Social Work at the University of Illinois at Chicago, whose prolific writings on the need for improved therapeutic and family programming for inmates established her as a leader in the field (Hairston 1988, 1995, 1996, 1998, 1999, 2003). In 1996 Hairston assisted the Child Welfare League of America in hosting its first National Institute on Children of Incarcerated Parents in Washington, D.C., and coedited a special issue of their journal, *Child Welfare*, devoted to the subject (Seymour and Hairston 1998). Again, much of this work centers on calls for policy change (i.e., the need to integrate the child-welfare and criminal justice systems so that practitioners can be alerted to children left behind after a parent's arrest) and on characteristic social-work concerns such as permanency planning, kinship care, and the facilitation of parent-child contact. An influx of articles and policy reports on families of children issued by nongovernmental organizations complemented the practical applications of much of this academic work (for a sample of these writings, see Hornick 1991; Lloyd 1992; Hostetter and Jinnah 1993; Osbourne Association 1993; NACRO 1993–94; Howard League 1994; NACRO 1994; Breen 1995; Lloyd 1995; Ramsden 1998; Child Welfare League of America 2002). Meanwhile, the absence of sociological input in the literature of this time period is striking: for instance, among the sixteen contributors to the edited volume *Children of Incarcerated Parents* (Gabel and Johnston 1995) there were six attorneys, two psychologists, and five scholars or practitioners of social work, but not a single sociologist. Such a dearth of sociological analysis left the broader impact of incarceration on social relations, networks, and norms largely unexplored.

Much work on children of inmates has highlighted the plight of those with imprisoned mothers (Bloom 1995; Johnston 1995; Jose-Kampfner 1995; Richie 2002). Likewise, although efforts have been made to institute programs designed to facilitate women's opportunities to parent their children during periods of incarceration (e.g., Williams 1996; Louima 2002; Nixon 2002), such programs are markedly less robust for men (Sheridan 1996). A fundamental reason for this strong focus on maternal incarceration, even though women are a small percentage of the carceral population, is that women usually are the primary caretakers of their offspring, and therefore children with inmate mothers are more likely than those with inmate fathers to experience domestic upheaval at the time of arrest and to require temporary guardianship arrangements (LeFlore and Holston 1990; Caddle and Crisp 1996; Mumola 2000; Covington 2003; Travis and Waul 2003). In addition, incarcerated women's custody of their children is directly jeopardized by the 1997 Adoption and Safe Families Act, which mandates the termination of one's right to be the legal parent of a child who has been in foster care for fifteen or more of the previous twenty-two months (Hagan and Coleman 2001). A notable work on incarcerated fathers is Anne Nurse's (2002) comprehensive study of juvenile fathers paroled from the California Youth Authority system. Combining survey data, participant observation, and in-depth interviews, Nurse skillfully documents a spectrum of obstacles that young men experience in parenting during and after their incarceration, ranging from transformations in their own behavior wrought by the correctional culture to children who do not recognize them or who have taken to calling their mother's new partner "Daddy."

At the beginning of the 1990s, Moira Peelo and her colleagues (1991, 312) noted that the scholarly attention given to female lawbreakers had not been matched by "specific consideration of offenders' wives." Two books, Laura Fishman's *Women at the Wall* (1990) and Lori Girshick's *Soledad Women* (1996), addressed this topic. Fishman, who identifies herself as an African American sociologist whose ex-husband was imprisoned, conducted unrecorded interviews during an undated twenty-four-month period with thirty convicts' wives, all of whom were white and living in Vermont. *Women at the Wall* provides a wealth of interview data and an analysis heavily influenced by Erving Goffman that uses the concepts of "courtesy stigma" and "moral career" (Goffman 1961, 1963) to examine women's justifications for men's criminality, the effects of their husbands' incarceration on them, and how dreams for futures as "traditional" housewives lead them to remain in marriages that have thus far proven highly unsatisfactory (see also Fishman 1986, 1988a, 1988b, 1995). However, given Fishman's decision not to record her interviews and to rely instead on handwritten notes (Fishman 1990, 300), it is difficult to determine the accuracy of the extensive quotations from her participants, some of which cover more than a page. Also, the demographics of Fishman's participants—exclusively white, living in a mainly rural state with an atypically low imprisonment rate—raise questions about the pertinence of her data to a phenomenon that is concentrated among people of color living in urban areas (Garland 2001; Western, Pettit, and Guetzkow 2002; Cadora, Swartz, and Gordon 2003).

In *Soledad Women,* a study of twenty-five wives of prisoners in central California, Lori Girshick (1996, 17) sets out to "explor[e] how the institutional practices of the prison system organize the experiences" of her research participants. Girshick met her interviewees—seventeen white women, five African Americans, and three Hispanics—in 1986 while visiting her husband during his incarceration at a medium-security prison in Soledad, 130 miles south of San Francisco. The book catalogs the range of activities and pressures associated with having an incarcerated partner, including the burdens of coping with "secret lives," financial hardship, and harassment at the hands of correctional authorities, with a penultimate chapter that reviews policy recommendations from previous research regarding prison visitation, alternatives to sentencing, and improved programs for inmates (Girshick 1996, 35–46, 59–67, 81–93, 109–16). In her brief conclusion, Girshick (1996, 117–21) sketches a new research agenda, with the admonition that "[t]he lives of prisoners' wives cannot be looked at separately from the issues of social power and social structure" and raises questions about the influence of class oppression, sexism, social control, and political resistance. Ironically, this critique identifies the shortcomings of her previous nine chapters, which read as a litany of complaints devoid of social context and provide no data on participants' income or employment, nor any discussion of such variables as ethnicity, education, or the length of men's sentences.

In contrast, Donald Braman's (2004) ethnographic study presents detailed socioeconomic portraits of the mothers, wives, sisters, and children of fifty inmates from the Washington, D.C. area. Arguing that the use of incarceration "as the primary response to social disorder . . . [has] strained and eroded the personal relationships vital to family and community life" (2004, 221), Braman portrays eleven case studies of the trauma and hardship suffered by the predominantly female kin of men whose drug addictions, involvement in the underground economy, or violent encounters land them behind bars—sometimes repeatedly. Yet Braman's contention that "criminal sanctions directly and indirectly affect the ability of family members to engage in . . . reciprocally supportive and socially generative relationships" (2004, 39) is weakened by a lack of evidence that families indeed would have been able to sustain such relationships if not for the intrusion of the criminal justice system in their lives, and by recurrent indications in his own data that some of his participants are less burdensome to their families when they are under state lock and key. The possibility that incarceration might paradoxically improve some men's abilities to engage in "the norm of reciprocity that inheres in family life" (Braman 2004, 221) is left unaddressed in the analysis, and hence unresolved for the reader.

A spate of edited volumes in recent years has heralded the growing recognition of the repercussive effects of incarceration on inmates, their families, and their residential neighborhoods—as well as the mushrooming of academic and policy interest in convening to discuss and define the scope of the issue. For *Invisible Punishment: The Collateral Consequences of Mass Imprisonment* (2002, 1), Marc Mauer and Meda Chesney-Lind assembled anthropologists, legal scholars, public policy analysts, sociologists, and other academics and advocates "to describe the effects of policies that have transformed family and community dynamics, exacerbated racial divisions, and posed fundamental questions of citizenship in democratic society." Taking an activist and openly critical bent, the contributing authors pronounce the impact of incarceration as entirely negative. Although some cases clearly support this stance—for example, Paul Farmer's (2002) observation that the substandard prison living conditions and negligent penal healthcare provisions that have hothoused rampant outbreaks of drug-resistant tuberculosis constitute a form of quasi torture—others make associations between criminal justice policies and severe hardship that might be better laid at the doorstep of America's decrepit and fast-vanishing social-welfare state. A second volume, by Jeremy Travis and Michelle Waul, emerged from a conference organized at the Urban Institute at the behest of the U.S. Department of Health and Human Services. Divided into sections on "the consequences of imprisonment and reentry for individual prisoners, their families, and the communities to which these prisoners return" (2003, x), the book suffers from the unevenness of many edited collections, but contains a noteworthy chapter by Craig Haney on the psychological impact of incarceration on inmates' attempts to adjust to society following their release from correctional institutions. Another highlight is Ross D. Parke and K. Alison Clarke-Stewart's treatment of the effects of parental incarceration on children, which considers custodial confinement "not [as] a single or discrete event, but a dynamic process that unfolds over time."

Editors Othello Harris and R. Robin Miller (2003) focus exclusively on the impact of incarceration on African American families, drawing on work from a range of disciplines in social science, medicine, and penology. Primarily a compilation of previously published material, the volume is marred by a lack of cohesion (and a surfeit of repetition), but occupies an important space through its specific concentration on the population most affected by the phenomenon of mass incarceration. A conference hosted by the Institute for Policy Research at Northwestern University provided the foundation for Mary Pattillo, David Weiman, and Bruce Western's *Imprisoning America: The Social Effects of Mass Incarceration* (2004, 3), which positions itself against the backdrop that "incarceration is a pervasive event in the lives of poor and minority men

[that] has become normalized, affecting large social groups rather than just the behaviorally distinctive deviants in the shadows of social life." The contributions from economists, sociologists, policy analysts, and other scholars constitute a strong and meticulously researched volume, notable for its dispassionate evaluation of the scope of incarceration's effects on family and civic life. Finally, a workshop organized by Christopher Mele and Teresa A. Miller resulted in an edited volume examining the "collateral civil penalties," that is, "sanctions on certain types of employment, housing, education, welfare eligibility, parental rights, and protections from deportation (for noncitizens)" (2005, 1), that affect people convicted of crimes, their kin, and their social networks. At its best, the book guides readers through the Kafkaesque labyrinth of civil sanctions attached under U.S. law to criminal charges, in the process raising important questions about the social control of the poor and people of color. However, the volume suffers from analytical dispersion and unevenness across chapters, and lacks what would have been a major contribution to the field, that is, a comprehensive outline of the major civil penalties, the circumstances under which they are imposed (including whether they are imposed at the local, state, or federal level and what variations occur among jurisdictions), and the typical duration of their imposition.

A Note on Popular Culture

Although it is not the focus of my research, the appearance in recent years of a plethora of popular-culture books concerning issues of prisoners' loved ones merits brief notice here. Despite the dearth of scholarly research on women with incarcerated partners, books such as Sheila Isenberg's *Women Who Love Men Who Kill* (1991), Jacquelynne Willcox-Bailey's *Dream Lovers: Women Who Marry Men behind Bars* (1997), and Angela Devlin's *Cell Mates/Soul Mates* (2002)—all of which consist essentially of in-depth case histories and long interview quotations—attest to the popularity of the subject among nonacademic authors. Another genre of the popular-culture literature is guide books, both those designed for inmates and families during incarceration and those addressing the postrelease period. Among the former, *Behind Bars: Surviving Prison* (Ross and Richards 2002) walks inmates through "four fatal legal mistakes (and how to avoid them)," the ins and outs of penitentiary food, work, and violence, and even provides a glossary of "slammer slang." Families can turn to *Behind the Walls: A Guide for*

Families and Friends of Texas Prison Inmates (Renaud 2002), which provides detailed information on such matters as the Texas Department of Criminal Justice's custody levels, telephone-call policies, and inmate health-care system. Once someone steps out of the institution's gates he can consult *How to Do Good after Prison: A Handbook for the "Committed Man"* (Jackson 2004). This manual, published by Joint FX Press: Books for Successful Reentry, instructs ex-convicts on "good parole habits" such as "thinking win-win" and "showing respect" when dealing with one's parole officer. Among poor parole habits: "Don't show up at the parole office wearing a head rag, stocking cap, or bandana." The same author offers a corresponding volume (published by the same press) for "the Prisonwife," *How to Love and Inspire Your Man after Prison* (Jackson 2003). Advising women to "encourage him to meet new people and make new friends" and to "maintain positive family ties" (Jackson 2003, 66), this book concludes with two "Happily-Ever-After-Prison Stories" to spur women on in their rehabilitative efforts.

Appendix 3: United States Carceral Population, 1980–2000

Year	Number of people in jail	Number of people in prison	Total number of people behind bars	Increase over previous year	Percentage increase over previous year
1980	183,988	319,598	503,586	—	—
1981	196,785	360,029	556,814	53,228	11
1982	209,582	402,914	612,496	55,682	10
1983	223,551	423,898	647,449	34,953	6
1984	234,500	448,264	682,764	35,315	5
1985	256,615	487,593	744,208	61,444	9
1986	274,444	526,436	800,880	56,672	8
1987	295,873	562,814	858,687	57,807	7
1988	343,569	607,766	951,335	92,648	11
1989	395,553	683,367	1,078,920	127,585	13
1990	405,320	743,382	1,148,702	69,782	6
1991	426,479	792,535	1,219,014	70,312	6
1992	444,584	850,566	1,295,150	76,136	6
1993	459,804	909,381	1,369,185	74,035	6
1994	486,474	990,147	1,476,621	107,436	8
1995	507,044	1,078,542	1,585,586	108,965	7
1996	518,492	1,127,528	1,646,020	60,434	4
1997	567,079	1,176,564	1,743,643	97,623	6
1998	592,462	1,224,469	1,816,931	73,288	4

(*continued*)

(continued)

Year	Number of people in jail	Number of people in prison	Total number of people behind bars	Increase over previous year	Percentage increase over previous year
1999	605,943	1,287,172	1,893,115	76,184	4
2000	621,149	1,316,333	1,937,482	44,367	2

Source: Calculated using figures from Bureau of Justice Statistics, U.S. Department of Justice, *Key Facts at a Glance, Correctional Populations 1980–2000, Number of Persons under Correctional Supervision* (http://www.ojp.usdoj.gov/bjs/glance/tables/corr2tab.htm).

Appendix 4:
Field Documents

CALIFORNIA STATE PRISON
SAN QUENTIN
MAINLINE QUARTERLY PACKAGE AUTHORIZATION

P L E A S E   R E A D   C A R E F U L L Y

    THIS FORM IS AN AUTHORIZATION TO SEND A QUARTERLY PACK-AGE TO A MAINLINE INMATE, WHO QUALIFIES, AT SAN QUENTIN STATE PRISON. THE ADDRESS LABEL ON THE REVERSE SIDE OF THIS FORM MUST BE ATTACHED TO THE OUTSIDE OF THE PACKAGE. THE WEIGHT OF THE PACKAGE IS NOT TO EXCEED (30) THIRTY POUNDS. THE ADDRESS LABEL MUST INDICATE A RETURN ADDRESS AND BE SIGNED BY THE SENDER AND RECEIVING INMATE AT THE AREAS PROVIDED. THE WEIGHT OF THE PACKAGE IS TO BE COMPLETED BY THE SHIPPER (US. MAIL, U.P.S., FED. EX., ETC.), AT THE AREA PROVIDED. MAINLINE INMATES, WHO QUALIFY, MAY RECEIVE ONE THIRTY POUND QUARTERLY PACKAGE PER CALENDAR QUARTER.

    PLEASE READ CAREFULLY THE SPECIFIC REQUIREMENTS REGARD-ING CLOTHING TYPES AND ALLOWABLE QUANTITIES. ANY ITEM IN-DICATING A VALUE LIMIT MUST INCLUDE A RECEIPT. TAKE NOTE OF ALLOWABLE FOOD ITEMS AND THE PACKAGING REQUIREMENTS INDICATED - ANY AND ALL ITEMS NOT SPECIFICALLY LISTED OR DESCRIBED IN THIS FORM ARE NOT AUTHORIZED AND WILL NOT BE ISSUED TO THE RECEIVING INMATE. UNAUTHORIZED ITEMS WILL BE, AT THE INMATES DISCRETION, MAILED OUT AT THE INMATES EX-PENSE, DONATED TO A CHARITABLE ORGANIZATION OR DESTROYED.

I. **CLOTHING ITEMS, GENERAL INFORMATION:** UNLESS OTHERWISE INDICATED, ALL CLOTHING ITEMS ARE TO BE WHITE OR LIGHT GRAY. ALL CLOTHING ITEMS MUST BE OF A SOLID COLOR WITH NO PATTERNS, PRINTS, LOGOS OR EXTERNAL WRITING. CLOTH-ING ITEMS THAT HAVE LININGS OR INSIDE POCKETS ARE NOT PERMITTED.

1. **ATHLETIC SHORTS:** (GYM SHORTS), ELASTIC WAIST BAND ONLY. LIMIT: (2).

2. **ATHLETIC SUPPORTERS:** LIMIT: ONE (1).
    A. **PROTECTIVE CUPS:** LIMIT ONE (1). FOR BASEBALL AND SOC-CER TEAM MEMBERS ONLY. RECEIVING INMATE MUST POSSESS DOCUMENTATION OF TEAM MEMBERSHIP.

3. **BELTS:** NOT TO EXCEED ONE AND ONE HALF INCHES IN WIDTH MAXIMUM SINGLE LAYER LEATHER. BLACK OR BROWN ONLY. PASS

THROUGH HOLE TYPE BUCKLE ONLY. BUCKLE NOT TO EXCEED TWO BY TWO INCHES. LIMIT: ONE (1).

4. **BATH ROBES:** NO HOODS. NO KARATE OR GEE TYPES ALLOWED LIMIT: ONE (1).
5. A. **BASEBALL STYLE CAP:** CLOTH OR CLOTH/NYLON MESH-COMBO ONLY LIMIT ONE (1).

   B. **WATCHCAP STYLE:** DARK BLUE ONLY. LIMIT: ONE (1).
6. **HANDKERCHIEFS:** LIMIT: FIVE (5)
7. **JEANS:** DARK BLUE DENIM ONLY. **NO** BRUSHED OR FADED MATERIAL, **NO** ACID OR STONE WASHED TYPES. **NO** LAYERED CONSTRUCTION OR QUILTED STITCHING. **NO** ZIPPERED OR EXTRA LEG POCKETS. PAINTER OR CARPENTER STYLES ARE NOT PERMITTED. NO BUILT IN BELTS OR BIB OVERALLS. BUGLE BOY AND CALVIN KLEIN BRAND ARE NOT AUTHORIZED. LIMIT: TWO (2).
8. **LONG UNDERWEAR:** (THERMALS), **NO** POCKETS. LIMIT: TWO (2) SETS.
9. **PAJAMAS: NO** HOODS. LIMIT: ONE PAIR.
10. **SOCKS:** WHITE ONLY. LIMIT: TEN PAIR.
11. **SUSPENDERS:** STRAPS NOT TO EXCEED ONE AND ONE HALF INCHES IN WIDTH. BLACK OR BROWN SOLID COLOR CLOTH ONLY. LIMIT: ONE PAIR.
12. **SWEAT PANTS:** ELASTIC WAIST BAND OR DRAWSTRING O.K. LIMIT: TWO PAIR.
13. **SWEAT SHIRTS:** PULLOVER TYPE ONLY, NO ZIPPERS, BUTTONS OR HOODS. **NO** POCKETS. LONG OR SHORT SLEEVE O.K. LIMIT: THREE.
14. **FOOTWEAR:**
A. <u>**ATHLETIC, TENNIS OR JOGGING TYPES:**</u> VALUE NOT TO EXCEED $60.00. WHITE OR BLACK ONLY. SMALL COLOR STRIPE, LOGO, OR PATTERN O.K. CAVITIES OR VOIDS, SEALED OR NOT, ARE NOT AUTHORIZED **(IE. WINDOWS IN SOLES). NO** PUMPS, POCKETS, ZIPPERS, OR VELCRO. **NO** METAL ARCH SUPPORTS OR FALSE INSOLES. **THE BRANDS ARE NOT AUTHORIZED:** BRITISH KNIGHTS, BUGLE BOYS AND CALVIN KLIEN. JORDAN'S ARE PERMITTED, HOWEVER THOSE MODELS DIS-PLAYING AN "XIV" LOGO ARE NOT AUTHORIZED. LIMIT: ONE PAIR.
B. <u>**SANDALS:**</u> SOLID RUBBER SOLES ONLY. STRAPS NOT TO EXCEED ONE AND ONE HALF (11/2) WIDTH. **NO** METAL ARCH SUPPORTS. BLACK OR BROWN ONLY. LIMIT: ONE PAIR.
C. <u>**SLIPPERS:**</u> SOFT SOLE, CLOTH ONLY. BLACK OR BROWN ONLY. LIMIT ONE PAIR.
D. <u>**CLEATS:**</u> BASEBALL OR SOCCER TYPE ONLY. **(NO HIGH TOPS)** RUBBER/PLASTIC "SPIKES" ONLY THAT ARE FIXED TO THE SOLE. FOR BASEBALL AND SOCCER TEAM MEMBERS ONLY. RECEIVING INMATE MUST POSSESS DOCUMENTATION OF TEAM MEMBERSHIP.
15. **UNDERSHIRTS: NO** FISHNET. T-SHIRTS OR A SHIRTS (TANKTOPS) O.K. **NO** POCK-ETS. LIMIT: SIX (6).
16. **UNDERSHORTS: NO** FISHNET. BOXER OR BRIEF TYPE O.O. LIMIT: SIX (6).

FOOD ITEMS

1. **GENERAL INFORMATION:**
   A. **APPROVED PACKAGING:** ALL FOOD ITEMS MUST BE IN FACTORY SEALED, TAMPER PROOF CONTAINERS. DELI WRAPPED, BAKERY OR HOMEMADE ITEMS **ARE NOT** PERMITTED. BOXES OR BAGS WITH GLUED OR ROLLED WIRE SEALS MUST HAVE INNER CONTAINER(S) OF SEALED PLASTIC WITH HEAT-CRIMPED EDGES. STYROFOAM PACKAGING (IE. CUP-A-NOODLES) IS NOT PERMITTED. **DO NOT SEND GLASS.**
   B. **WEIGHT LIMITS:** UNLESS OTHERWISE INDICATED, THE WEIGHT LIMIT PER PACKAGED ITEM IS (32) THIRTY-TWO OUNCES (TWO POUNDS).
   C. FOOD ITEMS **MUST NOT** REQUIRE REFRIGERATION.
2. **SPECIFIC ITEMS:**
   A. **CANDY** (SEE GENERAL INFORMATION) INCLUDES GRANOLA OR HEALTH BARS. NO HAND PACKED SEE'S TYPE. DO NOT SEND INDIVIDUAL CANDY BARS OR PIECES OF CANDY. NO BULK TYPE SUPERMARKET BIN CANDY.
   B. **CANNED GOODS: NO GLASS JARS.**
      1. CANNED MEATS, FISH, POULTRY: WEIGHT LIMIT: (16) SIXTEEN OZ. (1 LB) PER CAN.
      2. CANNED VEGETABLES, INCLUDING SALSAS: WEIGHT LIMIT SIXTEEN OUNCES PER CAN.
      3. PREPARED CANNED FOODS (IE. STEWS, SOUPS, PASTAS AND CHILI). WEIGHT LIMIT (16) SIXTEEN OUNCES (ONE POUND) PER CAN.

C. **CAKES, COOKIES AND PASTRIES:** (SEE GENERAL INFORMATION). NO POPPY SEEDS.

D. **CHEESES:** CLEAR PLASTIC FACTORY SEALED ONLY, WITH NO REFRIGERATION REQUIRED. WEIGHT LIMIT (16) SIXTEEN OUNCES (ONE POUND) PER ITEM.

E. **CRACKERS, CHIPS, PORK CRACKLINS, PRETZELS:** (SEE GENERAL INFORMATION). NO CANISTER (IE. PRINGLES) TYPE. **SEEDS & NUTS** (SEE GENERAL INFORMATION. **NO SHELLS.**

F. **CEREALS:**
   1. DRY: SINGLE SERVING BOXES ONLY, IN PACKS OF SIX OR MORE. FACTORY SEALED IN PLASTIC. DO NOT SEND INDIVIDUAL BOXES.
   2. INSTANT HOT: SINGLE SERVING PACKETS ONLY. FACTORY SEALED BOXES ONLY.

G. **DRIED MEATS, FISH AND POULTRY:** CLEAR PLASTIC FACTORY SEALED ONLY. FULLY COOKED WITH NO REFRIGERATION REQUIRED. WEIGHT LIMIT: 16 OZ. (1 LB.) PER ITEM.

H. **DRIED INSTANT FOODS:**
   1. NOODLES: (SEE GENERAL INFORMATION)
   2. SOUPS: POUCHES IN FACTORY SEALED BOXES ONLY. PAPER TYPE CUPS WITH TEAR-OFF PAPER SEALS MUST BE IN MULTI-PACKS FACTORY SEALED IN PLASTIC (IE. NILE & SPICE ISLAND). NO BOUILLON CUBES. NO STYROFOAM.

I. **HONEY:** CLEAR PLASTIC CONTAINERS ONLY. WEIGHT LIMIT 16 OZ. (1 LB.) PER CONTAINER.

J. **INSTANT DRINK MIX:**
   1. COLD: KOOLAID TYPE, MILK, ETC. (SEE GENERAL INFORMATION)
   2a. HOT: COFFEE, **INSTANT ONLY.** DRY OR LIQUID CONCENTRATE OK. PLASTIC JARS OR CONTAINERS ONLY. LIMIT: FIVE POUNDS. **NO** TEA BAGS PERMITTED.
   2b. TEA, **INSTANT ONLY.** NO TEA BAGS. NO LOOSE BULK TEA LEAVES.
   2c. CHOCOLATE, CIDER, ETC. (SEE GENERAL INFORMATION).

K. **SEASONED SAUCES:** (HOT, SOY, ETC.) PLASTIC CONTAINERS ONLY. WEIGHT LIMIT (16) SIXTEEN OUNCES PER CONTAINER.

MISCELLANEOUS ITEMS

1. **CALENDAR:** MAX. SIZE 12 INCHES BY 12 INCHES. NO METAL BINDING. NO NUDES. LIMIT:ONE.

2. **OCCASION / GREETING CARDS:** LIMIT: TWELVE.

3. **RELIGIOUS MEDALLION:** NO SHARP POINTS, STONES OR SETTINGS. SIZE LIMIT: ONE INCH BY ONE INCH. VALUE NOT TO EXCEED $100.00, INCLUDING CHAIN.

4. **SUNGLASSES:** ALL PLASTIC CONSTRUCTION ONLY. NO MIRRORED LENSES OR WRAP-AROUND TYPE. NO CLIP-ON'S. ONE PAIR ONLY. VALUE NOT TO EXCEED $15.00.

5. **TABLE GAMES:** LIMITED TO CHECKERS, CHESS (OPEN-BOTTOM PIECES ONLY), DOMINOES, MONOPOLY, PINOCHLE CARDS AND SCRABBLE. NO DICE OR ELECTRONIC GAMES. LIMIT: ONE GAME AND TWO DECKS OF CARDS. NOT TO EXCEED $25.00 IN VALUE.

6. **WATCH:** WRIST TYPE ONLY. NO STONES OR SETTINGS. FUNCTIONS MAY INCLUDE: TIME, DATE, ALARM AND STOP WATCH. VALUE NOT TO EXCEED $100.00. LIMIT: ONE.
   A. **WRISTBAND:** LIMIT: ONE.   B. **WATCH BATTERY:** LIMIT: ONE.

7. **WRITING MATERIALS:**
   A. PAPER, LINED OR TYPING, PAD OR REAM TYPE. LIMIT: 200 SHEETS. NO METAL BINDINGS.
   B. PENCILS: WOOD OR MECHANICAL - CLEAR PLASTIC CONSTRUCTION. LIMIT: FIVE IN FACTORY SEALED PACKS.
   C. PENS: CLEAR PLASTIC CONSTRUCTION. LIMIT: FIVE IN FACTORY SEALED PACKS.
   D. ENVELOPES: LIMIT: 100. STAMPS OR STAMPED ENVELOPES, LIMIT: 100.

San Quentin Mainline Price List
MARCH 2001

Last Name: _____   WRITE CLEAR

CDC# _____

House: _____

TOBACCO

SMOKING

Camels, Pack ⊗	5.15
Kools, Pack ⊗	5.15
Generic Non-Filter, Pack	3.05
Generic Filter, Pack	3.05
Bugler, 6oz Can	11.05
Bugler, .65oz Pouch	1.35
Kite, .65oz Pouch	1.35

SMOKELESS

Bowie, Fine Natural	3.80
Bowie, Long, Winter	3.80
Bowie, Chew	3.10

SMOKING SUPPLIES

Bugler Papers	.55
Cigarette Roller	2.25
Lighter	.95

POSTAGE

Postcard, Plain	.25
Stamped Envelope	.38
Stamps, Book of 20	6.80
One Cent Stamp	.01

WRITING SUPPLIES

Writing Tablet, Yellow	.85
28 Line Legal Paper	.10
Envelopes, Box of 50	1.10

Manila Envelope	.20
Ink Pen	.55

COSMETICS

HAIR CARE

VO5 Shampoo	1.45
VO5 Conditioner	1.45
Dandruff Shampoo,	2.95
S-Curl Kit	7.10
LPOM Relaxer Kit	7.25
S-Curl Activator	3.80
LPOM Hair Lotion	4.35
Black Orchid Pomade	1.15
Proline Hair Food	2.30
Murray's Pomade	2.50
Protein 29	2.65
Sulpher 8	2.95
Afro Comb	.65
Afro Pick	.65
Palm Brush	.80
Pocket Comb	.40
Hair Brush	1.80

DENTAL CARE

Colgate Toothpaste	2.05
Close-up Toothpaste	1.75
Ultrabrite Toothpaste	
Efferdent, Generic	3.05
Effergrip	3.50
Mouthwash	1.05

Toothbrush	.45
Dental Floss, Unwaxed	1.35

BODY CARE

Skin Care Lotion, 20oz	1.15
Cocoa Butter Lotion, 20oz	1.15
Baby Oil	1.50
Body Powder	1.15
Medicated Cream	1.05
Deodorant, Mennen	2.15
Antiperspirant, Mennen	2.15
Sunscreen	4.20
Cotton Swabs	.95
Shower Shoes	.90
Fingernail Clipper	.65
Wash Cloth	.45

COSMETICS

SHAVING

Disposable Razor	.25
Colgate Shave Cream	1.65
Depilatory Shave	3.25
Magic Shave, Gold	2.40
After Shave, Nonalcoholic	1.10

SOAP

Tone Soap	1.00
Ivory Soap	.35
Irish Spring Soap	.55
Dial Soap	.70

VITAMINS & DRUG

VITAMINS

Weight Gain Powder	7.90
Protein Powder	7.20
Ultrex Vitamins, 100 tabs	5.25
Vitamin C Complex, 100tabs	2.50
Amino Acid, 100 Tabs	6.50

OVER-THE-COUNTER

Ibuprofen, 50ct	2.50
Tylenol, Generic, 60ct	2.30
Aspirin, 110 tabs	1.55
Decongest. Antihs.Tab, 24/tabs	2.05
Liquid Antacid	4.00
Antifungal Cream	1.70
Pepto bismol, Generic	2.85
Hemorrhoidal Ointment	3.80
Alka Seltzer, 12 Tablets	3.30
Cough Drops	.70
Chapstick	1.35
Rolaids	.85
Saline Solution, 4oz	2.85
Medicated Foot Powder	2.10
Opti-FreeDisinfectant Sol.	13.05
B&L DailyCleaner	8.85
Wetting/Soaking Solution	12.70
B&L Concentrating Cleaner	8.20
Clerz-2 Lubricating Drops	9.75
Enzymatic Cleaner Tabs	9.75

MISCELLANEOUS

AAA Batteries (Alkaline)	2.90
AA Batteries	1.20
C Batteries	1.25
D Batteries	1.25
Combination Lock	7.00
Extension Cord (cell housing only)	2.35
Power Breaker Strip* (NO RC)	11.25
Tumbler W/Lid	2.05
Shoe Polish	1.80
Laundry Soap	1.35
Soap Box	.50
Bowl W/Lid	.65
P38 Can Opener	.50
Stinger (GP inmates)	5.25
Ear Bud, (ear phone)	1.45
Forks	.30
Spoons	.20
Acrylic Mirror	2.10
Pinochle Cards	1.50
Greeting Cards, circle letter	1.75
A B C D E F G H	

BEVERAGES

SOFT DRINKS

Mug Root Beer	.45
Pepsi Cola	.45
Diet Pepsi Cola	.45
Wild Cherry Pepsi	.45

COFFEE, TEA & DRINK MIX

Folgers, 8oz	5.60
Maxwell House Coffee, 3oz	2.35
Hot Cocoa Mix, Whipper	3.05
Orange Breakfast Drink	1.30
Instant Drink, Peach	1.90
Instant Drink, Fruit Punch	1.20
Tea Bag, 100/bx	2.50
Dry Milk	3.45

SNACK FOOD

BBQ Potato Chip, 6oz.	1.05
Sour/Crm Onion Chip, 6oz	1.05
Tortilla Chip, 16oz	1.50
Pork Cracklin, 2.5oz	.85
Chili Cheese Corn Chip, 12oz	1.15
Caramel Corn, 6oz	1.05
Meat Log	1.50
Beef & Cheese	.65
Snickers	.55
Three Musketeers	.55
Mars Bar	.55
Bag Candy, Allstars	1.25
Bag Candy, Jelly Beans	1.25
Bag Candy, Jolly Ranchers	1.25
Duplex Cookies, 5 oz	.45
Dunking Sticks, 6/pk	1.35
Bag Cookies, Chocolate Chip	1.15
Saltine Crackers	1.50
Snack Crackers	1.20
Raspberry Shortbread	1.55

CONDIMENTS

Mayonnaise	1.90
Mustard	.95
Crushed Chili Peppers	.60
Louisiana Hot Sauce	1.15
Picante Sauce	1.70
Strawberry Preserves	2.00
Sugar, Cube	1.05

(Continued)

Sugar Substitute, 100bx	1.75
Honey	2.25
Cheese Spread, Cheddar	1.60
Peanut Butter	2.10
BBQ Sauce	1.90

Food

Ramen, Chili	.20
Ramen, Beef	.20
Ramen, Creamy Chicken	.20
Jalapeno Peppers	1.20
Beef Stew	.80
Chunk Chicken	1.65
Vienna Sausage	.65
Roast Beef in Gravy	2.75
Mackerel (Jack)	1.00
Smoked Clams ↑	1.70
Smoked Oysters	1.90
Kipper Snacks	.85
Spam ☺ ⚡	1.95
Herring Steaks	.75
Tuna in Water	.90

Sardines ↑	.85
Chunk Chili ↑	1.05
Canned Whole Corn	1.10
Canned Mushrooms	1.00
Instant Rice	.95
Refried Beans, Instant	1.45
Rice & Beans, spicy	1.00
Instant Oatmeal	2.75
Bear Claws	2.70
Apple Horns	2.70
Cinnamon Rolls	1.45

Ice Cream

Ice Cream, Fudge Nut	1.25
Ice Cream, Vanilla	1.25
Ice Cream, Cookie & Cream	1.25
Ice Cream, Chocolate	1.25

Photo Project

Photo Ducat (visiting room only)	2.00
Photo Album	2.45

Legend

↑ Price Increase
↓ Price Decrease
☺ New Item
⊗ Discontinued Item when current stock is depleted.
⚡ Pending Approval
⚡ Limited Time Only
* must be engraves before issuance

Substitution Lines

References

Abraham, Laurie Kaye. 1993. *Mama Might Be Better Off Dead: The Failure of Health Care in Urban America.* Chicago: University of Chicago Press.

Arpaio, Joe, and Len Sherman. 1996. *America's Toughest Sheriff: How We Can Win the War against Crime.* Irving, Texas: Summit Publishing Group.

Associated Press. 2000. "Inmate Dies and 12 Are Hurt as Riot Erupts in California Prison." *New York Times,* February 24, A14.

Bakker, Laura K., Barbara A. Morris, and Laura M. Janus. 1978. "Hidden Victims of Crime." *Social Work* 23, no. 2: 143–48.

Bandele, Asha. 1999. *The Prisoner's Wife: A Memoir.* New York: Scribner.

Bartky, Sandra Lee. 1990. *Femininity and Domination: Studies in the Phenomenology of Oppression.* New York: Routledge.

Baum, Dan. 1996. *Smoke and Mirrors: The War on Drugs and the Politics of Failure.* Boston: Little, Brown.

Bauman, Zygmunt. 1995. *Life in Fragments: Essays in Postmodern Morality.* Cambridge, Mass.: Blackwell.

Beardsworth, Alan, and Teresa Keil. 1997. *Sociology on the Menu: An Invitation to the Study of Food and Society.* London: Routledge.

Becker, Gary S. 1991. *A Treatise on the Family.* Chicago: University of Chicago Press.

Bellah, Robert N., Richard Madsen, William M. Sullivan, Ann Swidler, and Steven M. Tipton. 1996. *Habits of the Heart: Individualism and Commitment in American Life.* 2nd ed. Berkeley: University of California Press.

Béranger, Dominique. 2000. *Mère, femme, fille, soeur, amie de détenu: Témoignages.* Paris: L'Harmattan.

Blake, Joe. 1990. *Sentenced by Association: The Needs of Prisoners' Families.* London: Save the Children.

Bloom, Barbara. 1995. "Imprisoned Mothers." In *Children of Incarcerated Parents,* edited by K. Gabel and D. Johnston. New York: Lexington Books.

Blumstein, Alfred. 1998. "U.S. Criminal Justice Conundrum: Rising Prison Populations and Stable Crime Rates." *Crime & Delinquency* 44, no. 1: 127–35.

Blumstein, Alfred, Jacqueline Cohen, and Daniel Nagin. 1977. "The Dynamics of a Homeostatic Punishment Process." *Journal of Criminal Law and Criminology* 67, no. 3: 317–34.

Bordo, Susan. 1993. *Unbearable Weight: Feminism, Western Culture, and the Body.* Berkeley: University of California Press.

Bourgois, Philippe. 1995. *In Search of Respect: Selling Crack in El Barrio.* Cambridge: Cambridge University Press.

Braman, Donald. 2004. *Doing Time on the Outside: Incarceration and Family Life in Urban America.* Ann Arbor: University of Michigan Press.

Breen, Peter A. 1995. "Families in Peril: Bridging the Barriers." *Corrections Today* (December): 98–99.

Brooks, G. R., and L. B. Silverstein. 1995. "Understanding the Dark Side of Masculinity: An Interactive Systems Model." In *A New Psychology of Men,* edited by R. F. Levant and W. S. Pollack. New York: Basic Books.

Brubaker, Rogers, and Fred Cooper. 2000. "Beyond Identity." *Theory and Society* 29, no. 1: 1–47.

Bulcroft, Richard A., and Kris A. Bulcroft. 1993. "Race Differences in Attitudinal and Motivational Factors in the Decision to Marry." *Journal of Marriage and the Family* 55 (May): 338–55.

Bunker, Barbara B., Josephine M. Zubek, Virginia J. Vanderslice, and Robert W. Rice. 1992. "Quality of Life in Dual-Career Families: Commuting versus Single-Residence Couples." *Journal of Marriage and the Family* 54, no. 2: 399–407.

Bunting, Sheila M. 2001. "Sustaining the Relationship: Women's Caregiving in the Context of HIV Disease." *Health Care for Women International* 22: 131–48.

Bureau of Justice Statistics. 1995. *State and Federal Prisons Report Record Growth during Last 12 Months.* Washington, D.C.: U.S. Department of Justice.

———. 1997. *Survey of Inmates of State and Federal Correctional Facilities.* Washington, D.C.: U.S. Department of Justice.

———. 2003. *Sourcebook of Criminal Justice Statistics.* Washington, D.C.: U.S. Department of Justice.

Bush, George W. 2001a. "Rallying the Armies of Compassion." Washington, D.C.: The White House.

———. 2001b. "Remarks by the President in Submission of Faith-Based Services Proposal." Washington, D.C.: Office of the Press Secretary, January 30.

Butzin, Clifford A., Steven S. Martin, and James A. Inciardi. 2002. "Evaluating Component Effects of a Prison-Based Treatment Continuum." *Journal of Substance Abuse Treatment* 22, no. 2: 63–69.

Caddle, Diane, and Debbie Crisp. 1996. *Imprisoned Women and Mothers.* London: Home Office.

Cadora, Eric, Charles Swartz, and Mannix Gordon. 2003. "Criminal Justice and Health and Human Services: An Exploration of Overlapping Needs, Resources, and Interests in Brooklyn Neighborhoods." In *Prisoners Once Removed: The Impact of Incarceration and Reentry on Children, Families, and Communities,* edited by J. Travis and M. Waul. Washington, D.C.: Urban Institute.

California Department of Corrections. 1999. *California Department of Corrections Visitor Handbook.* Sacramento: http://www.cdc.state.ca.us/facility/visitor-hb.htm.

———. 2000. "Facilities List." Sacramento: http://www.cdc.state.ca.us/facility.htm.

California Department of Corrections and Rehabilitation. 2005. "CDC Facts." Sacramento: http://www.corr.ca.gov/CommunicationsOffice/facts_figures.asp.

———. 2006. "Weekly Report of Population." Sacramento: http://www.cdcr.ca.gov/ReportsResearch/OffenderInfoServices/WeeklyWed/TPOP1A/TPOP1Ad060823.pdf.

Camp, Camille Graham, George Camp, and Bob May, eds. 2002. *The 2001 Corrections Yearbook.* Middletown, Conn.: Criminal Justice Institute.

Campbell, Beatrix. 1993. *Goliath: Britain's Dangerous Places.* London: Random House.

Cardon, Carole. 2002. "Relations conjugales en situation carcérale." *Ethnologie français* 32, no. 1: 81–88.

Carlen, Pat. 1982. "Papa's Discipline: An Analysis of Disciplinary Modes in the Scottish Women's Prison." *Sociological Review* 30, no. 1: 97–124.

———. 2005. "The Women's Imprisonment and Re-Integration Industries." Paper presented at A Prisão a Psiquiatria e a Rua, Lisbon, June 6.

Carlson, Bonnie E., and Neil J. Cervera. 1991a. "Inmates and Their Families: Conjugal Visits, Family Contact, and Family Functioning." *Criminal Justice and Behavior* 18, no. 3: 318–31.

———. 1991b. "Incarceration, Coping, and Support." *Social Work* 36, no. 4: 279–85.

Carter, Keith. 1996a. "Domestic Visits: A Forced Non-Relationship of Private Affection in a Semi-Public Place." In *Qualitative Research: The Emotional Dimension,* edited by K. Carter and S. Delamont. Aldershot: Averbury.

———. 1996b. "Masculinity in Prison." In *Gender and Qualitative Research,* edited by J. Pilcher and A. Coffey. Aldershot: Avebury.

Charles, Nickie, and Marion Kerr. 1988. *Women, Food and Families.* Manchester: Manchester University Press.

Cheal, David. 1996. "'Showing Them You Love Them': Gift Giving and the Dialectic of Intimacy." In *The Gift: An Interdisciplinary Perspective*, edited by A. E. Komter. Amsterdam: Amsterdam University Press.

Chesney-Lind, Meda. 2002. "Imprisoning Women: The Unintended Victims of Mass Imprisonment." In *Invisible Punishment: The Collateral Consequences of Mass Imprisonment*, edited by M. Mauer and M. Chesney-Lind. New York: New Press.

Chiang, Harriet. 2002. "Court Won't Let Inmate Ship Sperm to Wife." *San Francisco Chronicle*, November 19, A3.

Child Welfare League of America. 2002. *Making Children a National Priority*. Conference proceedings, hosted by Institute on Children and Families Separated by Incarceration, March 6–8, Washington, D.C.

Clark, Judith. 1995. "The Impact of the Prison Environment on Mothers." *Prison Journal* 75, no. 3: 306–24.

———. December 1995–January 1996. "Love Them and Leave Them: Paradox, Conflict, and Ambivalence among Incarcerated Mothers." *Zero to Three*: 29–35.

Clear, Todd R. 2002. "The Problem with 'Addition by Subtraction': The Prison-Crime Relationship in Low-Income Communities." In *Invisible Punishment: The Collateral Consequences of Mass Imprisonment*, edited by M. Mauer and M. Chesney-Lind. New York: New Press.

Cleaver, Eldridge. 1978. *Soul on Fire*. Waco: Word Books.

Clemmer, Donald. 1958 (1940). *The Prison Community*. 2nd ed. New York: Holt, Rinehart, and Winston.

Coffman, Keith. 2000. "Guards Charged with Brutalizing Inmates." *APBnews.com*, November 3.

Cohen, Erik. 1986. "Lovelorn Farangs: The Correspondence between Foreign Men and Thai Girls." *Anthropological Quarterly* 59, no. 3: 115–27.

Cohen, Stanley. 2002 (1972). *Folk Devils and Moral Panics*. 3rd ed. London: Routledge.

———. 1985. *Visions of Social Control*. Cambridge: Polity Press.

———. 1997. "Crime and Politics: Spot the Difference." In *Law, Society and Economy: Centenary Essays for the London School of Economics and Political Science 1895–1995*, edited by R. Rawlings. Oxford: Clarendon Press.

———. 2001. *States of Denial: Knowing about Atrocities and Suffering*. Cambridge: Polity.

Cohen, Stanley, and Laurie Taylor. 1974. *Psychological Survival: The Experience of Long-term Imprisonment*. New York: Vintage.

———. 1992. *Escape Attempts: The Theory and Practice of Resistance to Everyday Life*. 2nd ed. London: Routledge.

Cole, David. 1999. *No Equal Justice: Race and Class in the American Criminal Justice System*. New York: New Press.

Collins, Jan Clanton, and Thomas Gregor. 1995. "Boundaries of Love." In *Romantic Passion: A Universal Experience?* edited by W. Jankowiak. New York: Columbia University Press.

Collins, Patricia Hill. 1991. *Black Feminist Thought.* New York: Routledge.

Comfort, Megan, Olga Grinstead, Bonnie Faigeles, and Barry Zack. 2000. "Reducing HIV Risk among Women Visiting Their Incarcerated Male Partners." *Criminal Justice and Behavior* 27, no. 1: 57–71.

Comfort, Megan, Olga Grinstead, Kathleen McCartney, Philippe Bourgois, and Kelly Knight. 2005. "'You Can't Do Nothing in this Damn Place!' Sex and Intimacy among Couples with an Incarcerated Male Partner." *Journal of Sex Research* 42, no. 1: 3–12.

Conover, Ted. 2000. *Newjack: Guarding Sing Sing.* New York: Random House.

Corrado, Marisa. 2002. "Teaching Wedding Rules: How Bridal Workers Negotiate Control over Their Customers." *Journal of Contemporary Ethnography* 31, no. 1: 33–67.

Coulter, C. 1991. *Web of Punishment: An Investigation.* Dublin: Attic Press.

Council of Europe. 2002. *Statistique pénale annuelle du Conseil de l'Europe, Enquête 2000.* Strasbourg.

Covington, Stephanie S. 2003. "A Woman's Journey Home: Challenges for Female Offenders." In *Prisoners Once Removed: The Impact of Incarceration and Reentry on Children, Families, and Communities,* edited by J. Travis and M. Waul. Washington, D.C.: Urban Institute Press.

Crawley, Elaine. 2004. *Doing Prison Work: The Public and Private Lives of Prison Officers.* Cullompton, Devon: Willan Publishing.

Culberton, Robert G. 1975. "The Effect of Institutionalization on the Delinquent Inmate's Self Concept." *Journal of Criminal Law and Criminology* 66, no. 1: 88–93.

Cullen, Jim. 2003. *The American Dream: A Short History of an Idea That Shaped a Nation.* New York: Oxford University Press.

Cummins, Eric. 1994. *The Rise and Fall of California's Radical Prison Movement.* Stanford: Stanford University Press.

Currie, Dawn. 1993. "'Here Comes the Bride': The Making of a 'Modern Traditional' Wedding in Western Culture." *Journal of Comparative Family Studies* 24, no. 3: 403–21.

Currie, Elliott. 1998. *Crime and Punishment in America.* New York: Henry Holt.

Daniel, Sally W., and Carol J. Barrett. 1981. "The Needs of Prisoners' Wives: A Challenge for the Mental Health Professions." *Community Mental Health Journal* 17, no. 4: 310–22.

Davidson, Tyler. 1996. "Jail Date: Wives of San Quentin Inmates Protest Politicians' Efforts to Restrict the Family Visitation Program." *SF Weekly,* February 7–13, 6, 8.

Davis, Angela Y. 1998. "Race and Criminalization: Black Americans and the Punishment Industry." In *The Angela Y. Davis Reader,* edited by J. James. Oxford: Blackwell.

Davis, Ann. 1992. "Men's Imprisonment: The Financial Cost to Women and Children." In *Prisoners' Children: What Are the Issues?* edited by R. Shaw. London: Routledge.

Demello, Margo. 1993. "The Convict Body: Tattooing among Male American Prisoners." *Anthropology Today* 9, no. 6: 10–13.

DeParle, Jason. 2004. *American Dream: Three Women, Ten Kids, and a Nation's Drive to End Welfare.* New York: Viking.

DeVault, Marjorie L. 1991. *Feeding the Family: The Social Organization of Caring as Gendered Work.* Chicago: University of Chicago Press.

Devlin, Angela. 2002. *Cell Mates/Soul Mates: Stories of Prison Relationships.* Winchester, United Kingdom: Waterside Press.

Ditchfield, John. 1994. *Family Ties and Recidivism: Main Findings of the Literature.* Research Study 118. London: Home Office.

Donaldson, Greg. 1993. *The Ville: Cops and Kids in Urban America.* New York: Ticknor and Fields.

Douglas, Mary. 1970. *Body Symbols.* Oxford: Blackstone.

Downes, David. 2000. "The 'Macho' Penal Economy: Mass Incarceration in the United States—A European Perspective." In *Mass Imprisonment: Social Causes and Consequences,* edited by D. Garland. London: Sage.

Duncan, Greg J., Björn Gustafsson, Richard Hauser, Günther Schmaus, Stephen Jenkins, Hans Messinger, Ruud Muffels, Brian Nolan, Jean-Claude Ray, and Wolfgang Voges. 1995. "Poverty and Social-Assistance Dynamics in the United States, Canada, and Europe." In *Poverty, Inequality and the Future of Social Policy: Western States in the New World Order,* edited by K. McFate, R. Lawson, and W. J. Wilson. New York: Russell Sage Foundation.

Duncan, Martha Grace. 1996. *Romantic Outlaws, Beloved Prisons: The Unconscious Meanings of Crime and Punishment.* New York: New York University Press.

Dutton, Donald G., and Stephen D. Hart. 1992. "Risk Markers for Family Violence in a Federally Incarcerated Population." *International Journal of Law and Psychiatry* 15, no. 1: 101–12.

Eddy, J. Mark, and John B. Reid. 2003. "The Adolescent Children of Incarcerated Parents: A Developmental Perspective." In *Prisoners Once Removed: The Impact of Incarceration and Reentry on Children, Families, and Communities,* edited by J. Travis and M. Waul. Washington, D.C.: Urban Institute.

Edin, Kathryn. 2000. "What Do Low-Income Single Mothers Say about Marriage?" *Social Problems* 47, no. 1: 112–36.

Edin, Kathryn, and Maria Kefalas. 2005. *Promises I Can Keep: Why Poor Women Put Motherhood before Marriage.* Berkeley: University of California Press.

Egelko, Bob. 2001. "Court OKs Remote Fatherhood for Inmates." *San Francisco Chronicle,* September 6, A3.

Ehrenreich, Barbara, and Arlie Russell Hochschild, eds. 2003. *Global Woman: Nannies, Maids, and Sex Workers in the New Economy.* New York: Henry Holt.

Families and Corrections Network. 2001. *Directory of Programs Serving Families of Adult Offenders*. Washington, D.C.: National Institute of Corrections, U.S. Department of Justice.

Farmer, Paul. 2002. "The House of the Dead: Tuberculosis and Incarceration." In *Invisible Punishment: The Collateral Consequences of Mass Imprisonment*, edited by M. Mauer and M. Chesney-Lind. New York: New Press.

Faupel, Charles E. 1991. *Shooting Dope: Career Patterns of Hard-Core Heroin Users*. Gainesville: University Press of Florida.

Fausto-Sterling, Anne. 1995. "Gender, Race, and Nation: The Comparative Anatomy of 'Hottentot' Women in Europe, 1815–1817." In *Deviant Bodies*, edited by J. Terry and J. Urla. Bloomington: Indiana University Press.

Feeley, Malcolm M. 1992 (1979). *The Process Is the Punishment: Handling Cases in a Lower Criminal Court*. New York: Russell Sage Foundation.

Fenton, Norman, and Jessie Chase Fenton. 1961. *When a Man Wants to Go Straight: How Can His Family and Friends Help Him*. Sacramento: County Project in Correctional Methods, Institute for the Study of Crime and Delinquency.

Fields, Jason, and Lynne M. Casper. 2001. "America's Families and Living Arrangements: March 2000." In *Current Population Reports, 520–37*. Washington, D.C.: U.S. Census Bureau.

Fimrite, Peter, and Michael Taylor. 2005. "No Shortage of Women Who Dream of Snaring a Husband on Death Row." *San Francisco Chronicle*, March 27, A1.

Fishman, Laura T. 1986. "Prisoners' Wives' Interpretations of Male Criminality and Subsequent Arrest." *Deviant Behavior* 7: 137–58.

———. 1988a. "Prisoners and Their Wives: Marital and Domestic Effects of Telephone Contacts and Home Visits." *International Journal of Offender Therapy and Comparative Criminology* 32, no. 1: 55–66.

———. 1988b. "Stigmatization and Prisoners' Wives' Feelings of Shame." *Deviant Behavior* 9: 169–92.

———. 1990. *Women at the Wall: A Study of Prisoners' Wives Doing Time on the Outside*. Albany: State University of New York Press.

———. 1995. "The World of Prisoners' Wives." In *Long-Term Imprisonment: Policy, Science and Correctional Practice*, edited by T. J. Flanagan. Thousand Oaks, Calif.: Sage.

Fishman, Susan Hoffman, and Albert S. Alissi. 1997. "Strengthening Families as Natural Support Systems for Offenders." In *Social Work in Juvenile and Criminal Justice Settings*, edited by A. R. Roberts. Springfield, Ill.: Charles C. Thomas.

Flanagan, T. J. 1981. "Dealing with Long-Term Confinement: Adaptive Strategies and Perspectives among Long-Term Prisoners." *Criminal Justice and Behavior* 8, no. 2: 201–22.

Foster, Janet. 1990. *Villains: Crime and Community in the Inner City*. London: Routledge.

Foucault, Michel. 1977. *Discipline and Punish: The Birth of the Prison*. New York: Vintage.

Frazier, Mansfield B. 1995. *From Behind the Wall: Commentary on Crime, Punishment, Race, and the Underclass by a Prison Inmate*. New York: Paragon House.

Fritsch, Travis A., and John D. Burkhead. 1981. "Behavioral Reactions of Children to Parental Absence due to Imprisonment." *Family Relations* 30, no. 1: 83–88.

Fuchs, Ester R., Robert Y. Shapiro, and Lorraine C. Minnite. 2001. "Social Capital, Political Participation, and the Urban Community." In *Social Capital and Poor Communities*, edited by S. Saegert, J. P. Thompson, and M. R. Warren. New York: Russell Sage.

Fürst, Elisabeth L'Orange. 1997. "Cooking and Femininity." *Women's Studies International Forum* 20, no. 3: 441–49.

Gabel, Katherine, and Denise Johnston, eds. 1995. *Children of Incarcerated Parents*. New York: Lexington Books.

Gabel, Stewart. 1992. "Behavioral Problems in Sons of Incarcerated or Otherwise Absent Fathers: The Issue of Separation." *Family Process* 31, no. 3: 303–14.

Garfinkel, Harold. 1968. "Conditions of Successful Degradation Ceremonies." In *Prison within Society: A Reader in Penology*, edited by L. Hazelrigg. Garden City, N.Y.: Doubleday.

Garland, David. 1990. *Punishment and Modern Society: A Study in Social Theory*. Oxford: Oxford University Press.

———, ed. 2001. *Mass Imprisonment: Social Causes and Consequences*. London: Sage.

Gerber, Jurg, and Eric J. Fritsch. 1995. "Adult Academic and Vocational Correctional Education Programs: A Review of Recent Research." *Journal of Offender Rehabilitation* 22, nos. 1–2: 119–42.

Gibbs, Carole. 1971. "The Effect of the Imprisonment of Women upon Their Children." *British Journal of Criminology* 11, no. 2: 113–30.

Girshick, Lori B. 1996. *Soledad Women: Wives of Prisoners Speak Out*. Westport, Conn.: Praeger.

Glaser, Jordan B., and Robert B. Greifinger. 1993. "Correctional Health Care: A Public Health Opportunity." *Annals of Internal Medicine* 118, no. 2: 139–45.

Glaser, O. 1964. *The Effectiveness of a Prison and Parole System*. Indianapolis: Bobbs-Merrill.

Gluckman, Max, ed. 1962. *The Rituals of Social Relations*. Manchester: Manchester University Press.

Goetting, Ann. 1982. "Conjugal Association in Prison: Issues and Perspectives." *Crime and Delinquency* 28, no. 1: 52–71.

———. 1999. *Getting Out: Life Stories of Women Who Left Abusive Men*. New York: Columbia University Press.

Goffman, Erving. 1959. *The Presentation of Self in Everyday Life*. New York: Anchor Books.

———. 1961. *Asylums: Essays on the Social Situation of Mental Patients and Other Inmates*. Harmondsworth: Penguin Books.

———. 1963. *Stigma: Notes on the Management of Spoiled Identity*. New York: Simon and Schuster.

Goldberg, Eve, and Linda Evans. 1998. *The Prison Industrial Complex and the Global Economy*. San Francisco: AK Press Distribution.

Gonnerman, Jennifer. 2004. *Life on the Outside: The Prison Odyssey of Elaine Bartlett*. New York: Farrar, Straus and Giroux.

Goodrum, S., M. Staton, C. G. Leukefeld, J. M. Webster, and R. T. Purvis. 2003. "Staff Members' and Clients' Perceptions of a Prison-Based Substance Abuse Treatment Program." *Journal of Offender Rehabilitation* 37: 27–46.

Goodsell, Charles B. 1984. "Welfare Waiting Rooms." *Urban Life* 12, no. 4: 467–77.

Gordon, Diana R. 1990. *The Justice Juggernaut: Fighting Street Crime, Controlling Citizens*. New Brunswick: Rutgers University Press.

Gouldner, Alvin W. 1996. "The Norm of Reciprocity: A Preliminary Statement." In *The Gift: An International Perspective*, edited by A. E. Komter. Amsterdam: Amsterdam University Press.

Gowan, Teresa. 2002. "The Nexus: Homelessness and Incarceration in Two American Cities." *Ethnography* 3, no. 4: 500–534.

Grinstead, Olga, Bonnie Faigeles, Carrie Bancroft, and Barry Zack. 2001. "The Financial Cost of Maintaining Relationships with Incarcerated African American Men: A Survey of Women Prison Visitors." *Journal of African-American Men* 6, no. 1: 59–70.

Grinstead, Olga, Barry Zack, Bonnie Faigeles, Nina Grossman, and Leroy Blea. 1999. "Reducing Postrelease HIV Risk among Male Prison Inmates: A Peer-Led Intervention." *Criminal Justice and Behavior* 26, no. 4: 468–80.

Groves, Julian McAllister, and Kimberly A. Chang. 1999. "Romancing Resistance and Resisting Romance: Ethnography and the Construction of Power in the Filipina Domestic Worker Community in Hong Kong." *Journal of Contemporary Ethnography* 28, no. 3: 235–65.

Guy, Alison, and Maura Banim. 2000. "Personal Collections: Women's Clothing Use and Identity." *Journal of Gender Studies* 9, no. 3: 313–27.

Hagan, John, and Juleigh Petty Coleman. 2001. "Returning Captives of the American War on Drugs: Issues of Community and Family Reentry." *Crime & Delinquency* 47, no. 3: 352–67.

Hagan, John, and Ronit Dinovitzer. 1999. "The Collateral Consequences of Imprisonment for Children, Communities, and Prisoners." In *Prisons*, edited by M. Tonry and J. Petersilia. Chicago: University of Chicago Press.

Hairston, Creasie Finney. 1988. "Family Ties during Imprisonment: Do They Influence Future Criminal Activity?" *Federal Probation* (March): 48–51.

———. 1991. "Family Ties during Imprisonment: Important to Whom and for What?" *Journal of Sociology and Social Welfare* 18, no. 1: 85–104.

———. 1995. "Fathers in Prison." In *Children of Incarcerated Parents*, edited by K. Gabel and D. Johnston. New York: Lexington Books.

———. 1998. "The Forgotten Parent: Understanding the Forces That Influence Incarcerated Fathers' Relationships with Their Children." *Child Welfare* 77, no. 5: 617–39.

———. 1999. "Kinship Care When Parents Are Incarcerated." In *Kinship Care: Improving Practice through Research*, edited by J. P. Gleeson and C. F. Hairston. Washington, D.C.: CWLA Press.

———. 2003. "Prisoners and Their Families: Parenting Issues during Incarceration." In *Prisoners Once Removed*, edited by J. Travis and M. Waul. Washington, D.C.: Urban Institute.

Hairston, Creasie Finney, Shonda Wills, and Nancy Wall. 1996. *Children, Families, and Correctional Supervision: Current Policies and New Directions*. Conference proceedings, hosted by the Jane Addams College of Social Work and the Jane Addams Center for Social Policy and Research, University of Illinois at Chicago.

Hammett, Theodore M. 2000. "Health-Related Issues in Prisoner Reentry to the Community." In *Reentry Roundtable*. Justice Policy Center, October 12–13. Washington, D.C.: Urban Institute.

———. 2001. "Making the Case for Health Interventions in Correctional Facilities." *Journal of Urban Health* 78, no. 2: 236–40.

Haney, Craig. 2003. "The Psychological Impact of Incarceration: Implications for Postprison Adjustment." In *Prisoners Once Removed: The Impact of Incarceration and Reentry on Children, Families, and Communities*, edited by J. Travis and M. Waul. Washington, D.C.: Urban Institute.

Hann, H. 1983. "Paternalism and Public Policy." *Society* 20: 36–46.

Hannon, Ginger, Don Martin, and Maggie Martin. 1984. "Incarceration in the Family: Adjustment to Change." *Family Therapy* 11, no. 3: 253–60.

Harrell, Margaret C. 2001. "Army Officers' Spouses: Have the White Gloves Been Mothballed?" *Armed Forces and Society* 28, no. 1: 55–75.

Harris, Othello, and R. Robin Miller, eds. 2003. *Impacts of Incarceration on the African-American Family*. New Brunswick, N.J.: Transaction.

Harrison, Paige M., and Allen Beck. 2006a. *Prison and Jail Inmates at Midyear 2005*. Washington, D.C.: Bureau of Justice Statistics, U.S. Department of Justice.

———. 2006b. *Prisoners in 2005*. Washington, D.C.: Bureau of Justice Statistics, U.S. Department of Justice.

Hasenfeld, Yeheskel. 1972. "People Processing Organizations: An Exchange Approach." *American Sociological Review* 37 (June): 256–63.

Hassine, Victor. 1999. *Life without Parole: Living in Prison Today*. Los Angeles: Roxbury Publishing.

Hauser, Christine, and Christopher Drew. 2005. "Three Police Officers Deny Battery Charges after Videotaped Beating in New Orleans." *New York Times*, October 11, A16.

Hay, Carter. 1998. "Parental Sanctions and Delinquent Behavior: Toward Clarification of Braithwaite's Theory of Reintegrative Shaming." *Theoretical Criminology* 2, no. 4: 419–43.

Hedges, Michael, and Zeke Minaya. 2005. "Troops' Best Gift: Family Support; Soldiers Serving on the Texas National Guard Are Far from Home But Not Forgotten." *Houston Chronicle*, June 19, B1.

Hinds, Lennox S. 1982. "The Impact of Incarceration on Low-Income Families." *Journal of Offender Counseling Services Rehabilitation* 5, nos. 3–4: 5–12.

Hochschild, Arlie Russell. 1979. "Emotion Work, Feeling Rules, and Social Structure." *American Journal of Sociology* 85, no. 3: 551–75.

Hofstadter, Dan. 1996. *The Love Affair as a Work of Art.* New York: Farrar, Straus and Giroux.

Holmes, Mary. 2004. "An Equal Distance? Individualisation, Gender and Intimacy in Distance Relationships." *Sociological Review* 52, no. 2: 180–200.

Holt, N., and P. Miller. 1972. *Explorations in Inmate Family Relationships.* Research Report No. 46. Sacramento: California Department of Corrections.

Hornick, Leslie Goodman. 1991. "Volunteer Program Helps Make Inmates' Families Feel Welcome." *Corrections Today* 53, no. 5: 184–86.

Hostetter, Edwin, and Dorothea T. Jinnah. 1993. "Families of Adult Prisoners." Prison Fellowship Ministries. http://www.fcnetwork.org/reading/researc .html.

Howard League. 1994. *Families Matter: A Report by the Howard League for Penal Reform.* London.

Howarth, Glennys, and Paul Rock. 2000. "Aftermath and the Construction of Victimisation: 'The Other Victims of Crime.'" *Howard Journal of Criminal Justice* 39, no. 1: 58–78.

Hughes, James E. 1983. "My Daddy's Number Is C–92760." In *Children of Exceptional Parents*, edited by Mary Frank. Binghampton, N.Y.: Haworth Press.

Ignatieff, Michael. 1978. *A Just Measure of Pain: The Penitentiary in the Industrial Revolution.* London: Macmillan.

Ingraham, Chrys. 1999. *White Weddings: Romancing Heterosexuality in Popular Culture.* New York: Routledge.

International Centre for Prison Studies. 2006. *World Prison Brief.* Kings College, University of London, June 21, 2006; http://www.kcl.ac.uk/depsta/rel/ icps/worldbrief/world_brief.html.

Irwin, John. 1985. *The Jail: Managing the Underclass in American Society.* Berkeley: University of California Press.

Irwin, John, and James Austin. 2000. *It's About Time: America's Imprisonment Binge.* Belmont, Calif.: Wadsworth.

Isenberg, Sheila. 1991. *Women Who Love Men Who Kill.* New York: Simon and Schuster.

Jackson, George. 1970. *Soledad Brother: The Prison Letters of George Jackson.* New York: Bantam Books.

Jackson, Michael B. 2003. *How to Love and Inspire Your Man after Prison.* Willingboro, N.J.: Joint FX Press.

———. 2004. *How to Do Good after Prison: A Handbook for the "Committed Man."* Willingboro, N.J.: Joint FX Press.

Jacobs, James B. 1977. *Statesville: The Penitentiary in Mass Society.* Chicago: University of Chicago Press.

Johnson, Elizabeth I., and Jane Waldfogel. 2004. "Children of Incarcerated Parents: Multiple Risks and Children's Living Arrangements." In *Imprisoning America: The Social Effects of Mass Incarceration,* edited by M. Pattillo, D. Weiman, and B. Western. New York: Russell Sage Foundation.

Johnson, Jason B. 2000. "San Quentin Guard Appears in Court: Plea Delayed on Cocaine, Heroin Charges." *San Francisco Chronicle,* August 31, A18.

Johnston, Denise. 1995. "Jailed Mothers." In *Children of Incarcerated Parents,* edited by K. Gabel and D. Johnston. New York: Lexington Books.

Jorgensen, James D., Santos H. Hernandez, and Robert C. Warren. 1986. "Addressing the Social Needs of Families of Prisoners: A Tool for Inmate Rehabilitation." *Federal Probation* 50, no. 4: 47–52.

Jose-Kampfner, Christina. 1991. "Michigan Program Makes Children's Visits Meaningful." *Corrections Today* 53, no. 5: 130–34.

———. 1995. "Post-Traumatic Stress Reactions of Children of Imprisoned Mothers." In *Children of Incarcerated Parents,* edited by K. Gabel and D. Johnston. New York: Lexington Books.

Katz, Michael. 1996. *In the Shadow of the Poorhouse: A Social History of Welfare in America.* New York: Basic Books.

Kauffman, Kelsey. 1988. *Prison Officers and Their World.* Cambridge: Harvard University Press.

Kirsch, Irwin S., Ann Jungeblut, Lynn Jenkins, and Andrew Kolstad. 2002. *Adult Literacy in America: A First Look at the Findings of the National Adult Literacy Survey.* Washington, D.C.: National Center for Educational Statistics.

Klein, Shirley R., and Stephen J. Bahr. 1996. "An Evaluation of a Family-Centered Cognitive Skills Program for Prison Inmates." *International Journal of Offender Therapy and Comparative Criminology* 40, no. 4: 334–46.

Komter, Aafke. 1996. "Women, Gifts and Power." In *The Gift: An Interdisciplinary Perspective,* edited by A. Komter. Amsterdam: Amsterdam University Press.

Landry, Bart. 1988. *The New Black Middle Class.* Berkeley: University of California Press.

Leach, Edmund. 1982. *Social Anthropology.* New York: Oxford University Press.

LeBlanc, Adrian Nicole. 2003. *Random Family: Love, Drugs, Trouble, and Coming of Age in the Bronx.* New York: Scribner.

LeFlore, Larry, and Mary Ann Holston. 1990. "Perceived Importance of Parenting Behaviors as Reported by Inmate Mothers: An Exploratory Study." *Journal of Offender Counseling Services Rehabilitation* 14, no. 1: 5–21.

Lévi-Strauss, Claude. 1996. "The Principle of Reciprocity." In *The Gift: An Interdisciplinary Perspective*, edited by A. E. Komter. Amsterdam: Amsterdam University Press.

Lewis, Charles. 1998. "Working the Ritual: Professional Wedding Photography and the American Middle Class." *Journal of Communication Inquiry* 22, no. 1: 72–92.

Lichter, Daniel T., Diane K. McLaughlin, George Kephart, and David T. Landry. 1992. "Race and the Retreat from Marriage: A Shortage of Marriageable Men?" *American Sociological Review* 57 (December): 781–99.

Liebling, Alison. 2000. "Prison Officers, Policing, and the Use of Discretion." *Theoretical Criminology* 4, no. 3: 333–57.

Light, Roy. 1993. "Why Support Prisoners' Family-Tie Groups?" *Howard Journal* 32, no. 4: 322–29.

Lipset, Seymour Martin. 1996. *American Exceptionalism: A Double-Edged Sword.* New York: W. W. Norton.

Lipsky, Michael. 1980. *Street-Level Bureaucracy: Dilemmas of the Individual in Public Services.* New York: Russell Sage.

Lloyd, Eva. 1992. *Children Visiting Holloway Prison: Inside and Outside Perspectives on the All-Day Visits Scheme at HMP Holloway.* London: Save the Children.

———. 1995. *Prisoners' Children: Research, Policy and Practice.* London: Save the Children.

Louima, Gariot. 2002. "For Mothers in Prison, a Bittersweet Family Day." *Los Angeles Times,* May 31.

Lowenstein, Ariela. 1986. "Temporary Single Parenthood: The Case of Prisoners' Families." *Family Relations* 35, no. 1: 79–85.

Lupton, Deborah. 1996. *Food, the Body and the Self.* London: Sage Publications.

Lynch, James P., and William J. Sabol. 2004. "Effects of Incarceration on Informal Social Control in Communities." In *Imprisoning America: The Social Effects of Mass Incarceration*, edited by M. Pattillo, D. Weiman, and B. Western. New York: Russell Sage Foundation.

Lynch, Mona. 2001. "Rehabilitation as Rhetoric: The Ideal of Reformation in Contemporary Parole Discourse and Practices." *Punishment and Society* 2, no. 1: 40–65.

Maksymowicz, Duszka. 2000. *Femme de parloir.* Paris: L'Esprit frappeur.

Malinowski, Bronislaw. 1996. "The Principle of Give and Take." In *The Gift: An Interdisciplinary Perspective*, edited by A. E. Komter. Amsterdam: Amesterdam University Press.

Mann, Leon. 1969. "Queue Culture: The Waiting Line as a Social System." *American Journal of Sociology* 75, no. 3: 340–54.

Martin, Dannie M., and Peter Y. Sussman. 1993. *Committing Journalism: The Prison Writings of Red Hog*. New York: W. W. Norton.

Martin, Mark. 2005. "Bill Would Close San Quentin State Prison." *San Francisco Chronicle*, April 22, B3.

Matthews, Jill. 1983. *Forgotten Victims: How Prison Affects the Family*. London: NACRO.

Mauer, Marc. 1999. *Race to Incarcerate*. New York: New Press.

Mauer, Marc, and Meda Chesney-Lind, eds. 2002. *Invisible Punishment: The Collateral Consequences of Mass Imprisonment*. New York: New Press.

Mauss, Marcel. 1921. "L'expression obligatoire des sentiments: Rituels oraux funéraires australiens." *Journal de psychologie* 18: 425–34.

Mayer, Susan. 1995. "A Comparison of Poverty and Living Conditions in the United States, Canada, Sweden, and Germany." In *Poverty, Inequality, and the Future of Social Policy: Western States in the New World Order*, edited by K. McFate, R. Lawson, and W. J. Wilson. New York: Russell Sage Foundation.

McCall, Nathan. 1994. *Makes Me Wanna Holler: A Young Black Man in America*. New York: Vintage Books.

McCosh, John. 2001. "Costs of State Prisoners' Collect Calls Soaring." *Atlanta Journal-Constitution*, October 18, 1D.

McDermott, Kathleen, and Roy D. King. 1992. "Prison Rule 102: 'Stand by Your Man.' The Impact of Penal Policy on the Families of Prisoners." In *Prisoners' Children: What Are the Issues?* edited by R. Shaw. London: Routledge.

McEvoy, Kieran, David O'Mahony, Carol Horner, and Olwen Lyner. 1999. "The Home Front: The Families of Politically Motivated Prisoners in Northern Ireland." *British Journal of Criminology* 39, no. 2: 175–97.

McLaughlin, Diane K., and Daniel T. Lichter. 1997. "Poverty and the Marital Behavior of Young Women." *Journal of Marriage and the Family* 59 (August): 582–94.

Meigs, Anna S. 1991. *Food, Sex, and Pollution*. New Brunswick, N.J.: Rutgers University Press.

Mele, Christopher. 2005. "The Civil Threat of Eviction and the Regulation and Control of U.S. Public Housing Communities." In *Civil Penalties, Social Consequences*, edited by C. Mele and T. A. Miller. New York: Routledge.

Mele, Christopher, and Teresa A. Miller, eds. 2005. *Civil Penalties, Social Consequences*. New York: Routledge.

Merton, Robert K., and Elinor Barber. 1976. "Sociological Ambivalence." In *Sociological Ambivalence and Other Essays*. New York: Free Press.

Miller, Jerome G. 1996. *Search and Destroy: African-American Males in the Criminal Justice System*. New York: Cambridge University Press.

Miller, Walter B. 1958. "Lower Class Culture as a Generating Milieu of Gang Delinquency." *Journal of Social Issues* 14, no. 3: 5–19.

Mills, C. Wright. 1940. "Situated Actions and Vocabularies of Motive." *American Sociological Review* 5, no. 6: 904–13.

Mina, Denise. 2003. "Why Are Women Drawn to Men Like This?" *Guardian,* January 13, 8–9.

Moerings, Martin. 1992. "Role Transitions and the Wives of Prisoners." *Environment and Behavior* 24, no. 2: 239–59.

Morris, Pauline. 1965. *Prisoners and Their Families.* London: George Allen and Unwin.

Mumola, Christopher J. 2000. *Incarcerated Parents and Their Children.* Washington, D.C.: Bureau of Justice Statistics.

Mundow, Anna. 2001. "The Business of Prison." *Irish Times,* May 12.

Murcott, Anne. 1983. "'It's a Pleasure to Cook for Him': Food, Mealtimes and Gender in Some South Wales Households." In *The Public and the Private,* edited by E. Gamarnikow, D. H. J. Morgan, J. Purvis, and D. Taylorson. London: Heinemann.

NACRO. 1993–94. *Outside Help: Practical Information for the Families and Friends of People in Prison.* London: National Association for the Care and Rehabilitation of Offenders.

———. 1994. *Opening the Doors: Prisoners' Families.* London: National Association for the Care and Rehabilitation of Offenders.

Nieves, Evelyn. 2000. "Police Corruption Charges Reopen Wounds in Oakland." *New York Times,* November 30, A18.

Nixon, Kamille. 2002. "Moms in Prison: 'Get on Bus' Program Helps Keep Families in Touch." *Catholic San Francisco,* August 30, 23.

Nurse, Anne M. 2002. *Fatherhood Arrested: Parenting from within the Juvenile Justice System.* Nashville: Vanderbilt University Press.

Osbourne Association. 1993. *How Can I Help? Working with Children of Incarcerated Parents.* New York.

Owen, Barbara. 1998. *"In the Mix": Struggle and Survival in a Women's Prison.* Albany: State University of New York Press.

Page, Joshua. 2004. "Eliminating the Enemy: The Import of Denying Prisoners' Access to Higher Education in Clinton's America." *Punishment and Society* 6, no. 4: 357–78.

Pager, Devah. 2003. "The Mark of a Criminal Record." *American Journal of Sociology* 108, no. 5: 937–75.

Parke, Ross D., and K. Alison Clarke-Stewart. 2003. "The Effects of Parental Incarceration on Children: Perspectives, Promises, and Policies." In *Prisoners Once Removed: The Impact of Incarceration and Reentry on Children, Families, and Communities,* edited by J. Travis and M. Waul. Washington, D.C.: Urban Institute.

Patterson, Orlando. 1998. *Rituals of Blood: Consequences of Slavery in Two American Centuries.* New York: Basic Books.

Pattillo, Mary. 1999. *Black Picket Fences: Privilege and Peril among the Black Middle Class.* Chicago: University of Chicago Press.

Pattillo, Mary, David Weiman, and Bruce Western, eds. 2004. *Imprisoning America: The Social Effects of Mass Incarceration*. New York: Russell Sage Foundation.

Paylor, Ian, and David Smith. 1994. "Who Are Prisoners' Families?" *Journal of Social Welfare and Family Law* 2: 131–44.

Peelo, Moira, John Stewart, Gill Stewart, and Ann Prior. 1991. "Women Partners of Prisoners." *Howard Journal* 30, no. 4: 311–27.

Petersilia, Joan. 1999. "Parole and Prisoner Reentry in the United States." In *Prisons*, edited by M. Tonry and J. Petersilia. Chicago: University of Chicago Press.

———. 2003. *When Prisoners Come Home: Parole and Prisoner Reentry*. New York: Oxford University Press.

Pettit, Becky, and Bruce Western. 2004. "Mass Imprisonment and the Life Course: Race and Class Inequality in U.S. Incarceration." *American Sociological Review* 69 (April): 151–69.

Phillips, Jenny. 2001. "Cultural Construction of Manhood in Prison." *Psychology of Men and Masculinity* 2, no. 1: 13–23.

Phillips, Susan A. 2001. "Gallo's Body: Decoration and Damnation in the Life of a Chicano Gang Member." *Ethnography* 2, no. 3: 357–88.

Piven, Frances Fox, and Richard Cloward. 1993 (1971). *Regulating the Poor: The Social Functions of Welfare*. New York: Pantheon.

Plummer, Ken. 1995. *Telling Sexual Stories: Power, Change and Social Worlds*. London: Routledge.

Podger, Pamela, and Peter Fimrite. 2001. "State Report Envisages Condos at San Quentin: General Services Examines Options for Relocating Prison, Replacing It with Housing, Transit Stops." *San Francisco Chronicle*, July 4, A17.

Prasad, Monica. 1999. "The Morality of Market Exchange: Love, Money, and Contractual Justice." *Sociological Perspectives* 42, no. 2: 181–214.

Purdum, Todd S. 1999. "Former Los Angeles Officer Sets Off Corruption Scandal." *New York Times*, September 18, A9.

Ramsden, Sally. 1998. *Working with Children of Prisoners*. London: Save the Children.

Renaud, Jorge Antonio. 2002. *Behind the Walls: A Guide for Families and Friends of Texas Prison Inmates*. Denton: University of North Texas Press.

Reuters. 2000. "Prison Guards Charged in Sperm-Smuggling Caper." October 12.

Richards, Martin, Brenda McWilliams, Lucy Allcock, Jill Enterkin, Patricia Owens, and Jane Woodrow. 1994. "The Family Ties of English Prisoners: The Results of the Cambridge Project on Imprisonment and Family Ties." Occasional Paper No. 2. Cambridge: Cambridge University, Centre for Family Research.

Richie, Beth E. 1996. *Compelled to Crime: The Gender Entrapment of Battered Black Women*. New York: Routledge.

———. 2002. "The Social Impact of Mass Incarceration on Women." In *Invisible Punishment: The Collateral Consequences of Mass Imprisonment*, edited by M. Mauer and M. Chesney-Lind. New York: New Press.

Rideau, Wilbert, and Ron Wikberg. 1992. *Life Sentences: Rage and Survival behind Bars*. New York: Times Books.

Ritter, John. 2001. "Bell Could Toll for San Quentin: Because of Rising Maintenance Costs, California Could Close State Prison—Much to the Delight of Developers." *USA Today*, March 14, 3A.

Robinson, K. M. 1997. "Family Caregiving: Who Provides the Care, and at What Cost?" *Nursing Economics* 15, no. 5: 243–47.

Rock of Ages Prison Ministry. 2003. "Our Labor." http://www.RockOfAges Ministry.com.

Rolston, B., and M. Tomlinson. 1986. "Long-Term Imprisonment in Northern Ireland: Psychological or Political Survival?" In *The Expansion of the European Prison Systems*. Working Papers in European Criminology No. 7. Belfast: European Group for the Study of Deviance and Social Control.

Ross, Jeffrey Ian, and Stephen C. Richards. 2002. *Behind Bars: Surviving Prison*. Indianapolis: Alpha.

Rothman, David J. 1971. *The Discovery of the Asylum: Social Order and Disorder in the New Republic*. Boston: Little, Brown.

Rotter, Joseph C., and Marsha E. Boveja. 1999. "Counseling Military Families." *Family Journal: Counseling and Therapy for Couples and Families* 7, no. 4: 379–82.

Sabo, Don, Terry A. Kupers, and Willie London, eds. 2001. *Prison Masculinities*. Philadelphia: Temple University Press.

Sachs, Susan. 2001. "U.S. Decides Not to Prosecute Four Officers Who Killed Diallo." *New York Times*, February 1, B1.

Sack, W. H., J. Seidler, and S. Thomas. 1976. "The Children of Imprisoned Parents: A Psychosocial Exploration." *American Journal of Orthopsychiatry* 46: 618–28.

Schafer, N. E. 1991. "Prison Visiting Policies and Practices." *International Journal of Offender Therapy and Comparative Criminology* 35, no. 3: 263–75.

———. 1994. "Exploring the Link between Visits and Parole Success: A Survey of Prison Visitors." *International Journal of Offender Therapy and Comparative Criminology* 38, no. 1: 17–32.

Schlosser, Eric. 1998. "The Prison-Industrial Complex." *Atlantic Monthly*, December, 51–77.

Schneller, D. P. 1978. *The Prisoner's Family: A Study of the Effect of Imprisonment on the Families of Prisoners*. San Francisco: R&E Research Associates.

Schwartz, Barry. 1975. *Queuing and Waiting: Studies in the Social Organization of Access and Delay*. Chicago: University of Chicago.

Scott, Marvin B., and Stanford M. Lyman. 1968. "Accounts." *American Sociological Review* 33: 46–62.

Scull, Andrew. 1977. *Decarceration: Community Treatment and the Deviant— A Radical View.* Englewood Cliffs, N.J.: Prentice-Hall.

Seidman, Steven. 1993. *Romantic Longings: Love in America, 1830–1980.* New York: Routledge.

Seymour, Cynthia B,, and Creasie Finney Hairston, eds. 1998. *Children with Parents in Prison* (special issue of *Child Welfare* magazine). Washington, D.C.: Child Welfare League of America.

Shakur, Sanyika. 1998. *Monster: The Autobiography of an L.A. Gang Member.* Boston: Addison-Wesley.

Shaw, Roger. 1987. *Children of Imprisoned Fathers.* London: Hodder and Stoughton.

———, ed. 1992. *Prisoners' Children: What Are the Issues?* London: Routledge.

Shelton, Allen. 1994. "My Bloody Valentine." *Studies in Symbolic Interaction* 16: 191–211.

Sheridan, John J. 1996. "Inmates May Be Parents Too." *Corrections Today* 58 (August): 100–103.

Shichor, D. 1992. "Myths and Realities in Prison Siting." *Crime & Delinquency* 38, no. 1: 70–87.

Shida, Kiyoshi. 1999. "The Shintoist Wedding Ceremony in Japan: An Invented Tradition." *Media Culture & Society* 21, no. 2: 195–204.

Sidel, Ruth. 1998. *Keeping Women and Children Last: America's War on the Poor.* 2nd ed. New York: Penguin.

Sidenvall, Birgitta, Margaretha Nydahl, and Christina Fjellstrom. 2000. "The Meal as a Gift: The Meaning of Cooking among Retired Women." *Journal of Applied Gerontology* 19, no. 4: 405–23.

Simmel, Georg. 1950. "The Stranger." In *The Sociology of Georg Simmel*, edited by K. Wolff. London: Free Press.

Simon, Jonathan. 1993. *Poor Discipline: Parole and the Social Control of the Underclass, 1890–1990.* Chicago: University of Chicago Press.

———. 2000. "The 'Society of Captives' in the Era of Hyper-Incarceration." *Theoretical Criminology* 4, no. 3: 285–308.

Skidmore, Paul. 1999. "Dress to Impress: Employer Regulation of Gay and Lesbian Appearance." *Social & Legal Studies* 8, no. 4: 509–29.

Sloop, John M. 1996. *The Cultural Prison: Discourse, Prisoners, and Punishment.* Tuscaloosa: University of Alabama Press.

Sniezek, Tamara. 2003. "Getting Married: An Interactionist Analysis of Weddings and Transitions into Marriage." PhD diss., University of California at Los Angeles.

Spain, Daphne. 1992. *Gendered Spaces.* Chapel Hill: University of North Carolina Press.

Sparks, Richard. 2002. "Out of the 'Digger': The Warrior's Honour and the Guilty Observer." *Ethnography* 3, no. 3: 556–81.

Sparks, Richard, Anthony E. Bottoms, and Will Hay. 1996. *Prisons and the Problem of Order.* Oxford: Clarendon Press.

Spence, Donald P. 1982. *Narrative Truth and Historical Truth: Naming and Inter-pretation in Psychoanalysis.* New York: W. W. Norton.

Spiro, M. 1979. *Gender and Culture: Kibbutz Women Revisited.* Durham: Duke University Press.

Stack, Carol B. 1974. *All Our Kin: Strategies for Survival in a Black Community.* New York: Harper and Row.

State of California. 2003. *California Code of Regulations, Title 15. Crime Preven-tion and Corrections. Division 3, Department of Corrections. Chapter 1: Rules and Regulations of the Director of Corrections.* Sacramento.

Stone, Bonnie Domrose, and Betty Sowers Alt. 1990. *Uncle Sam's Brides: The World of Military Wives.* New York: Walker and Company.

Swan, A. 1981. *Families of Black Prisoners: Survival and Progress.* Boston: G. K. Hill.

Sward, Susan, and Bill Wallace. 1998. "Three California Prisons under Intense Federal Investigation." *San Francisco Chronicle*, March 28, A7.

Swidler, Ann. 2001. *Talk of Love: How Culture Matters.* Chicago: University of Chicago Press.

Sykes, Gresham. 1958. *The Society of Captives: A Study of a Maximum Security Prison.* Princeton: Princeton University Press.

Sykes, Gresham, and David Matza. 1957. "Techniques of Neutralization: A Theory of Delinquency." *American Sociological Review* 22, no. 6: 664–70.

Thompson, P., and Pauline Morris. 1972. *Report on the Work of the Prisoners' Wives Service.* London.

Tonry, Michael. 1995. *Malign Neglect: Race, Crime, and Punishment in America.* New York: Oxford University Press.

———. 1999. "Why Are U.S. Incarceration Rates So High?" *Crime & Delinquency* 45, no. 4: 419–37.

———. 2001. "Punishment Policies and Patterns in Western Countries." In *Sentencing and Sanctions in Western Countries*, edited by M. Tonry and R. S. Frase. New York: Oxford.

Travis, Jeremy, and Michelle Waul. 2003. "Prisoners Once Removed: The Chil-dren and Families of Prisoners." In *Prisoners Once Removed: The Impact of Incarceration and Reentry on Children, Families, and Communities*, edited by J. Travis and M. Waul. Washington, D.C.: Urban Institute.

———, eds. 2003. *Prisoners Once Removed: The Impact of Incarceration and Reentry on Children, Families, and Communities.* Washington, D.C.: Urban Institute.

Turner, Castellano, and Barbara Turner. 1983. "Black Families, Social Evalua-tions, and Future Marital Relations." In *Black Marriage and Family Therapy*, edited by C. Obudho. Westport, Conn.: Greenwood Press.

Ungerson, Clare. 1983. "Women and Caring: Skills, Tasks and Taboos." In *The Public and the Private*, edited by E. Gamarnikow, D. H. J. Morgan, J. Purvis, and D. Taylorson. London: Heinemann.

Van Gennep, Arnold. 1909. *Les rites de passage.* Paris: Maisonneuve.

Vercoe, Kate. 1968. *Helping Prisoners' Families*. Report of a NACRO survey under supervision of Pauline Morris and R. L. Morrison. London: NACRO.

Wacquant, Loïc. 1996. "A Marriage in the Ghetto" [Un mariage dans le ghetto]. *Actes de la recherche en sciences sociales* 113 (June): 63–84.

———. 1998. "Inside the Zone: The Social Art of the Hustler in the Black American Ghetto." *Theory, Culture & Society* 15, no. 2: 1–36.

———. 1999. *Les Prisons de la misère*. Paris: Raisons d'Agir Editions.

———. 2000a. "Deadly Symbiosis: When Ghetto and Prison Meet and Mesh." *Punishment and Society* 3, no. 1: 95–134.

———. 2000b. "The New 'Peculiar Institution': On the Prison as Surrogate Ghetto." *Theoretical Criminology* 4, no. 3: 377–89.

Wallack, Todd. 2002. "No-Bid Contract for Jail Phones: Davis Donors Got Deal Despite State's Promises." *San Francisco Chronicle*, June 2, A1.

Western, Bruce, Leonard M. Lopoo, and Sara McLanahan. 2004. "Incarceration and the Bonds between Parents in Fragile Families." In *Imprisoning America: The Social Effects of Mass Incarceration*, edited by M. Pattillo, D. Weiman, and B. Western. New York: Russell Sage Foundation.

Western, Bruce, Becky Pettit, and Josh Guetzkow. 2002. "Black Economic Progress in the Era of Mass Imprisonment." In *Invisible Punishment: The Collateral Consequences of Mass Imprisonment*, edited by M. Mauer and M. Chesney-Lind. New York: New Press.

Westlake-Chester, Tina. 1995. "The Processes and Problematics of Coordinating Events: Planning the Wedding Reception." Paper presented at Qualitative and Ethnographic Research Conference, McMaster University, Hamilton, Ontario, May 30, 1995.

White, Hylton, and Pamela Reynolds. 1994. *In the Shadow of the Island: Women's Experience of Their Kinsmen's Political Imprisonment 1987–1991*. Pretoria: Human Sciences Research Council.

Willcox-Bailey, Jacquelynne. 1997. *Dream Lovers: Women Who Marry Men behind Bars*. Kent Town, South Australia: Wakefield Press.

Williams, Elizabeth Friar. 1996. "A Tie That Binds: Fostering the Mother-Child Bond in a Correctional Setting." *Corrections Today* 58, no. 6: 80–81.

Wilson, William Julius. 1987. *The Truly Disadvantaged: The Inner City, the Underclass, and Public Policy*. Chicago: University of Chicago Press.

Zalba, Serapio R. 1964. *Women Prisoners and Their Families*. Monograph of the California Department of Corrections. Clifton Park, N.Y.: Delmar.

Zimring, Franklin E., Gordon Hawkins, and Sam Kamin. 2001. *Punishment and Democracy: Three Strikes and You're Out in California*. New York: Oxford University Press.

Zinoman, Peter. 2001. *The Colonial Bastille: A History of Imprisonment in Vietnam, 1862–1940*. Berkeley: University of California Press.

Zoellner, Tom. 2000. "Phone Woes Take Toll on Inmates: Meltdown Leads to Costly Calls from S.F. County Jail." *San Francisco Chronicle*, July 31, A17.

Index

abuse. *See* domestic violence
Adoption and Safe Families Act
    (1997), 217–18
African Americans: gender
    relations among, 141–42;
    incarceration rates among,
    6–7; mass incarceration and,
    141, 149, 151; stigmatization of
    prisoners' families and, 216
Aisha's story: conjugal visits and,
    119–20, 120n13; decision mak-
    ing and, 95–96; food and, 87,
    107; interviewee recruitment
    and, 204; phone calls and, 89;
    relationship choices and, 132,
    133, 134, 140, 145–46; religion
    and, 134; sex and celibacy
    and, 145–46; socioeconomic
    background and, 208; wedding
    and, 116
Alice's story: institutionaliza-
    tion and, 102; interviewee
    recruitment and, 204; packages
    and, 83, 87; phone calls and,
    91; plea bargaining and, 188;
    reactions to deviance and, 153;
    relationship choices and, 150,
    153–54; socioeconomic back-
    ground and, 153, 208
Almodóvar, Pedro, 93n23
ambivalence, sociological, 12–13,
    16, 185
Andal, Dean, 117
Ann's story: domestic violence
    and, 178, 179; interviewee
    recruitment and, 204; relation-

ship choices and, 168, 169,
    170–71, 170n15, 178, 179;
    socioeconomic background
    and, 170–71, 208; substance
    abuse and, 178
Austin, James, 7n4

Bandele, Asha, 73, 129n3
Bangú prison (Brazil), 118n11
Banim, Maura, 55, 55n25
Barber, Elinor, 12
Barlinnie Special Unit (Scotland),
    118, 118n11
Bartky, Sandra Lee, 77, 86, 86n16
Basalisa's story: interviewee
    recruitment and, 204; phone
    calls and, 89–90; race and,
    142; relationship choices
    and, 132, 133, 134–35, 140,
    142, 143; religion and, 134;
    socioeconomic background
    and, 208
Bauman, Zygmunt, 25, 92–93
Behind Bars (Ross and Richards),
    221
Behind the Walls (Renaud), 221–22
Bernice's story: appointment
    scheduling and, 41; inter-
    viewee recruitment and, 204;
    interview structure and, 205–
    6; letter writing and, 72–74;
    packages and, 82–83; presence
    creation and, 94–95; race and,
    142; relationship choices and,
    132, 133, 140, 142; socioeco-
    nomic background and, 208

251

Made in the USA
Monee, IL
28 March 2021